RACETRACKER

LIFE WITH
GRIFTERS AND GAMBLERS...

John Perrotta

ISBN: 1502767945
ISBN 13: 9781502767943
Library of Congress Control Number: 2014918715
CreateSpace Independent Publishing Platform
North Charleston, South Carolina

For my brother Robert

FOREWORD

John Perrotta, a bonafide Jersey boy with a wandering soul, was not necessarily destined to sink himself hip deep in the world of thoroughbred racing, consorting with an array of colorful characters with names like Peaches, Snake, Pockets and The Schnoz. But that's where he ended up, and oh what stories he could tell.

Perrotta's journey took him far and wide, to racetracks large and small, wheeling and dealing in search of fast horses worthy of strutting their stuff in world-class events like the Kentucky Derby, the Irish Derby and the Breeders' Cup. Sometimes he caught them, sometimes they got away, but there was always a good story waiting at the end of the day.

Perrotta followed the money and he followed the dream, two forks in the same road that led him to the side of movers and shakers like Frank Stronach, the Austro-Canadian auto parts magnate who collected racetracks and racehorses as if they were trading cards. Like Robert Brennan, the empire builder in both thoroughbreds and finance who ended up cooling his jets behind bars. Like David Milch, the mercurial screenwriter and passionate consumer of all things racing, whether he was buying expensive horses at auction or boxing them in thousand dollar exactas.

Talk about good stories to tell.

Thankfully, Perrotta has told them in *Racetracker*, his heartfelt memoir dedicated in its title to the "racetrackers" he has known. They are the keepers of the thoroughbred flame with whom the author shares a kinship born of cold mornings and hot coffee at the rail, of bitter disappointments and soaring glories in the afternoons, of evenings spent in the company of fellow travelers searching for the best of the breed – or at least the winner of the next race.

By rough count, Perrotta has held down more racetrack jobs than Doan's has little liver pills. At one time or another he was a hotwalker, ticket-taker, elevator operator, racing journalist, jockey's agent, stable agent, track official, racehorse owner, racehorse breeder, racetrack executive and head of operations for one of the largest racing stables in the land.

Such a rich C.V. gives Perrotta the right to lead the reader down a number of intriguing paths. Armed with alarming recall, the author hacks through the dense brush of thoroughbred commerce, a game not recommended for the timid, to reveal a world in which the actual handlers of horseflesh – the breeders, trainers, the jockeys, the grooms – are fascinating in their own right and often enobled by their association with the animal, even when they're trying to cash a bet.

The nobility of the horseplayer is another matter entirely, and here is where Perrotta's tale glows with the hot light of having spent time in the trenches in league with the characters who are convinced they can beat the game. Some of the gambles, both won and lost, are every bit as dramatic in Perrotta's hands as the races on which they ride.

It becomes clear, as the journey of the book unfolds, that Perrotta's love affair with the sport can be best described as eternal. He loves it, warts and all, and it is the warts that give *Racetracker* that rarest gift for the reader – the rich entertainment of a true story well told.

--Jay Hovdey

Burlington, Vermont
August 31, 1955

On the fourteen-inch screen of my grandfather's black and white television, the horses and jockeys approaching the starting gate look like toys, hard to compare to Roy Rogers's Trigger or Gene Autry's Champion, or even my favorite, Hopalong Cassidy's Topper, handsome as he is in full color on my school lunch box. Grandpa is content in his easy chair with the vibrating seat, smoking a cigar and it's no secret that my Dad is excited, sipping a can of Pabst Blue Ribbon, he and I parked on the couch while he explains:

"Nashua's the better one, I think, that's him with Arcaro, even if Swaps did beat him in the Derby, and Swaps didn't even show up for the Preakness and the Belmont, but a match race always goes to the horse in front and Swaps is all speed, since that's how they train them in California."

He's on the edge of the couch as the horses leave the starting gate.

"Oh boy oh boy," says my Old Man.

"Oh boy oh boy," says I, unaware of what will become a permanent shift in my perspective.

I.

"MAMAS, DON'T LET YOUR BABIES GROW UP TO BE COWBOYS / LET 'EM BE DOCTORS AND
LAWYERS AND SUCH..."

--WILLIE NELSON

My friend David Milch likes to quote Mark Twain: "Every man I ever met,
I met on the river." To me, the racetrack was that place, my river.

For most, the racetrack world is sometimes quaint, sometimes mysterious, and though often confusing, a nonetheless fascinating niche of the
world at large. It can offer an occasional amusement or diversion from
the somber business of everyday life, much like a circus or a carnival, with

pretty ponies, jugglers and clowns living a gypsy-style existence that one might never imagine rational people embracing as a serious avocation.

Hopefully, when introduced to this alternate universe, the reader will gain some understanding of how many an ordinary citizen makes that conscious decision to shuck the "real" world and spend a lifetime at the track, rising before sunrise in order to hurry off to this place where individuality is its own reward, where one's limitations are set only by oneself, and where the center of the universe becomes... a horse.

The reader will find plenty of stories on the following pages describing practices "outside the law," strictly speaking. They took place in a time when the climate of horse racing could be likened to the Wild West of the American frontier. As in the land of the Cowboys and Indians, racing was exciting and mysterious, full of danger and romance, style and secrecy, and for those reasons the sport has always held its own cachet among those who seek to escape the mundane.

Of course, that was then, and this is now... and my spinning of these yarns is neither intended to condone nor condemn any rule-breaking which took place outside normal societal standards, but merely to enlighten and entertain the reader with the idea that they happened, and in their moment were tolerated as clever ploys, just part of the game, like bootleggers during Prohibition. To put it in perspective, most of these tales took place in an era when no one wore seatbelts, you could smoke anywhere you wanted and no one even thought twice about asking the bartender for a "to-go" cup to take their martini on the road. It was a time when everyone "knew" when someone was taking an edge, but no one cared to prove it.

As a microcosm of the world at large, horse racing contains proportionally just the same amounts of good and evil, nobility and crudeness, altruism and villainy as the rest of the planet.

Yet for some lovers of the sport, unwilling to admit its flaws like an ardent admirer denying his beloved's pock-marked complexion, horseracing is and always has been a noble sport of kings, undertaken with high-born notions of lords and ladies, pure and grandiose, dedicated to blind and steadfast devotion to the noble beast. To some the acres encompassing the track are as much a sacred piece of ground as the Vatican.

Closer to the truth, yes, racing can be a sport of kings and the privileged, but more likely it picks up its a share of beggars and bums, rascals and scallywags along the way, depending with whom you're rubbing elbows at any given time.

Such is the nature of swiftly passing time, as one day I was a kid "bringing in the hay" on the farms of Monmouth County, New Jersey, only to find myself a lifetime later having broken bread and shed tears with an amazing troupe of characters hereafter to be referred to, with affection, as "racetrackers."

Until I turned fifteen, my family lived in one of a few country homes surrounding Armand Hammer's Shadow Isle Farm near the village of River Plaza, New Jersey, where the international tycoon raised his champion Black Angus cattle. A dozen of them wandered the acres surrounding our house and once they knew you, you could walk among them just like you can a herd of horses. No barbed wire guarded those fields, only the two strands of electrified wire that cordoned the perimeter, and we delighted in finding ways to dupe visiting city-kids into touching them and getting a scary but harmless jolt.

The cattle fields were our playground and we became skilled at the art of "cow chip tossing"... a farmer's sport of flinging the piles of dried manure like they were Frisbees.

Hammer was best known for heading the Occidental Petroleum Company during the early days of the Libyan oil boom and reputedly key to much of America's negotiations during those tense Cold War days. He whisked off to Russia in his private plane during the '60s and 70's to repair international relationships between the east and west and was either a hero or at the center of Cold War espionage, depending on whose version you believe. He let us kids fish off his dock on Shadow Lake and swim in his pool at the farm, so he was okay with us.

Many hooked on horseracing refer to it as being "bitten by the bug" or "getting it in your blood," and my personal involvement with the track wasn't fostered by any particular interest in horses, since I was a cow-guy, but rather that it was the best (and only) place to gamble in those days.

Actually, horses were hardly ever my cup of tea as a kid. I took riding lessons from old lady Armstrong at her Shoestring Stables in Middletown, but I soon lost enthusiasm for the equestrian sports as she constantly berated me for talking too much and at one point bluntly told me I'd be better off taking up boating than trying to master horses.

So much for positive reinforcement.

Credit or blame for the gambling affinity, however, goes to my old man, a mild-mannered physician who was known for his soothing bedside manner. He found the track a respite from the stress of the operating room at Riverview Hospital in Red Bank and took most of his Wednesdays and Saturdays every spring, summer and fall at Monmouth Park and the other Jersey racecourses.

My dad grew up in Burlington, Vermont, where racing in those days consisted of a weekly sweepstakes on TV run by the IGA supermarket chain and a fortnight of harness heats at the Chittenden County Fair held in nearby Essex Junction every August. Where he and his brothers and sisters got the inclination remains a mystery, but since all my cousins are also confirmed track junkies, I have to imagine there is a genetic link somewhere.

The Jersey Shore area was pastoral, sparsely populated and many of the local horsemen were Dad's patients, welcoming us to farm visits on the weekends as he had more than likely set a broken arm or delivered one of their kids.

The film version of Frank Loesser's *Guys and Dolls* was released in 1955, staring Hoboken boy Frank Sinatra and there couldn't have been a better advertisement for horseracing. Monmouth Park, Garden State and Atlantic

City were all quality meets and the "tops" from New York shipped down regularly for stakes races, capturing the imagination of the local populace hoping for the adrenaline rush of an anticipated gamble in the company of a Nathan Detroit or a Sky Masterson.

Housewives and gas station attendants alike saved up all year to have "action" money for Monmouth. Even Helen who ran the snack bar at the beach club had a bet runner, and she guaranteed to get your wagers down for the Daily Double if you put up your picks and your cash by noon.

Post time at Monmouth was a genteel two P.M., allowing folks to hit the beach for a few hours with the family or put in a half-day at work before fabricating their excuses for an afternoon absence and even miss the business traffic on the way home since the races didn't finish until after six.

One random Saturday in June when I was maybe fourteen my father decided I could pass for the requisite sixteen and join him on the grandstand apron where he preferred to observe the action, eschewing the jacket and tie crowd he was with on a daily basis, indulging his alter ego as an incognito fan in khakis and a golf shirt.

Keep in mind that Dr. Perrotta wore a tie to dinner even at home when we ate at the kitchen table.

Something many racing fans have in common is that they first tagged along to the races with a parent or grandparent, and cashed the first bet they ever placed, or had placed for them, like the race had been fixed just for them. Mine was exactly that and came on that summer day at Monmouth Park on the back of a horse named Parka, trained by the classic horseman and Hall of Famer Jimmy Croll whose path I would come to cross many times thereafter.

I once tried to figure out how many races I must have watched since that day in June at Monmouth with my dad, the day I "broke my maiden." Closest I can come is somewhere in excess of 50,000. That constitutes a lot of ground covered and most of it observed through 10x50 binoculars.

The majority of those races would be ordinary in the scope of things, and most of them deservedly forgotten, save the instances where I either had a large bet riding or had the chance to observe true greatness, but as they say, "you never forget your first time."

I think I netted about fifteen bucks, just enough to open the door to a gambling life.

II.

"A MAN WHO DOESN'T MAKE A BET EVERY DAY MIGHT BE WALKING AROUND LUCKY AND NOT EVEN KNOW IT."

--VARIOUSLY ASCRIBED TO SINGER/PHILOSOPHER JIMMY DEAN AND OTHERS

Once that door was open, so to speak, it never closed. My high school was for boys-only, run by the DeLaSalle Christian Brothers in Lincroft, New Jersey, and built on the site of the old Greentree-Whitney farm. It housed students in racehorse barns that had been converted to classrooms and it still had an overgrown one-mile Thoroughbred track lurking at its center. C.B.A. established itself early on in the sport of track and field, developing scores of All-American runners, all of whom trained in the same covered track where Greentree champions Twenty Grand, Devil Diver and Tom Fool had their early gallops for the classic trainers Jimmy Roe and John Gaver, Sr.

It's most likely that the spirit of long-gone thoroughbreds quietly seeped into our pores in those barns as more than a few of us ended up lifers in the horse game, some as trainers or track administrators, plenty turning lifetime gamblers and although maybe not all that reputable, at least a furlong better than the two who were missing from class reunions because they were fugitives from murder charges. Rumor had it that one did his wife's lover in with an axe. If only he'd gone to the track and cashed a bet...

The year my fifteenth birthday and Easter vacation coincided, my parents splurged on a week and a half at the Rockefeller family's Dorado Beach Resort in Puerto Rico. The brochure boasted of sandy beaches and balmy sunsets, tropical drinks with umbrellas and girls in bikinis, but the hotel casino was what caught my eye.

I studied up on roulette, read everything I could find in the library on odds and betting systems, spending time during math classes working on my strategy, and with at least as much resolve as Ivanovich in Dostoyevsky's *The Gambler*, I went south, set on beating the wheel.

Resort casinos in the Caribbean were merely entertainment for the guests, not Vegas-style caverns intent on emptying your pockets. And in the way that bars in France feel about the drinking age, in Puerto Rico they're not all that concerned about how old the players might be.

The first night there, we wandered to the tiny casino after dinner, where there might have been a half-dozen blackjack tables, a couple of craps tables and a pair of roulette wheels, all manned by slick-looking guys in tuxedos. I feigned ignorance of every game as I let my old man instruct me on the finer points of craps and blackjack.

Sean Connery had already imprinted my generation with the image of the coolest cat ever... "Bond... James Bond," and I imagined myself trading judo-chops with bad guys and seducing some of those sultry vixens under the tropical moonlight.

"Don't take insurance, don't split anything but aces or eights. Don't play the props or the 'Don't Pass' and remember, the casino has an edge at every game."

Dad didn't even consider roulette and scoffed at the suckers trying to beat the wheel of fortune.

In craps the house edge comes from "craps" itself, the expression for when the dice come up two ones or one-two or a pair of sixes. In blackjack it comes from the tie hand when they don't have to pay you, even when you have a perfect 21.

"To push is not to lose," the dealers say, smiling but not mentioning that it's also not to win.

And in roulette, their edge comes from the zero and the double zero, making the simple odds against you actually 37 to 1, rather than the 35 to 1 they pay on those rare instances when you are lucky enough to have the little white ball fall in the slot with your number.

"Take the even-money chances and raise your bets when you have their money," said my old man as he scooped his winnings from the blackjack table. He and mom eventually lost interest and when they decided to head to bed, I promised to "be along shortly." Of course, had I lost my stake right there and then, most of the stories that follow this one wouldn't be here and I'd have been doomed to a boring, respectable life.

I stuck with my resolve to play red or black, progressing my bets when I was ahead, sticking to basics and the couple of hundred that I ended up in front after a week of ups and downs merely served to reinforce my conviction that "it ain't gambling if you know what you're doing."

I went back to Jersey feeling like I'd uncovered a long-lost formula for alchemy.

Guys who are inclined to gamble seem to gravitate toward each other, and during the school year when Monmouth was dormant, those of us who did would find a way to make it to the harness track at Freehold.

It was close, only a dozen miles away, and the Standardbreds or "sulkies" carried us for gambling action until "flat racing" at Monmouth re-opened late in June and we would have more betting capital from summer jobs.

The more we hung at the fence at Freehold, the more my pal Peter became convinced that the drivers were our edge in a game not altogether on the level and he studied them accordingly, deciding that one named Howie Camden was tipping someone off when he was "live" by switching the whip to his left hand as the horses passed the stands for the post parade.

Coincidence or true conspiracy, we made a few good hits when those horses came in and were sure we had found the key to the mint, contriving a way to cut classes regularly whenever he was driving. It also probably didn't hurt our chances that Camden was one of the best from the Stanley Dancer school of harness drivers and had a couple of world records on his resume. Howie was probably just left-handed.

My father had little or no interest in Standardbreds, but he began to take me with him and his friend Sal on their Saturday treks to bet on the Thoroughbreds at Garden State or Atlantic City or Aqueduct, all tracks only an hour or so drive from home.

Sal Viati was an older guy who owned a popular tavern in town, off the boat from Italy about thirty years but he still spoke with an accent so thick you couldn't understand him most of the time, and he was strictly a numbers player who didn't even buy a Racing Form.

Dad, on the other hand, spent hours studying the Racing Form and was a damn good handicapper, so it about drove him insane when Sal would hit a big Daily Double or an exacta playing "seven an' ah-six-ah, six-ah an' ah-seven-ah." His favorite numbers. "Look, Doc, I'm-ah got'em again-ah!"

Or another crony, Adam Kretowicz, who went to the races mainly for the social aspect, prospecting for clients for his real estate brokerage and principally played names. Adam was pure Polish and proud of it, playing anything that hinted at that ethnicity. He'd cash big on names like Warsaw Princess or Gdansk Gal and have my old man talking to himself.

When Monmouth opened for the summer in June, we'd have to drive to the train station in Red Bank every evening after dinner and get a "Telly" as soon as it hit the newsstand. Entries were made the day before, not two or three days out like they are nowadays, and for horseplayers it was like opening a Christmas present, guaranteed a surprise or two in every issue.

Racing and boxing were the two sports the Morning Telegraph specialized in and we were fans of both. It was the eastern counterpart to the Daily Racing Form until the two papers merged in the 80's, leaving the Form sole possessor of the role of horseplayers' "Bible."

It always struck me as funny that my old man and his pals had to make a clandestine trip to the barbershop on the way to the track to pick up passes.

You'd think a Doctor and a guy who owned a successful restaurant could afford the price of admission but I guess to those who grew up during the Great Depression, they considered the four bucks it cost to get into the clubhouse might be better invested at a mutuel window where it at least had a chance to turn into something significant, and besides, it was the principle of the thing.

Hard to figure how barbers got the franchise on holding racetrack passes...

During the summer of my sixteenth year I was a busy guy, saving up for my first car and splitting my time between farm work, cutting and stacking hay, and bell-hopping at a venerable hotel in Sea Bright, New Jersey called the Peninsula House, another bastion of upper-class chic on the order of The Breakers in Palm Beach or the Del Coronado near southern California's beachside track, Del Mar.

The "P" House has long since burned down, but in those days it was top-shelf for summer lodging. Huge porches and Atlantic Ocean breezes gave respite from the stifling city heat of New York and Newark. Guys in seersucker suits bought gin and tonics for those silly New York virgins Springsteen later sang about.

I was the kid with the crew cut who schlepped suitcases, pocketing half-a-buck tips and phone numbers of all the cute girls one could hope to meet. It was kind of like fishing in a stocked pond.

Checking in for the season was one of the many guests who lived in the city but liked to call the hotel home for the summer (known in Jersey as going "down the Shore") and who brought along his son Danny, my age, and the key to this particular tale is that you can get a license to work at the track when you're sixteen. And the main reason jockeys look so young? They are.

Danny's old man, "Hap" Donnelly, was a Racing Commissioner, accounting for how his son came to be a member of that elite Monmouth Park valet parking squad, an ultra well-paid platoon of car-jockeys who had "connections."

The Commissioner took a liking to me, since I was a clean-cut working stiff and pretty soon he gave me an endorsement of sorts with track management, thus providing me entree to my first "real" job on the track where I got licensed as a hotwalker for the backstretch in the morning and as an usher for the admissions department during race-time, allowing me to retire from farm work and bell-hopping and rub elbows with real jockeys and trainers in the track kitchen.

The trainer's preliminary instructions for apprentice hotwalkers: "Lookit, kid. See that clock? Take this horse's lead shank and keep turning left when you get to the end of the shedrow until the big hand's pointing straight up... "

That's it -- the principal talent required is knowing which way is left.

For some, the hotwalker's job is an entryway, a stepping stone into the world of the backstretch and for sure the job that every great and most every not so great horse trainer started out with. It's the entry-level job at the track that fresh candidates line up for at the stable gate of every track each morning before dawn. You'd think a slight premium should be due those who have been around the block before and are reasonably sober over those totally inexperienced, but it's a one-size-fits-all type of position, mainly owing to the lack of technical knowledge required.

For others, hotwalker is the lifetime landing spot, a destination that brings little recognition, no glory and certainly few financial rewards to speak of.

Just about anybody that works at the track and amounted to anything started by walking "hots," and if you haven't been stepped on, bitten or kicked by a racehorse, likely you'll never develop the needed empathy required to become a true racetracker.

It has stayed with me all my adult life, making me suspect the true qualifications of anyone professing racetrack expertise without the hotwalker box ticked off on their resume.

Sometimes I imagine I can still feel the outline of that black and blue welt the size of a hand, just about covering my right shoulder blade, left by one of Charlie Sanborn's two-year-olds that first summer at Monmouth.

One thing you never do get on a farm is the tactile essence of the racetrack, the sounds and the smells and sights only witnessed on the backstretch from well before dawn on into the night... the "tuh-tuh, tuh-tuh, tuh-tuh" of hoofbeats as early gallopers glide by in near darkness or the crack of a rider's whip as they urge one on in a workout.

The track "kitchen" is what each facility refers to its own dining hall, the cafeteria or employee's eating place where the people who make their living taking care of race horses will always end up at some point in the day.

As Napoleon noted, "An army marches on its stomach," and the backstretch crew on the racetrack is no different. Trainers, grooms and hotwalkers, jockeys and exercise people and owners all pass through the kitchen at sometime during the morning, be it for a quick coffee before their day begins, pre-dawn, or during one of the intermissions of training time that come when harrows smooth the track surface, simply called "the break."

More than just a dining hall, most track kitchens do some part in funneling that life-blood called cash into the system, turning over payroll or personal checks and extending whatever credit may be appropriate to those who've established it. The kitchen is also one of those great symbols of equality in racing, where well-heeled owners and down-at-their-heels stable workers share Formica-topped tables and eat off cafeteria trays.

I've visited most of them, but the one at Oaklawn Park in Hot Springs, Arkansas should be the standard to measure all others by. You could have dinner there and the fried catfish would probably be better than you can find in any local restaurant.

Breakfast is the most important meal on the backstretch since all the action there begins before dawn and lasts until they close the track around ten or ten-thirty to prepare it for the days' racing.

Richard Anderson, known as "The Frenchman," was the proprietor of a number of kitchens at Monmouth, Atlantic City and Hialeah. His advice to "Eat your betting money, but never bet your eating money," became a rule that savvy racetrackers come to live by.

To this day I have difficulty passing the racetracker's standard, a bacon-egg-and-cheese sandwich on a hard roll. It'll warm you on a chilly morning and you'll get it wrapped in tinfoil the same way at Keeneland or Belmont or Arlington or Santa Anita.

Since the hotwalker's main responsibility is to walk the recently exercised horse until it is suitably "cooled out" which usually takes about thirty minutes, allowing the animal a few sips of water each round and then holding it for the groom during a bath, it's a perfect occupation for anyone seeking a low stress occupation. The Monmouth backstretch used to be well populated with teachers on their summer hiatus.

Holding horses for the vet or blacksmith or while the trainer and his assistant do a "leg check" of each of their charges also comes under the list of hotwalker's duties. Washing water buckets and feed tubs, raking the shedrow and sprinkling it with water to keep down the dust are a few more tasks to be done before they quit for the day, usually well before noon.

The mechanical version of the hotwalker, designed to eliminate the human, may work for cheap but it can't tell if a horse is tying-up (cramping) or getting his leg over the shank, and you won't find them around the Old School trainers.

Truth be known, a kid of sixteen who likes to gamble will do anything to get in the track for free...

III.

"I'M SHOCKED... SHOCKED TO FIND THAT GAMBLING IS GOING ON IN HERE!"

--CAPTAIN RENAULT (CLAUDE RAINES) FROM *CASABLANCA*

When the original Monmouth Park opened in 1870, it ran a successful summer race meet with few interruptions until 1894, when the good people of New Jersey decided that legal gambling was the wage of sin and a state prohibition on betting put the track out of business.

After WW II businessman Amory L. Haskell, textile magnate Philip Iselin and a bunch of friends decided their favorite indulgence had been unjustly vilified and set out in June of 1946 to resurrect the resort area track. Haskell is the man the million-dollar event held there each August is named after. It catches a bunch of good three-year olds and occasionally the Kentucky Derby winner as they all try to keep alive their hopes of becoming the sophomore champion.

Haskell also held a major steeplechase event every fall on his estate in Middletown called the Monmouth Hunt, attracting ten thousand tailgaters to half a dozen races for a non-betting outdoor party. The Hunt became so popular in the 80's that it would actually out-draw the "real" races at Monmouth Park on the few occasions they ran the same weekend. Technically there's no betting, but folks run their own pools and it's not that hard to find a bookmaker if you really need to back a live one.

Steeplechase and Hunt races, where the horses run undulating courses and jump fences or obstacles, are not as popular in this country as they are in Ireland, England and France, but if you want excitement either as a rider or a fan, they're hard to beat. All the steeplechase riders I ever knew had a fairly eccentric nature, likely due to the number of times they came off their horse and landed on their head.

The hunt races are longer than those on the "flat," usually at least two or two and a half miles, and follow the lay of the land, over hill and dale with fences either fixed or made of brush, and the ones in Europe can have huge fields, sometimes as many as thirty horses. The National Steeplechase and Hunt Association oversees the sport in the U.S. and their events at Fair Hill, New Jersey, the Horse Park in Lexington, Kentucky, and at Saratoga determine their Eclipse Award winner.

The Cheltenham Festival in Gloustershire, England attracts some of the largest crowds of any sporting event in that country as the Irish take on the Brits and both bet with reckless abandon. It is held on the week of St. Patricks Day each March and those who fancy jumpers consider it their Mecca, lining up ten deep at the bookies betting queue and every year without fail the Irish land a coup.

Understandably, much of the excitement comes from watching the spills, and in some races there will be only one or two horses to finish with a rider on their back.

My grandparents on my mother's side emigrated at the turn of the century, along with many of the other Irish and English who came to take jobs as domestic help. They landed in Rumson, New Jersey on a lovely piece of land on the banks of the Navesink River called the Borden Estate, named after the retired Army General who owned it.

My grandfather Tom Pratt had made a natural transition from his Old Country occupation of carriage driver to that of chauffeur as folks traded their horse-drawn rigs for automobiles. Part of his duties still included driving the General and his guests to the Hunt meets in vintage carriages stored on the estate.

Grandmother Johanna's twin sister Mary and her husband Joe Clancy came along as part of the package. Uncle Joe was a former jump-rider in Ireland and trained forty steeplechase horses for the General. Broken up badly from spills during his riding career, he needed the aluminum crutches braced to his arms to get around and stayed fortified with John Jameson's best whisky.

I'd have to visit him occasionally with my mother and between the heavy brogue and the drink, everything he said sounded like "Arrahghhgh, gash ganaff ahgh," to a little kid and was more than slightly horrifying. I saw him on and off for at least ten years and I don't think I ever understood a word he said. But Uncle Joe had a reputation as a top man with a horse and brought his jump-riders over from Ireland and schooled them in the old country way of training.

Steeplechase has never really caught on in this country as a betting game and the fact that the horses fall fairly often distresses the fans, so most young men and women seeking a career with horses will quickly gravitate to flat racing. Other than teaching the horses to jump fences, the basic principles of horsemanship are the same for flat or steeplechasing; get them in condition and keep them happy and healthy. The transition to flat racing isn't that difficult.

During the period of that betting prohibition and through the early years of the twentieth century, Monmouth County served as training grounds for many of the top New York stables. Two of Uncle Joe's best riders were the Harraway brothers, Albert and Tom. They later went on to become a couple of the Jersey circuit's better trainers and at one time or another I walked hots for both. Tom was the more accomplished of the two and trained influential stakes horses at Monmouth and the Maryland tracks, including one notable colt named Talc that won a bunch of stakes races and made an excellent stallion.

Lots of green grass and plenty of hay and straw made the Monmouth county area ideal for private stables to prepare their racers to compete at their home tracks on Long Island.

Col. L.S. Thompson was one of the builders of the original Monmouth Park and established his Brookdale Farm about eight miles away in Lincroft. They had their own bleachers and on the occasional Sunday morning Dad would take me with him to watch horses breeze on the mile track.

That farm later became Brookdale Community College and for a couple of summers during the years I was a jockey agent I got a kick out of teaching a "Horseracing 101" course there. Turnout was pretty good and I'd have trainers and jockeys from Monmouth Park sit in, answering questions from the class. My favorite was when the little old lady asked me if gelding horses made any difference. My answer; "If they'd done it to me early enough I could have been at least Governor." She mulled it over for a few moments contemplation and smiled as she nodded in agreement... "I see..."

Within sight of the Atlantic Ocean and benefitting from the lovely ocean breezes, Monmouth was nirvana to summer expatriates in those days before air conditioning made summer heat and humidity of the city bearable. Those of us who lived there year-round took it for granted, but the "Bennies" from the city flocked to the beachfront like it was the cure to what ailed them.

Some of the wealthier families that could afford the huge summer homes in Monmouth Beach and Long Branch, Elberon and Deal also had a penchant for racehorses and the track's Clubhouse was a paradigm for fashions of the day.

Ladies always wore dresses to go racing; men wore suit and tie and usually a hat as well. Straw boaters, homburgs, fedoras and the occasional dandy in a Panama hat. No baseball caps...

The New York trainers liked to platoon their horses back and forth to the shore for a break and use the races there for "schooling" before returning to Long Island in the fall when purses were more lucrative. This is usually referred to in instructions to the jockey as "giving him an easy one" or "not beating him up," but shouldn't be considered in the same light as "holding" a horse intentionally to set him up for a bet.

They thought experience was the best teacher in those days, and tried to develop horses slowly as not to blow their minds before true talent had a chance to exhibit itself. Horses are creatures of habit and the long-term value of properly developing demeanor was valued much more than being "undefeated."

Only the rare and gifted horse will win at first asking in good company and jockeys were often instructed to tuck their horses in behind the field in order to allow them to feel some dirt thrown back in their faces, even horses they knew were good ones. Trainers felt that horses that went to the lead too soon could get "speed crazy" and never learn to rate or relax, rendering them ineffective in the longer "route" races where the big money was to be made and that was what they were doing, looking forward down the road toward that goal of eventually increasing their income.

Being in the right place at the right time usually trumps ability or intellectual superiority when it comes to moving ahead in life and such was my luck when during my second summer at the track I was offered the operator's job on the private elevator that serviced the exclusive Parterre section at Monmouth. That tiny conveyance only held about eight but it exited right at the door to the executive suite on the fourth floor.

My stellar clientele was not only the track owners, Philip and Betty Iselin, who were the embodiment of style and grace at the time, he in Saville Row chalk striped suits and she, adorned in Chanel, but included their huge circle of high society friends. Of course, they had their share of phonies and hangers-on, but for the most part it was a bunch with a lot of class and a lot of money to go with it.

These were the "guys" and "dolls" immortalized in Frank Loesser's play, and they were Damon Runyon's walking, talking racetrackers and rounders in the flesh. Each Saturday a sampling of Iselin's entourage showed up for a day of racing, wining and dining in the private Parterre boxes that overlooked the track, that era's version of the super-boxes and executive suites found in ballparks and stadiums today. It was a dream-walk to a kid with an active imagination, schmoozing with celebrities and entertainers. I got to spend numerous four-floor elevator rides with the likes of David Willenz, the New Jersey Attorney General who prosecuted and brought Bruno Hauptmann to justice in the Lindbergh kidnapping trial, a very serious man with a wry sense of humor, and his most unlikely pal Irving Caesar, the famous songwriter of *Tea for Two, Swanee,* and believe it or not, *Just a Gigolo.* He penned over 700 songs, many of which became modern standards.

I most looked forward to Mr. Caesar's visits, as he embodied Broadway and the entertainment world, both of which would be fascinating to any high school kid, then or now. He was about five-foot four, silver-grey hair parted down the middle and always sported a three-piece suit and a bowtie, with a white carnation in his lapel and the stub of a cigar in his mouth.

About the only way you could get him to break out in song was to say "hello" to him, and with any luck he'd do a dance routine, too.

Phil Iselin was tight with other big shots like "Sonny" Werblin, best known for exploits like his coup in acquiring the immortal Joe Namath to quarterback his New York Jets football team and later building Giants' Stadium and the Meadowlands race track, turning that worthless swampland into a goldmine. Iselin and Werblin each had stables of their own and it wasn't a secret that they valued a trip to the winner's circle right up there with their biggest business accomplishments, perhaps even more. No doubt all of that crew were tough businessmen to have acquired such success, but every one of them always had time for a few words with the kid who ran the elevator.

I never met the original Nicely Nicely or Nathan Detroit, but the source of their inspiration rode that lift with me on a weekly basis. No Sarah Brown or Harry the Horse, but Barry Brown and Harry the Hat for sure.

Charles Engelhard was the international mineral magnate who spurred Ian Fleming's imagination to create the character Goldfinger for one of his James Bond stories. He raced horses all over the world and was one of the richest men on the globe, so when he coughed a huge entourage jumped. Most of his horses raced in New York, but occasionally his trainer Mack Miller would send one down to Monmouth on a Saturday for an allowance or stakes race.

They didn't come any bigger in racing circles than Engelhard, who raced Halo and Hawaii and Tentam under his Craigwood Stable silks and won the English Triple Crown with the great Nijinsky. He may have been a harsh and ruthless businessman, but when he came to the track it was for a good time and he usually had it.

One particular Saturday at the end of June, his bodyguard told me I should bet everything I had in my pockets on a horse named Assagai -- "Send it in, kid..."

Assagai was trying stakes company for the first time, but he'd had one victory on the turf and they felt he was destined for greatness there and I sent it in at seven-to-one, (thank you very much for the winner). Obviously the bodyguard figured whatever I could afford to put through the windows wasn't going to have any effect on his odds. Assagai went on to win the United Nations Handicap and the Man o' War that year and ended up the Champion grass horse of 1966.

A huge advantage to the independence of running such a one-man operation as a private elevator is that you can hide your Morning Telegraph under the cushions of a bench on the bottom floor for consultation between ups and downs, well out of the scrutiny of prying eyes. Then it's only a matter of passing your bets to another one of the ushers working the private boxes on one of the in-between floors.

Every Saturday Steve Mermelstein would show up with his father and his father's friends. He was my age and another budding degenerate, bored stiff at hanging with a bunch of old guys, so we would handicap between races and bet together and chat up whatever girls were around, promoting them for the big social event of the summer known as the Charity Ball.

Steve and I "agreed to agree" on a horse in the feature every week and run a show parlay, which meant our horse only had to finish third but we'd carry every winning bet forward, taking nothing out until the end of the season if we made it that far.

He held the cash so I couldn't be tempted to get creative and blow it during the week and we went thirteen straight bets, rolling our four bucks into eight hundred-eighty before Walter Blum got left at the gate on a filly named Lady Pitt that was nine-to-five in the Monmouth Oaks and busted us out by running fourth. She'd go on to be Champion three year-old filly that year, but it didn't do us any good as we ripped up a pile of losing tickets and cursed whatever gambling gods were in charge of torturing young horseplayers.

Horses that run on the Saturday cards are obviously a different caliber than those filling the more mundane races during the week. The Saturday Maiden Special Weights, Allowance races and Stakes all had plenty of shippers from New York as Monmouth was considered the testing ground for quality of both horses and riders on the way up.

Besides Jorge Velasquez, we saw Sandy Hawley, Braulio Baeza, Angel Cordero, Jr., Jacinto Vasquez, Pete Anderson, Jean Cruguet and Heliodoro Gustines at Monmouth to ride future legends like Verbatim, Gallant Bloom, Ta Wee, Summer Guest, Alma North, and Majestic Light.

Plenty of the local riders were good enough for the big-time but had families and preferred to stay closer to home where they could be big fish in a smaller pond. You could count on Sam Boulmetis, Walter Blum, Phil Grimm and Frank Lovato or Mike Miceli for plenty of winners during the week and a few times on the weekend if they had the right horse.

If you were stuck going into the last race, the local knowledge dictated: "Go home with Culmone," and it seemed that Joe would bail us out more often than not.

As they say, "When the legend becomes fact, print the legend..."

Boulmetis and Blum both became stewards when they retired. Tracks often made ex-riders into officials, based on the "fox watching the hen-house" logic that they had probably either committed or witnessed every misdeed possible and would be able to easily spot an attempt to thwart the principles of racing. There were no steward's certification programs and their credentials came from the University of Life Experiences.

Johnny Rotz, Bill Boland and Bill Hartack also stepped into the Steward's Stand shortly after retiring from illustrious riding careers. All conceded that they were no angels but nonetheless dedicated themselves to their new vocations with evangelical zeal and served the sport well for decades.

I attended Steward's School at the University of Louisville in 2008 and Hartack was in my class, even though he'd been working as an official for twenty-five years. He had a wry, cynical wit and his questions always had a barb.

Former jocks can detect the most skillful rider holding a horse and see right through his excuses and it's easy to understand how some who had made those same transgressions themselves often made the best stewards although I did know a few over the years to become a bit self-righteous. Kind of a "born-again" thing...

The CIA also used this same methodology when it enlisted the most world's successful cocaine smuggler, John Pernell Roberts, to run guns to Nicaraguan rebels for them when they needed to overthrow that government.

The recount of Roberts' life in his autobiography, *American Desperado*, makes interesting reading, especially to us racetrackers who remember him owning and racing horses on the Florida circuit in the '80's and '90's under his Mefisto Stable colors. He may have been a bloodthirsty killer outside the gates, but hanging around the racing office, he was just one of the guys.

Jockeys, it is often said, are pound-for-pound the fittest and strongest of all athletes. I would wholeheartedly subscribe to this premise, with an addendum. Some of them are also mentally "men of steel."

Jockey autobiographies make fascinating reading and I have a few personal favorites including *Never Look Back* by Billy Pearson. A popular rider in the 1940s and 50s when filmmakers and movie stars frequented the track, Pearson was a close friend of John Huston and had a unique career. He took up pre-Columbian art as a hobby since his riding took him across the border often (racing in Tijuana) and managed to amass a valuable collection and considerable knowledge of what could only be considered an esoteric topic. Television loved sports stars and when Pearson got on "The $64,000 Question" quiz show, he made it right to the end and his final hurdle was on -- guess what? -- pre-Columbian art. He nailed the winning answer and took home the money, winning over a hundred thousand during his stint as a contestant, quite a pile of cash in those days.

Other riders' stories contain great life lessons in persistence and tenacity. Julie Krone stands 4-10½, but anyone who ever saw her ride knows she is not only the best woman jockey ever, she is simply one of the best jockeys ever... period. Her autobiography, *Riding For My Life* is fascinating reading, especially the chapter titled "Fights, Fights, Fights." Whenever we cross paths, I like to kid Julie about how I almost became her agent when she came to New Jersey and she ribs me right back that even I probably couldn't have slowed her down.

Read Jerry Bailey's *Against the Odds* or Garrett Gomez's autobiography and you'll quickly realize that the jockey's game isn't all fun and games.

The best ones often have to battle a multitude of demons on their way to success and the personal price isn't cheap.

Pete Axthelm's account tells of Steve Cauthen's incredible journey from minor-league Midwestern tracks first to Chicago and then on to New York where he broke every record. The story of his stardom and Triple Crown fame astride Harbor View Farm's Affirmed is entitled *The Kid*.

Steve's agent, Eddie Campbell, had a gift for spotting talented riders and teaching them their trade at an early age. Eddie was a true racetracker who took a pass on the big show, content to stay home with his family on the Ohio/Kentucky circuit, sending riders like Cauthen and Ronnie Hirdes on to Chicago or New York when he deemed them ready. An American racetrack classic, it's a story all horseracing lovers should read.

IV.

"MONEY WON IS TWICE AS SWEET AS MONEY EARNED."

--FAST EDDIE FELSEN (PAUL NEWMAN) FROM *THE COLOR OF MONEY*

Many of the friends I made during my stint at the University of Vermont became followers of the Grateful Dead on their concert tour, venturing to all parts of the country and were proud to be known as "Dead Heads."

I, on the other hand, became a "Dr. Fager-Head," cutting school to watch that super-horse win races from age two in '66 all the way through his epic year of 1968. A true devotee, I made it to almost half of his twenty-two starts, and never saw another horse cross the finish line in front of him.

Dr. Fager was disqualified and placed last in the field of four in the Jersey Derby when Manny Ycaza sawed off the field, nonetheless a real injustice since he could have pulled a beer wagon and still won by daylight. I was hooked forever as a Thoroughbred fan when I saw him romp home in the World's Playground at Atlantic City, the Cowdin and Champagne at Aqueduct and the Vosburgh, which he took twice, his second time in the final start of his career.

Funny enough, I don't think I ever bet on him, since his odds were always "prohibitive." Against three horses in the Whitney at Saratoga, he paid five cents on the dollar... an okay return on investment for bankers but no good for horse race gamblers.

The "Doctor's" accomplishment of capturing four titles in one season: Champion Handicap Horse, Champion Sprinter and Champion Grass Horse as well as Horse of the Year, plus setting the world record for a mile likely will never be repeated.

"Gentleman" Johnny Rotz could have ridden him one-handed in the '68 Roseben Handicap at Aqueduct when he whistled away from Tumiga and Diplomat Way at odds of 1 to 5. I'd hitchhiked down from Vermont for the race and when I cashed a daily double, I hopped a DC-3 flight out of LaGuardia to get back to college, and my folks were none the wiser.

Across the state from Garden State Park, about forty-five minutes drive with its own exit off the Expressway was the boutique meet at Atlantic City Race Track, founded after WWII by John Kelly, Sr., father of movie star Grace Kelly, who'd later become the Princess of Monaco. Some of Kelly's partners were Frank Sinatra, Bob Hope and bandleader Xavier Cugat and the track was known for frequent celebrity visits as well as a mobster hang-out long before Atlantic City became the gaming capital of the East.

Horsemen loved the one-mile turf course and for as long as the track was open, champion grass horses including Mongo, Parka, Assagai, Manila, Hawaii, Fort Marcy, and Mac Darmidia made at least one start there.

My favorite of Dr. Fager's performances was his victory in the 1968 United Nations Handicap at Atlantic City Race Course. The lot was full and my father and I had to park on a sidewalk when we went to see the "Doctor" make his only start ever on the grass carrying 134 pounds including Braulio Baeza against the previous years' grass champ Fort Marcy.

Odds-on, Dr. Fager took the lead at the start, went head-and-head for a mile and got passed mid-stretch but still came back to outgame Advocator, winning by a neck from a horse he had conceded twenty-two pounds.

Truckin, like the do-dah man indeed...

My college job in Vermont was another plum; cub sports reporter for the *Burlington Free Press* when I attended the University as a pre-med student, learning that an aversion to science would be a major obstacle to my ever becoming a doctor. But I felt right at home in the newsroom and was soon adopted by the veteran journalists. They taught me how to take my own action photos and how to develop them and I got daily bylines for stories on high school baseball, basketball, football and anything that even resembled a sport.

I've heard Vermont described as "nine months of winter and three months of bad skiing," and when the temperatures average well below zero for weeks at a time, you realize where they came up with that sentiment. Regardless of the weather, outdoor sports rule in Vermont, including cross-country skiing, ice fishing and snow-mobiling. When the maple syrup runs in the spring, even that gets competitive.

I can only blame the free lift pass that came along with my press credentials for giving me the incentive to ski my way out of school after a year. The Vietnam War was in full gear and I became prime draft bait, which didn't bother me that much, but horrified my father.

He'd spent a lot of time teaching me how to hunt and fish, and bought me my first shotgun when I was nine, so I had no fear of guns and thought nothing of a stint in the army, but he had been a Major in the Medical Corps during WW II and done front-line surgery on infantry men and was dead set against his only son being in the line of fire.

He quickly arranged for me to enroll at St. Michael's College in Winooski, Vermont, switching to an English major in their Liberal Arts program, and I resolved to have a career as a sportswriter.

As fortune would have it, the Draft Board took the whole military issue out of play when it went to a lottery system to select draftees and I drew number 231, which gave me about the same chance of being called by them as I did of getting a call from Brigitte Bardot.

The sports editor at the *Burlington Free Press* was a rough and tumble guy named Don Filion and his mast read, "Fillin' In." He was a prototype of the classic newspaper man portrayed in the movies, tough on the outside with a heart of gold and he provided great guidance and inspiration, even teaching me how to smoke and type without taking the cigarette out of my mouth, among the other acquired skills a good hack needed.

Racing was a viable and vibrant sport in those days and since I was the only one who knew the way to Green Mountain Park, and knew it well, Don appointed me as his racing editor. He took great pride in the fact that we correctly nailed the winner, Dancer's Image, ridden by Bobby Ussery, as my pick for the 1968 Derby winner.

Amazingly, only five years later I would become Ussery's agent.

For live racing action in Vermont you had but two choices. Blue Bonnet Raceway in Montreal was about two hours to the north across the Canadian border where the season alternated night races between harness horses and thoroughbreds, or Green Mountain Park in Pownal, Vermont, three hours to the south, which was owned by the Rooney family of Pittsburgh Steelers and Yonkers Raceway fame and also held a night venue.

Jonesing for action, we'd occasionally trek north, but even though it was a longer ride, we much preferred a road trip south to the domestic brand where you could find shippers from Suffolk, Rockingham or any New York track.

Green Mountain Park was one of those tracks that racetrackers love for the way it looks and smells and the way it makes you feel right at home.

Opened in the early '60's and nestled in a verdant valley near the conjunction of Vermont, New York and Massachusetts, it was ideally positioned in theory to pull bettors from a radius that included Saratoga and the New York Capital region of Albany about fifty miles to the west.

Unfortunately most of those fans must have been saving their money for the "Spa" and the crowds never materialized at Green Mountain, and it struggled along, converting to a greyhound track before finally shutting the doors forever in 1976, finally succumbing to pressure from animal rights groups who painted those races as dog-abuse.

Green Mountain joined Narragansett, Lincoln Downs and Rockingham Park as another of the great New England venues that didn't make it. Narragansett had just under 45,000 attendees back in the 1940's and Lincoln's big crowd of 35,000 in the early '50's overshadowed Green Mountain's 12,000 in 1965, so I guess the handwriting had been on the wall for a couple of decades as they closed one by one.

Another of the other reporters I looked up to as a mentor was a young guy from Cincinnati named Chris Hapner. He was only a few years older than me and when he eventually split town to take a job in Tampa I figured heading south made sense to me too and I began to seek opportunities in that direction.

After a year and a half at the *Free Press*, I came to the conclusion that I must certainly have acquired at least as much knowledge as guys who'd put in twenty years there, so I quit school, intent on chasing a job I'd got wind of with the *Palm Beach Post Times* in Florida. One of my Jersey pals agreed to make the drive with me, and the week after Thanksgiving, much to my parents' dismay, we beat it south, young men driving non-stop in pursuit of the Promised Land.

I found myself a cheap motel in Delray Beach with a couple of plastic flamingos on the front lawn and settled in to become a Floridian. I ate oranges off the tree and oysters on the half-shell and fished off the beach for pompano.

At the *Post Times* interview I passed muster and was offered a spot on the staff as a business reporter, giving me something to mull over. Did I want to change direction and start covering planning board meetings and traffic court? Fortunately or unfortunately, Tropical Park in South Miami opened Thanksgiving weekend, so I begged off starting the job until the following week, citing the importance of getting "settled in" to my new digs.

For quite a while I had been following the moves of a Suffolk Downs trainer named Tony Cataldi, a pretty slick conditioner who'd occasionally ship a live one in to Aqueduct to score at a big price. He was running a horse called Johnny Boy II in the last race at Tropical with New England's leading rider Tony DeSpirito up.

Namesake or not, Johnny Boy II was one of those consistent horses that always gave you a run for your money and I loved him, figuring he'd go off at a decent price, so I hit the highway to South Miami with nothing else on my mind but to bet on him. The $12.80 payoff price on the win end gave me a better than 5-1 boot to my gambling bankroll and suddenly the prospect of desk work on a business beat became dramatically less attractive when I left Tropical with over a grand in my stash.

I took a shot at Dania Jai-alai later that night, 'cause when you're lucky, you're lucky and you better keep at it until you're either fat or not lucky any more, and besides, it was on the way home. I parlayed three small quinellas and finished the day twenty-nine hundred ahead.

When I woke up the next morning feeling the glow of that invincibility of a young man who's got a pocket full of cash, I contemplated the future for a few hours before I made my call to the editor's desk, begging off... "Sorry but some pressing family business has come up."

The job I passed on paid a whopping hundred-sixty five bucks every two weeks--before taxes.

Vagabond life suited me fine, but I needed a good story line for my parents as my old man's patience was beginning to wane. He wanted me to pursue a profession and since I had already convinced him that the Fourth Estate was just that, soon I found myself back taking classes part-time at the University of Miami and gambling full-time.

Through a friend from Jersey I met half-a-dozen other young gambling degenerates just like myself, all Jewish guys from Manhattan, hipsters whose conversations were punctuated with "baby," or "far out," or "groovy," and I crashed with them in Miami until I could find a place of my own.

We wore bell–bottoms and white shoes, and Travolta's Tony Manero in Sat*urday Night Fever* was the role model for the part we all imagined we were playing.

Most of the guys worked boiler-room phone-sale jobs, pitching underwater real estate on the long-distance lines to folks in Wisconsin or Michigan or Ohio who had a dream of someday retiring to the beach. A couple of them were rich kids, going to school to beat the draft and enjoying the "sex, drugs and rock n' roll" lifestyle of South Florida, but it was the gambling culture that held us together like glue.

And to be sure, it was pretty much non-stop action we lived in, going to whatever pari-mutuel sport was open, playing gin rummy constantly and holding a poker or crap game once or twice a week for the college kids who drifted in on weekends.

Henry Penso was a plus sized Jewish kid from New York's lower east side and even to this day the best gin player I've ever seen, taking our money like we were his own personal ATMs. He was an mnemonist, possessing what's usually referred to as a photographic memory and it enabled him to remember every card coming out of the deck and calculate the likely contents of his opponent's hand. We all kept trying to beat him, but I came to refer to my sessions as "lessons," since I had to pay for everything I learned. Most guys he treated like fish, letting them win a little and lose a lot, but we were track buddies too, so he didn't fish out the pond and generally left me enough cash to stay in action.

At the end of the spring semester I was ready to head home to New Jersey, and the day before I was going to leave I took my '66 Mustang to one of the car dealers on 27ᵗʰ Ave. and sold it for 900 bucks.

Fortunately for me, Henry had a weakness for craps, and as they say, "the dice have no memory." We rolled the "devil's dominoes" that night and I got back $1,500 of my money that Henry had been holding from our weekly gin lessons. That gave me a bankroll for the summer up north and I planned to come back to finish my last year at U of M in the fall.

There were no casinos in Florida yet, but there was plenty of pari-mutuel action between Tropical, Hialeah and Gulfstream for thorough-breds, Pompano Park for Harness and the Greyhound racing action at Biscayne and Flagler, Miami Beach and Hollywood Kennel Clubs. The Jai Alai frontons in Miami and Dania did their thing five nights a week, putting on twelve games a night, mostly for packed houses.

Most of the time we struggled out of bed at the crack of noon to seek sustenance at Pumpernicks or Wolfies, the New York Deli-style joints that were open late and catered to the clubbing crowd. Sometimes breakfast was a reprise in the same place we might have ended up at late the night before, fresh from oversized speakers blaring Led Zeppelin, Stones or Beatles, Cream or Iron Butterfly, or maybe as mellow as Leonard Cohen, and occasionally when someone made a nice score and wanted to celebrate, we'd hit an upscale spot.

One January night I scored a grand at Miami Jai-alai and got to play the big shot, hosting a table of eight at the steakhouse around the corner from our digs in North Bay Village on the 79ᵗʰ Street causeway. Our timing was good too, since the following night three mobsters died in a "Scarface" shootout scene at the same table we had occupied only 24 hours before and it did occur to me that my luck had held up for more than one night.

Eventually my friend Michael and I moved out of "boy's camp" and found an apartment on Miami Beach where we could run our own "cut" poker game two nights a week, dealing twelve hours of five and seven-card stud from 6 p.m. to 6 a.m., establishing a steady clientele of car salesmen, well-heeled college kids, and action-junkie stockbrokers.

We provided the place, the cards and refreshments and did the dealing, taking a few bucks (our "cut") from each pot. We took turns sitting in as the game wound down and could usually extract a little from the tired players and the ones who were chasing a losing night. It provided rent money and a steady bankroll for our daily trips to Tropical, Hialeah or Gulfstream, since those guys trying to get "even" usually just get "even worse..."

South Florida was rapidly developing, undergoing a growth explosion, and when the Seminole Indians finally got their first break in the gaming business it was for bingo.

The Seminoles are the only Native American tribe never to sign a peace treaty with the U.S. government but they had been scraping out a living out on Highway 441 in West Hollywood selling tax-free cigarettes and hand-made trinkets and wrestling alligators until they won the right to open a bingo hall in 1979.

It took them until '94 to get into the casino business as a joint venture with the Hard Rock corporation and since their "sovereign nation" status exempts them from taxes, they suddenly made so much money that they were able to buy a majority position in the public company and now the tribe owns Hard Rock International. Their thousand room hotel stays full of folks there to party and play slots, poker and table games, but it all started with tax-free cigarettes and bingo. And wrestling alligators.

To serious gamblers, bingo is basically a game for little kids or old folks to play at the church auditorium. You'll never see ESPN covering a bingo game. But poker is a different story and it's an American tradition, familiar to everyone from soda jerks to presidents.

The key to winning at poker is often the same as the key to winning in life, being that sometimes the hands you fold can ultimately prove more important than those you play out. Knowing when to dump that pair of aces when the odds have turned against you will put you way ahead of that guy who feels he has to hang on to them until the bitter end.

Most gambling pursuits are ongoing games, meaning that when one hand is over they'll deal another and when one race is over, another will follow. As the judge says in court, "Next case..."

We'd start in early evening and play all night and during a memorable marathon session, one of the regulars in our game, a car-guy named Kevin, kept leaving the table to call the hospital in Coral Gables where his wife was all set to have their first baby. He figured there was no point to just hanging out in a hospital waiting room when he could be missing his chance to get lucky.

Kevin was what poker players refer to as a "calling station," meaning that he would play most hands to a showdown even if he had little or no chance, necessitating that luck intervene and bail him out when he did win a hand. Unfortunately, luck doesn't usually work that way and on the night in question he was stuck for over a grand, desperate to get it back before he had to split to the delivery room.

About dawn when he finally tapped out for three thousand and had to quit, he called the hospital to say he was on his way, and they told him to take his time, he already had a new baby daughter.

Sundays were problematic except during football season since parimutuels like horse and dog racing and Jai-alai weren't permitted to operate on the Lord's Day in Florida until 1986 and we had to invent ways to gamble.

Several of the guys who didn't have jobs would cash in a pint at the blood-bank on a regular basis to supplement their gambling bankrolls, but at one time or another all of us were on a first name basis with most of Miami's finest pawnbrokers.

Since a lot of the time we were passing the same money around among ourselves, part of the trick to staying ahead was running up enough new guys, the "fresh blood," who were "learning" how to bet and utilize them to provide cash flow until they either gave up or realized how expensive the lessons were.

An early Fall Sunday afternoon my degenerate friends and I got the inspiration to back Henry as our two-legged horse in a head-to-head eating contest at the Dunkin Donuts on US 1 in Coral Gables.

Henry downed two dozen crème-filled, and washed them down with a quart of milk, easily putting away the red-neck punk from Homestead and starting a weekly competition that drew more sharpshooters than Billy the Kid on Saturday night and generated a healthy betting pool of a couple of hundred in cold cash every time.

He whipped all comers for about a month, until the NFL season got started, which was a good thing anyway as Henry was starting to get nauseous at the smell of deep-fried dough.

Every weekday afternoon plus Saturday they ran nine races at Tropical Park and we'd catch at least the last three. After the New Year we'd follow those horses across town to Hialeah and around 10 p.m. each evening we'd head for Miami Jai-alai over near the airport for the last three games.

In any pari-mutuel sport, the best quality (and best betting opportunities) are the races or games at the end of the card, since they're the best horses or the best competitors and those usually perform more closely to form than do lesser ones, the idea being to keep the bettors there to the end so they will either keep betting the money they're ahead or keep trying to recoup their losses.

Pari-mutuel gambling establishments don't care who wins or loses, since it's not you against the house and they are simply taking a commission (hence "take-out") on every bet and the amount they make depends on the total bet by all players, which is referred to as the "handle." If all the money bet at the end of the day totals a million dollars, the house has deducted approximately two hundred thousand in "take-out" from which it pays taxes and contributes to the purses. The balance (roughly half) is their operating profit. If they handle a million, it's about a hundred grand to their bottom line.

The difference between tracks or other types of pari-mutuel gambling games is that you are continually playing against all the other players and the house is taking that cut, as opposed to when you play in a casino, it's them against you and although there's no "cut," they always have a slight advantage over the player on every bet. They can win all the money and clean out the players, while the pari-mutuels are simply re-distributing the betting capital while taking a commission. Thus, casino gambling can be viewed as "zero-sum" gaming, whereas racing's pari-mutuels are "non-zero-sum" since the house never ends up with all the money at the end of the day.

The three-walled court they play Jai-alai on is called a fronton and the Miami season traditionally opened the day after Christmas. When the game was at its peak, the joint was packed to the gills with tourists every night, but you could get in free after the ninth game and always find a great seat near the front where someone who came early had tapped out and left. My crew preferred the first few rows right at the screen, in order to be sure the players could hear our exhortations or entreaties or insults as the case might have been.

Jai-alai originated in the Basque region of Spain and was first introduced as a gambling sport in Florida in 1935; four years after horse and dog racing were legalized to stimulate the economy following the Great Depression.

It's a version of three-wall handball and the pros can literally run six feet up a vertical side-wall, catch and throw the ball (*pelota*) from the basket-like *cesta* attached to their hand before landing back on their feet.

The incredible speed of the ball (over 100 mph) and the athleticism of the players, along with the quickly changing chance of any number combination winning makes Jai-alai possibly the most exciting game of all to gamble on.

It never did catch on as a big money betting game as the win pools are too small and any significant wager like a bet as small as fifty dollars to win on any team might make them the favorite, skewing the odds, but for low-budget grinders who like to play quinellas and perfectas there's nothing better.

Jai-alai has always been an "entertainment-first" type of gambling, carried on the back of the customer primarily looking for a night of fun. It isn't at all like the racetrack, where you could bet a lot and still not influence the odds since the pools are large, but as they say, "it's a living."

The second season I was in Miami I had a number system that I came up with based on the new scoring method they started that season called the "Super Seven" which doubled points after the first round. I realized it gave an edge to the higher post positions for exacta payoffs and came up with a set of numbers to play blind, meaning it didn't matter to me who the players were.

All the guys I hung with had their own *cestas* and we'd play a few times a week at Mendiola's fronton in South Miami where they let amateurs play with a rubber ball so as not to kill each other with the goatskin rocks the pros use. We'd play straight twelve point games for a buck a point and pretend to be Basques, soon realizing how hard it is and understanding how maybe those guys weren't stiffing when the ball pops out of their *cesta*.

The competitors in the late games were mostly Basques and the best in the world all came to play the Miami fronton. To them it was the same as playing baseball in Yankee Stadium or tennis at Wimbledon. The top is the top.

Churruca, Juaristi, Asis, Chimela, Arriaga, Mendiola and Bengoa were such fierce competitors you didn't have to worry much about them fixing the games, they were too proud and just wanted to beat each other.

To the pride of all my Jewish gambling pals, one of the best players in the world turned out to be a kid named Joey Cornblit. Jai-alai players go by their last name, but he used Joey. Go figure.

My gambling system for Jai-alai was only about numbers, so it wouldn't matter that much to me if they did tie one up once in a while. Bettors always think the players screw up on purpose just when you need that point to win, but that's just part of the self-loathing perspective all gamblers subject themselves to occasionally and to some it's the only way they have to vent their pent-up frustration with luck or life in general.

I played only cold exactas with the system and for one season the patron saint of gamblers was in my corner as I'd walk in with about fifty bucks capital for the night and hit on at least one of the three or four games. I broke even one night, and the rest of the time I walked out a winner, anywhere from five bucks to two hundred, and twice topping a thousand, a lot of cash in those days.

One thing about gambling systems one should always keep in mind, is that they all work occasionally, even the old ladies' favorite at the track, that of sticking a hat pin through the eye of the horse on the cover of the program and betting every number with a hole in it. That system went out of style with the hat pin.

Guaranteed it shows a profit once in a while, just part of the coincidental nature of the gambling universe. My Jai-alai system was good for that first season when they changed the scoring system and never worked again after that.

For whatever reason, that ship had sailed...

V.

"IF YOU CAN'T DAZZLE THEM WITH BRILLIANCE, BAFFLE THEM WITH BULLSHIT."

--W.C. FIELDS

Eventually I amassed enough credits at the University of Miami and my parents were happy enough with my B.A. in Philosophy, deluding themselves that a respectable career as a teacher might be in the future for their only child. I even bought into the storyline myself for a while, taking some graduate courses in case I should move on to a Master's, but reality set in before that notion took me over. As a friend used to say, the Philosophy degree qualified me to pontificate, if nothing else.

I graduated on the half-year in January, and took off on a road trip to Mexico with my girlfriend Bonnie and my former Vermont roommate Bruce. Peter Fonda's 1969 classic film *Easy Rider* inspired us to our Quixotic quest and we headed from Miami up the Florida panhandle on the Gulf coast trail across Alabama and Louisiana toward Houston, Corpus Christi and Brownsville, Texas, making a bee-line for the shortest way south of the border, our original destination being Mexico City.

We might have made it, had I invested in some quality tires instead of the recaps I grabbed in Miami that forced us to keep our speed under sixty since the vibrating front end of that '67 Camaro quivered enough to loosen the fillings in your teeth. When we finally cut our odyssey short, nearly out of cash and patience, it was in the desperate Gulf Coast oil-town of Tampico where we became enchanted with the local market place, eating our meals there until each of us had acquired a bout of Montezuma's revenge.

It was another adventure just to get back to Miami in one piece, playing out more like an episode of *Survivor* than a vacation, and Bonnie and I soon after migrated to New Jersey for the summer.

Bonnie and I were married there in August and made the decision to head back to Miami based on the rumor that there was huge demand for unemployed philosophers. By then I had determined a career as a free-lance writer might suit a young degenerate of my ilk and began pounding the keys of my portable Smith-Corona typewriter, churning out material that produced an astonishing collection of rejection letters, mostly polite but all to the point.

Ultimately I did manage to find gainful employment as a social worker for Dade County and persisted writing free-lance articles about racing, for various trade journals and in my mind I was well on my way to living my dream until "the money ran out."

Like many other sports, racing provides unique stories and it's rife with superstitions and rituals virtually impossible to explain.

I became fascinated with the habitual gamblers, those at the track every day who will wear the same clothes, park in the same spot, eat the same food and go to the same betting window for weeks while on a winning streak, and when lady luck turns, they'll blame the most innocuous occurrence for their losses.

One of the oldest of track traditions has always been to remove the cover sheet of your program or a page from the Racing Form and place it on an empty seat to stake your claim. Racing fans would consider this sacrosanct and never sit on another's' papered seat at the risk of the evil luck it might bring. Upon close inspection, most of the gambler's odd habits begin to look like closet cases of OCD.

The first racetrack idiom I remember having tossed at me when I first went to work at Monmouth was the "Holy Ghost," which attributed divine intervention when a winning number would repeat a third time, thus Father, Son and... Holy Ghost!

Many a handicapper, having forgotten to bring his writing instrument, purchases a "lucky pencil" with his track program. They're usually only lucky for the day of purchase if they work at all, but they get credit for any good fortune, nonetheless.

And you'll never catch a racetracker picking up a coin that isn't 'head's-up'.

There's nothing worse than having someone sit next to you eating peanuts in the shell. Many gamblers don't realize they're the kiss of death but believe me, you have no chance of cashing a ticket as soon as that guy cracks open the bag.

And for owners, even casting an admiring glance at the trophy before a stakes race can completely extinguish your chances of getting your hands on it after the race.

Nobody needs bad luck at the track, so anything you can do to create good karma is desirable, like always leaving the change for the cashier when you cash a ticket, or rubbing small children on the head. My kids all learned early on never to take the coins on a winning bet, be it twenty cents or eighty. Not really a tip, but strictly for the karma. If you hit a big lick or the clerk takes time to fill out your IRS report for a winning exotic bet, it's probably a good idea to pitch him a few bucks.

The mutuel clerks are a breed unto their own, and come in two varieties: the guys who are there to *take* bets and the guys who are there to *make* bets. The practice of punching your own tickets is called "betting out of the box" and has spelled the end of many a career.

Clerks originally had to make their cash drawer reconcile at the end of the day, depending on whether they cashed or sold, counting receipts by hand and balancing it with a cash-register-like machine. Since computers were introduced to both sell and cash, it's a lot simpler, but at the end of the day they still need to balance the till or they're going to have the shortage docked from their pay at the end of the week. Every mutuel manager can tell a story of the clerk at their track who thought he'd take down an easy score by making a substantial show bet on a big favorite, only to miss and then continue to keep doubling his bets until he ran out of races. Those guys end up working for free to pay off such errors in judgement and plenty of them just disappear into the night, never to return.

The superstitious disdain among gamblers and gangsters for fifty-dollar bills is probably easy enough to understand since they look similar to twenties and more than a few punters found themselves short when their mutuel clerk may have neglected to give the correct change for a double sawbuck.

I was selling tickets at the Meadowlands the first season it was open for harness racing, when one night a lunatic gambler was so desperate to bet on a hot tip, he brought gold coins, five and ten and twenty dollar gold pieces to the window where the sellers took them at face value. He was buying twenty-dollar tickets with coins worth thousands. Of course, the clerks pocketed them and put their own cash in the box as the nag finished up the track, last.

Before touch-screen machines made betting like a computer game, punters had to put up their money, call their bet specifically... "Gimmie ten across the board on the five horse," at which the seller punched one ticket for win, place and show and gave them change. That would have been referred to as the "six dollar combo" window.

A favorite tactic of less scrupulous clerks was the "drop" by which they'd throw partial payment of the change on the counter and lean over like they'd dropped something, hoping the bettor took the ticket and the money and didn't check the amount, thereby getting "dropped."

Most mutuels clerks are honest though, and plenty have made good money over the years touting.

A tout is someone who gives a tip on a horse in exchange for either a bet or a cash payoff when the horse wins. The most common tactic of race track touts is to give a different horse to several clients who have no chance of comparing notes. That way the tout is covered with multiple chances in the same race. Makes it less of a gamble, right?

"C'mere buddy. Five winners on top yesterday. I got something for you."

Or whispered behind the back of a weathered hand, "Sacco's going with his filly in the fifth. Bet twenty for me and come back and see me when he wins."

The standard methodology of the tout, cast your bread upon as many waters as possible.

I've never given much credence to the newspaper touts since they pick three horses every race, even in the short fields, and they always take credit for their third choice as if they had nailed a winner.

Or the guys with the "information services" who advertise in the back of the Racing Form, promising to give you double-digit payoffs if only you'd send them $19.95. They're the same guys who text you with an alert that they have a stone-cold cinch for next weekend's football games. Just send some cash... Yeah right.

Logic dictates that if they really knew who was going to win they'd keep it to themselves. Just follow them to the parking lot and check out what kind of car they're driving. Odds are, it's that dirty twelve year-old Honda with a dented fender.

Bettors always cringe when the guy in front of them in line bets the same number they intend to, or you hear someone in your vicinity calling out the same combination you have marked on your program to bet.

"Gimme a two dollar exacta box, five-eight," he'll say. Just shoot me.

There's nothing worse than calling the wrong numbers in your bet and having the seller punch a ticket you didn't want. If you don't buy it, you know it's coming in, so you have to take it. And when the lines are clogged up right before post time, you can't change because the one you switch to will move slower than the one you were in before and you'll get shut out for sure. Usually it's some novice, trying to get betting instructions from the seller at two minutes to post that gets you shut out.

In Jersey, winners of the nightcap would scratch their heads and suspect collusion for a low payoff when any variation of the combination of the numbers 1-3-7 would come up in the trifecta. That's because the union that all mutuel clerks in Jersey belong to is Local 137 and they all box it in the last race. It's "their number."

The racetrack is still the best place to watch grown men rush in, recklessly abandoning all vestige of self-discipline, frantic to grab onto any piece of information they might garner and rely on it as if it were gospel, no matter how dubious the source. What do they say? -- never play cards with a guy nicknamed "Doc" or "Lucky." The same admonition goes around the horses.

But nonetheless, those captains of industry, those men so cunning and calculating in their chosen field, revert to naïve fools, anxious to subject themselves to the judgment of characters they wouldn't trust to wash their car, just as soon as they pass through the race track turnstiles: "Jack's Green Card, get your Lawton here," was like a siren's song to some of those guys.

My buddy Tony's father sold tout sheets just inside the grandstand gate at Monmouth. He was a little guy, maybe five-four, with a stunning resemblance to Jimmy Durante, but instead of being called "Schnoz" he was known around the track simply as "The Hat."

In gambling parlance, "a red-boarder" is the expression for the guy who can always give you the winner *after* the results are posted, the term coming from the fact that the tote board payoff numbers are composed of little red lights, and The Hat was the ultimate red-boarder.

Give him any result and he'd give you the reason he should have bet it. Three and three in the Daily Double? "Of course," he'd say. "Jesus Christ! Jesus Christ was thirty-three when he died! I shoulda' had it!"

Tony himself was known both on and off the track by his own nickname of "Stomps" which was only a slight aberration of an alleged familial relationship with the infamous Johnny Stompanato, a handsome mob bodyguard whose claim to fame was being stabbed to death by Lana Turner's daughter during his volatile relationship with the movie actress.

Stomps was convinced that he carried his father's luckless legacy to the gambling ring, often telling friends that if he loved a bet they should go the other way and bet against, and usually that would be true.

It became to be affectionately known as the "Hat" system. If he picked a winner, odds were it would get disqualified or at best end up in a dead-heat.

Stomps moved west in the late 70's and worked the mutuels at Golden Gate Fields and Bay Meadows, but proved that persistence can be rewarded in curious ways when he began sending in his losing lottery tickets to a bonus pool created by the California Lotto.

When his name was drawn at random from thousands of other "losers," Tony was selected to go on the lottery channel on cable television and spin a wheel, winning $75,000! Unbelievably, six months later he was selected again and spun for another $95,000. Talk about a good loser...

Although the crowd has dwindled significantly since racing had its heyday, every track still has a number of "regulars" or "rounders" that attend daily.

A very few are those professional gamblers whose discipline allows them to grind out a living by betting on more winners than losers, while others are just content to avoid the sturm und drang of society, living in the anonymous lifestyle that allows them to avoid the world at large in exchange for a world inside the track gates, not dealing with rules in general other than post-times, not concerned with the economy or taxable events.

For the most part, rounders can survive from week to week between scores if they have an alternate source of income or a sponsor to pay the rent. Then it's just a matter of getting lucky once in a while, hitting a trifecta or a Pick 6. Lots of regulars come and go, but the ones with staying power usually have the bigger picture sorted out in their minds.

The most common way to survive in this "under the radar" lifestyle is by serving as a "ten-percenter," taking that amount as commission from patrons who hit a bet that requires filling out a W-2G report for the IRS. The rule stipulates that if a win exceeds 300-1 (for a dollar), the person cashing the ticket must fill out a form with the cashier, including their John Hancock and social security number. Adding insult to injury, 'Uncle' also withholds a portion of the cash payout should you win over five thousand on any individual bet.

Since lots of folks have diverse reasons for not wishing to admit that they are gambling, let alone winning, every track has a number of regulars willing to take responsibility for such activity, in return for the aforementioned percentage, and nobody's boss or spouse is any the wiser.

Huge jackpots generated by pools like the Pick 6 have served to create reputations for some of these ten-percenters when they've taken credit as the handicapper of record for million dollar wins that they had little or nothing to do with. They attend the track daily, saving and documenting those losses, which are deducted from the big score at tax time and receive their big payoff when Uncle Sam rebates them the withholding.

The greatest ploy of the most sophisticated ten-percenters is to sign and collect and then kick back a fee to the winner, thus allowing him to collect more than he normally would if he had cashed the ticket himself since he'd be unable to document the colossal losses to get back the withholding.

For example, if you hit a million dollar bet and the tax-man withholds thirty percent, you receive $700,000 and Uncle will keep the $300,000 he hits you for at the window unless you are able to prove that you lost more than that and claim it back at tax-filing time. On the other hand, a ten-percenter can sign for the ticket, give you your $700,000 and pay you another $150,000 for the privilege, since he can file for the losses and get back $300,000, netting each of you an extra $150,000.

After all, Uncle isn't there to bail you out when you lose...

VI.

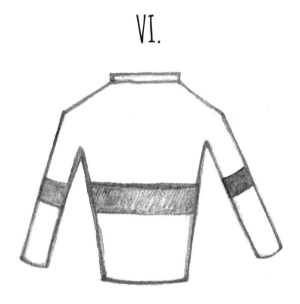

"WINNER, WINNER, CHICKEN DINNER..."

--LAS VEGAS CRAPS TABLE CHANT

I kept writing blurbs and fillers for sports magazines, principally the erst-while *Turf and Sport Digest*, and since most of my work was horseracing re-lated, when I managed to land a feature in that publication about a jockey named Frank Iannelli, my career course suddenly altered direction.

Iannelli was a naturally talented rider who had made his way onto the Jersey-Florida circuit from the school of hard-knocks on the New England tracks, notably Suffolk Downs in Boston where he'd been contract rider for trainer Clyde Locklear. Locklear was an old school trainer who valued having his own rider to carry out his orders and he taught his bug boys to be tenacious and ice cold fearless. When I met him, Frank was occasional- ly riding second call for Jimmy Croll behind the famous 'gate' rider Walter "Mousey" Blum and a skilled British import, Michael Hole.

Frank had won the Sorority stakes at Monmouth on a two-year-old filly of Croll's named Forward Gal the previous year and was on his way to acceptance from the New York/New Jersey circuit trainers and owners who wintered in Florida.

He was good-looking, charming and clever but unfortunately, the New England background in those days carried a strong stigma of larceny and Frank had all the classic habits possessed many other pro athletes... wine, women and song... as well as a playful desire to one-up the suckers.

Racetrackers lived the high-life, freely spending and indulging themselves at the restaurants and nightclubs with names like Sneaky Pete's across the high- way from Gulfstream and the infamous 500 Club in Atlantic City or Frank's Continental near Monmouth Park. Joe Sonken's Gold Coast bistro on the Intercoastal in Hollywood Beach was well known to be favored by both race- trackers and Chicago mobsters. It was the best place near Gulfstream to go for stone crabs if you didn't want to make the fifteen mile trek to the original Joes Stone Crab restaurant in Miami Beach and occasionally the back dining room would be closed for "private meetings," the parking lot filled with black limos and swarthy drivers in dark glasses who just might have doubled as extra bodyguards.

"Mister Joe" was a gregarious little man with a pot belly and twinkle in his eye, a Chicagoan who table hopped with a lit cigar in his mouth and glad- handed with the best of them. He had an English bulldog that he loved and kept with him at all times and images of bulldogs were visible all over the joint. Late one night he hopped into his Lincoln Continental, parked "mob style" fac- ing out, after maybe a few too many glasses of Dago red which might have in- fluenced him to put the car in reverse by mistake and when he hit the gas the car ended up tail first in the Intercostal Waterway. Joe managed to escape, but the pooch didn't make it and the Gold Coast was closed for a week in mourning.

Trainers, jocks and agents all drove big Cadillac sedans and wore expensive clothes, tipping like Broadway swells and in many places in the horse racing world where purses are minimal, some felt compelled, even entitled, to occasionally influence the outcome of a race in order to supplement earnings just to get by. Some trainer-jockey combinations would hold a horse for an entire season to set up the bet since many of them would just as soon hold a horse to cash a bet later than earn the winning purse on the spot.

"He could hold an elephant off a pile of peanuts," was how one Naragansett jockey agent used to describe his rider.

Plenty of jockeys in those days were well versed in the use of a "machine" which was racetrack vernacular for an electrical device. Highly illegal and alternatively referred to as a "joint," a "buzzer," a "battery," or a "machine," it was usually a little larger than a nine-volt battery and easily concealed in the jockey's cuff, secured by the rubber bands they wear to keep air from going up their sleeves during a race.

Designed to stimulate the horse with a timely shock, the activity is appropriately known as "plugging one in."

Many a horse with some talent considered an underachiever was often tried in morning works with the device and a skilled "machine rider" could occasionally wake one up with it since the horses' reaction could be unpredictable and it would be wise to know that before employing in an actual race when the money is down.

Frank came home one day with a custom made whip that had the battery in the handle, to this day the only one of its kind I've ever seen. The rider needed only to keep two brass tacks in his mouth and discreetly insert them in the butt of the whip before the horses went in the gate, and it delivered its jolt when the handle was pressed to the horses' neck. He thought it was great sport to chase everyone around, giving them a zap, until someone wrestled it away from him and the fear in his eyes told what he thought of its power.

This whip was so skillfully made no one could tell it from an ordinary one but it packed a jolt like a mini-taser and they would have had to take it apart or x-ray it to find the battery. Although it couldn't hurt a thousand pound horse, it certainly got his attention. It also helped avoid suspicion since the rider could switch his whip from hand to hand, something impssible to do with an ordinary machine.

When purses began to rise and the prize money for stakes races rose into the hundreds of thousands, many a rider packed a machine just for the sake of staying competitive, but some were particularly adept and were well known to all around the backstretch as "joint-riders," and every owner and trainer in America was aware of their existence, winking at what today no longer gets even tacit approval.

I'd usually make a few runs north or south every season, driving a trainer or jockey's car for a free plane ticket and a couple hundred dollars, and before one of those trips a top rider called me from New York.

"Could you go see Felix for me before you leave?" he said. "The shoe repair place on Palm Avenue? Yeah, in Hialeah... he's got something I need you to bring me. No, it's not a pair of boots."

Drugs were rampant in South Florida, the cocaine/reefer capital of the world at the time, so I felt compelled to ask.

"I'm not getting strip-searched by some Georgia cop for you to get your supply of nose-candy," I said.

But he swore no pharmaceuticals were involved and when I got to Felix's shop, a weathered old Cuban handed me a package the size of a two-pound box of chocolates.

The old man hadn't bothered to seal the box with anything but a piece of string, so when I got home I untied it and lifted the lid to take a peek inside, only to find half-a-dozen "machines," which I promptly delivered upon my arrival in Queens.

You could stand at the top of the stretch at Aqueduct and when the horses turned for home it sounded like a swarm of bumblebees.

When a maiden named Valhol won the 1999 Arkansas Derby his jockey Billy Patin became the poster-boy for machine riders.

Track maintenance found an electrical device on the Club House turn and when they reported it to the Stewards, Patin was picked up on camera discreetly dropping something in exactly the same spot when the horses galloped out post-race.

A close-up camera on the live national ESPN TV broadcast of the race clearly showed the crime and the wireless ESPN mike Patin wore provided the machine's buzzing, audio style.

Patin got a five-year suspension, imposed by the Oaklawn Park stewards.

"Machine Mania" again gripped racing press after Funny Cide's 2003 Kentucky Derby win, when an over-zealous Frank Carlson of the *Miami Herald* was so convinced he had a scoop and couldn't wait to get the proof when he imagined a shadow in the close up of a photo of Jose Santos' hand to be a machine. Frank was a pretty savvy racetrack journalist, so it was surprising that he would jump to that conclusion so quickly.

Upon not too much further inspection this was found to be completely incorrect, but not until trainer Barclay Tagg and Santos had their feet held to the fire to defend their integrity, while a pretty good writer flushed his credibility.

Talk about not letting the truth get in the way of a good story.

Even before that time I believe the use of electricity as an accessory had dropped off significantly since the proliferation of video surveillance and the use of machines at major tracks today would be rare or at least uncommon. I couldn't say the same about smaller venues where small purses cause more cut-throat competition and some riders might rationalize the need to use one as an aid to cash a bet to supplement income.

Ironically, the amount of shock delivered to a thousand pound animal by one of these illegal devices is probably a lot less painful than being struck repeatedly with a (legal) whip. They don't draw blood and they're not nearly as distressing to spectators and the shocks they give are more like those from the collars used to train dogs than that of a cattle prod.

I'm not advocating machine use by any means, but I think one thing racing should do to improve its chances with the uninitiated would be to minimize whip use by riders. The sight of a jockey slashing away on a tired horse in the stretch is a severe turn-off, especially for first time race watchers.

England has a limit on what way and how many times a rider may hit a horse during a race (no more than 12 times in the final quarter mile) and the officials there regularly do extensive reviews of their criteria. It is acknowledged that there is a legitimate use for the whip, "for safety and encouragement," but it is necessary to specify what that is and they delineate the appropriate design and control of it, so as not to compromise the welfare of the horse during the race.

Their regulations have teeth in that officials are able to withhold riding fees and the jockey percentage of purse monies and in extreme cases riders may be suspended.

VII.

"MONEY TALKS, BULLSHIT WALKS."

--SAM ZELL

Impressed with my flattering magazine article about him, and since his current agent Steve Vaonakis would be heading back home to Maryland at the end of the Gulfstream meet, Frank decides that it would be a great idea that I become his agent for the next season in Florida and puts on a full-court press to convince me to do so.

The high life of sports celebrity can be intoxicating to the un-initiated. We dine and dance nightly in Miami hot spots, with hus-tlers and gangsters and information-seeking hangers-on picking up every check and providing a seemingly endless supply of top-quality Colombian "flake" and Jamaica's finest weed to keep the party rolling. I stop by to see Frank outside the jock's room at Hialeah and he tells me, "Mister D's taking us to the Playboy Club on Collins Avenue."

I'd seen the same character pounding the hundred-dollar window at Hialeah and heard his reputation as a credit-card scammer. When I point this possible character defect out to Frank, he summarily dismisses it with, "Nah, you got the wrong guy. He's okay. He's cool."

That night we drink champagne from flutes of Waterford crystal and red wine from glasses as big as goldfish bowls at a table set for twenty-four including half-a-dozen jockeys, several with the compulsory five-eleven blonde and at least as many agents and sundry minor racetrack officials in attendance for a free roll.

I'm in the company of New England's leading rider, Anthony DeSpirito, who competed with Willie Shoemaker for top winner in the '50's and had been on the Ed Sullivan Show. He could have played Jake LaMotta in Raging Bull instead of DeNiro and wouldn't have had to do much acting. Tony's stunning wife Doris is parked between us and I immediately suspect she might be much too charming for anyone's good.

By 2 a.m., all the racetrackers are out way past their bedtime, obviously way over-served with cabernet sauvignon and pharmaceuticals when Tony sticks a .38 pistol in my face, recommending that any thoughts of mine toward reciprocating Mrs. DeSpirito's cordiality would be a real bad idea.

I draw on five and a half years of college experience referencing Roget's Thesaurus and make use of every assuring phrase I can muster and it couldn't have been more than three or four days later before my heartbeat returns to normal.

Anyway, the hustler/hanger-on "Mister D" picks up the check and hammers stolen credit cards for a several thousand dollar tab *including exorbitant tips. The next week it's the talk of the track when several FBI agents escort him from the Club House at Hialeah in a set of shiny handcuffs. Welcome to the fast lane.*

Since I had no practical experience to qualify me for the agent game other than a general working knowledge of racing and some reasonable handicapping skills, Frank and I agree to meet up at the Fall meet at Garden State Park in Cherry Hill, NJ, where I could hang with his local agent, Jimmy Martino, in order to learn the ropes.

Jimmy didn't go to Florida for the winters and I wasn't getting paid for the internship, so the arrangement seemed equitable for all and he proved a capable coach, teaching me the intricacies of the "condition book," so named since it contains the qualifications of eligibility for entering horses and the races offered for the next two weeks or so. Other than knowing the rules and regulations, which differ from state to state but have certain commonalities, the job isn't very complicated.

The principal business of being a jockey agent is similar to that of any other agent in the entertainment business with a few notable exceptions. Most theatrical agents work on a commission or percentage, usually around ten percent, and represent a number of clients. Jockey agents get twenty-five percent, but are restricted to handling no more than two riders, one apprentice and one veteran, or two veterans, also referred to as journeymen. Otherwise, the principal is to get your client on stage as much as possible, win as many races as you can.

The ostensible reason for the "two rider" restriction is to prevent any one agent from having too much control over any given race, either by having too much input or by preventing other jockeys from competing. It's not really about the possibility of anyone "fixing" a race, but in any event, the system works to keep a balance of mounts vs. riders and hasn't changed for nearly a hundred years.

As a new kid on the block, the only way I got to represent top riders was to take their books as they were nearing the end of their careers, like Bobby Ussery, Mike Miceli and Frank Lovato, and they would round up my commission to thirty percent since they wanted to be selective and not ride too many horses and still allow me to make a living.

Usually an agent likes to represent a "bug boy" along with the older rider if for no other reason than to avoid turning down any business. If the horse is a real long shot with not much of a chance you can persuade the trainer to take the apprentice since he gets the five, seven or ten pound weight break that comes with him. Sometimes horses run off with bug boys and win at a big price as the kid is just hanging on and doesn't do too much to interfere... a willing passenger if you will.

Apprentices have limited chances at first, thus they will ride anything they can get on, even if it's a 50 to 1 shot with no chance or a horse that's been eased in his last start, the kind no established rider wants to deal with.

Since they provide a weight advantage for the horse they ride it's usually fair compensation, as the learning period takes longer for some than others and very few "bug boys" would be any match for the best older riders without it.

Occasionally a rider at the end of his career will get tired of fighting the scales and turn agent. Many make great agents, since they formed alliances with top trainers over the years and know the game inside out. Angel Cordero, Jr. had a series of spills and hung up his saddle at age forty-nine with over seven thousand winners. He took the book of fellow Puerto Rican Johnny Velazquez and mentored him to a Hall of Fame career, principally riding first call for Todd Pletcher's dynamic stable.

Todd was smart enough to realize early on that Velazquez came with an asset no other jock had, Angel's experience. Angel was the only agent who could get on horses in the morning and check them out, giving valuable feedback to both the trainer and his rider.

Mike Gonzalez, Richard DePass and Danny Neid are only a few of the good riders who made the transition to agent and have done so with success over the past dozen years.

The top ten riders at most meets will ride approximately seventy-five percent of the horses, leaving remaining twenty-five percent of the mounts to the less popular or new faces on the scene.

The agent's primary function is to solicit mounts based on the schedule of races published by the Racing Secretary in the condition book every ten days to two weeks and arrange his rider's work day to have the best chance of picking up "live" mounts.

Some agents provide more services than others, looking after the riders' financial affairs, travel arrangements and giving their jockeys assistance and counsel on personal issues as well. They basically handle all the business affairs of their rider, seeking and booking his mounts, anticipating conflicts and attempting to position their rider to win as many races possible.

Due to the relationship I had with trainer John Forbes as his stable agent, I had C.C. "Chuckie" Lopez' book basically from day one and soon realized he had no concept of money. We easily won the Monmouth and Meadowlands meets and he was top jockey in New Jersey for the year. Chuckie was in heaven, living his dream, and the financial rewards that came along with it didn't concern him. After he bought his fourth or fifth new car in about six months, I put him on an allowance, taking him to the bank with his paychecks to buy CDs so that when the gold rush was over, at least he'd have some savings built up.

Jockeys usually begin their careers as soon as they are able to be licensed at age sixteen and the relationship between agent and jockey can be special, with agents and riders often developing father-son or big brother-little brother relationships that may last years, usually until a new wife or girlfriend gets involved and it becomes "time for a change."

As the rider gets older he may change venues, move to another part of the country and make multiple agent changes. Generally speaking there is no standard formal agreement between riders and agents and business is done on a handshake, and backstabbing can be expected to happen in even the most successful collaborations.

When a jockey becomes successful the agent needs to be even more selective in the horses he agrees to ride and provide some rest time between races. When I had leading riders like Chuckie, I didn't have to look for mounts, they came looking for me.

Everyone would like to ride all favorites, but there's only one in each race. Taking a call with one trainer and dropping him when you get a better mount is referred to as "spinning" him. Top agents have been known to take great pleasure in spinning those trainers who tortured them in the past, the ones who didn't realize the ladder up might also go down and trainers who finally reach the pinnacle of their success have likewise shown themselves to be sadistic bullies, either by a character assassination or outright ultimatum to the jock, forcing him to sack his agent in order to keep on a barnful of good horses.

Occasionally even top riders have to ride long shots, usually due to the relationship with the trainer, in order to demonstrate faithfulness, but a skillful jock's agent always tries to ride the best horse in every race, and will spin a trainer for a better chance. The best agents can do this without losing mounts and often jump off and on horses, geting back on to ride the second place finisher next time and only allowing lesser riders to have a chance if they should get lucky and win the race.

Confirming the mount is referred to giving a "call" and a top rider will commonly have a first and second call, with another rider named to "sit behind" him, since as Broadway Danny Rose says, "you can't ride two horses with one behind."

Because races are drawn and published in the Daily Racing Form anywhere from forty-eight to seventy-two hours in advance, agents need to anticipate changes and stay in close contact with both the trainers and the Racing Office.

In essence, it's another selling job and the best jockey agents are usually street-smart super salesmen with much of their business created from many years of relationships with the trainers.

When a trainer doesn't want to use a certain jockey, they usually blame the owner, saying "I got overruled... his [wife, girlfriend, kid, etc.] says I have to use [insert leading rider's name]."

When an agent doesn't want to ride for a trainer he gets evasive -- "I gave a half-a-call to Orseno, I'll have to check with him and get back to you" -- which really means he's got to check the Past Performance charts before committing. Nowadays there are computer packages that allow agents to quickly check their iPad to evaluate a prospective mount while they're on the phone, just as long as they can keep the conversation going long enough.

Like many other occupations on the track, jockey agents are required to take a written test, based on the rules of racing and pass the scrutiny of the stewards before being licensed. Although many have a minimum of formal education, they are easily the most savvy and informed individuals working the backstretch, since their livelihood depends on maneuvering through daily sessions of constantly changing situations, dealing with the uncertainty.

Horses get sick or injured and have to scratch and you have to find another mount. Some trainers get mad or miffed when they lose a race and some switch riders like they change their shirts, so agents need to think on their feet and find another mount for their jockey. Some trainers are particularly insecure or have self-esteem issues and fear being made to look foolish, so they'll use their power to intimidate agents and take them to the stewards for not honoring a call, since there's no specific contractual agreement for mounts other than a verbal one and it's easy for them to cancel commitments. Whereas, if the agent does so, he'll have to kiss off any chance of riding for that barn in the future. A cancelled call on either side requires compensation but in most cases it's a losing battle for the agent and rider.

When I eventually took the steward's certification course at the Racing Officials Accreditaion Program at the University of Louisville, I believe the reason I was able to ace the final exam was from my days as a jockey's agent, when I learned both the written and unwritten rules of the game.

The Garden State meet ended just after Thanksgiving, and Frank and I headed to Tropical Park in South Miami where I took my first test for an agent's license. Interestingly the application had no place to list educational institutions attended, but did require detailed disclosure of any illegal transgressions, arrests and felonies in particular.

As winter racing in the north didn't exist in those days, Florida tracks attracted a mix of top class New York stables and a miscellany of small to mid-size outfits from all over the country, as well as a fair-sized Canadian contingent. I used the shoe-leather approach, going barn-to-barn soliciting mounts and soon learned not to take rejection personally.

Tropical Park wasn't nearly as famous as Hialeah, but they did run the first legal betting race there in 1931 (Hialeah had illegal betting since opening in 1925) and it was a gem of a little track, unfortunately located directly in the path of residential real estate development and far from the beachfront resorts that the tourists preferred.

There were seventy-two jockeys with tack in the jockeys' room at Tropical that winter, so if you figure nine races with an average of eight starters, there's not a lot of mounts to go around after the top jockeys take four or five out of each race.

And they came from all over the map, the best of the best -- Braulio Baeza, Jacinto Vasquez, Eddie Maple, Larry Adams, Angel Cordero, Jr. and Jorge Velasquez were the top New York riders, but Sandy Hawley, Ron Turcotte and Jeff Fell were there from Canada, Earlie Fires and Don MacBeth from Chicago, and Mike Hole, Carlos Marquez, Mike Miceli and Craig Perret represented the Jersey contingent. Donald Brumfield shipped in from Kentucky and Charlie Maffeo, Tony DeSpirito and Phil Ernst brought their tack from Suffolk Downs in Boston. I managed to book a ride here and there, but after a month we were still winless. The agent business is all about relationships and as a rookie playing in the big leagues for the first time, I was way behind the guys who had worked the circuit for years.

The only saving grace was the fact that some stable riders didn't head south for the winter, as it wasn't worth the expense if they had a family, and occasionally a good horse might come available if you got your rider on him for a morning work.

There were three tracks in South Florida and since many horsemen had winter homes there, most would stable at the one closest to where they lived. New York trainers favored Hialeah, the premier meet where

Kentucky Derby hopefuls got sorted out in races like the Everglades and Flamingo Stakes and the best Handicap horses got their year started in the Widener.

Trainers from the New Jersey, Maryland, Chicago and Kentucky circuits lived in Hollywood, the town between Gulfstream and Ft. Lauderdale, since they'd usually stay for the full season in Florida before heading home or maybe to the short spring meet at Keeneland. I had to concentrate on those guys since some would stay until the end of Gulfstream in April and ship to Garden State before Monmouth opened in June.

The smaller outfits camped out around Tropical where the track owner Saul Silberman, known affectionately as "Little Caesar," was one of those bigger than life characters that bet with both hands and loved the action.

Prior to the advent of computers as the mechanism of exchange, betting windows began with the two-dollar standard, on up to five, ten, fifty and hundred dollar sellers. If you wanted to bet more, the mutuel clerk would have to keep punching them in one at a time in whatever denomination he sold until your tickets totaled the amount you put up.

Rumor had it that Silberman had a mutuel machine in his office that wouldn't shut off until the horses passed the quarter pole, but the track often favored closers and he lost a bundle anyway.

Mutuel tickets were heavy stock paper almost like cardboard, and they came in colors to distinguish their denomination and category: Win, Place, and Show. The fifty and hundred dollar tickets had black stripes on the sides and smaller yellow tickets were for Daily Doubles and all had various codes to discourage counterfeiting.

Occasionally bettors will throw away a winning ticket before a race is made official when there's a jockey's claim of foul or a steward's inquiry and the order of finish of the race gets changed. Every year hundreds of thousands of dollars is lost in this way and the money reverts to the state in most situations.

After the meet closed at Tropical Park Silberman would let the fraternities from the University of Miami sweep the track after closing day and cash the winnings left on the ground, turning up thousands of dollars worth of uncashed tickets.

For most, it was the only way they would ever make money at the track.

To many racetrackers, the initial appeal of racetrack life stems from its transient nature. Conceptually the track and the circus are easy to compare since racetrackers "pick up their tents" and move on from meet to meet just as circus people do.

Horses and jockeys fill the Big Top, and the gamblers, touts and patrons provide an entertaining sideshow. I know the prospect of being able to make a living working outdoors and moving to the sunny south every winter held great appeal to me and was a significant factor in my deciding how to make a living.

Among my running mates those days were a racing journalist named Jack Will, the popular writer/commentator Pete Axthelm, and Warren Brubaker, a Chicagoan who'd passed the bar but preferred the paddock to a courtroom.

Jack was might have been the best racing writer other than Joe Hirsch, but whereas Hirsch hung with the bon vivants and the likes of quarterback Joe Namath and always put himself in the right place at the right time, Jack had a few more dubious habits and it seemed like he preferred to regularly put himself in a jam.

One of his duties at the *Morning Telegraph* was to write a terse comment on the horses in the morning line, like "should better last" or "may do later" or "not today." It's the first place racetrackers look to see what the world at large thinks of their chances. And also the place where owners check when trying to rationalize their irrational investments. They love to quote the comments about their horse when they're favorable and scoff at them when they're not.

It was a spring meet at Garden State and one of the horses entered in a cheap claimer had taken Jack's money a few times and he still had a bitter taste in his mouth when he was writing his comments, so he tagged the horse with "always in the shithouse."

Nowadays in the era of full frontal nudity and regular use of the "F-word" on premium TV this might get by, but in the '70's it was enough to get him canned although it did make him cause célèbre and the idol of many racetrackers thereafter.

Pete Axthelm was a brilliant guy who wrote for *Sports Illustrated* and did television coverage that included thoroughbred racing. A Yale graduate, Pete was the first to acknowledge that his personal demons of drink and gambling would likely do him in and in the end he was right, but in the meantime he loved to hang at the grandstand bar, suck up the degenerate atmosphere and debate handicapping selections with the rest of us, garnering "local flavor" for his writing.

He fought a losing battle with cirrhosis of the liver and tried to quit drinking when ordered to do so by the doctors but eventually stood by his decision that he would "rather die in color than live in black and white." Pete was only forty-seven and everyone who knew him was crushed at the premature departure.

When they convinced Calder to name an annual turf event "The Pete Axthelm Stakes," Warren Brubaker and Jack Will decided to honor their lost friend by finding a horse each year to compete in Pete's racing silks. They would hunt for a three-year-old that was competitive, lease him for the day, run him in the "Axe Stable" silks and hope for the best. Jack borrowed a nice horse named The Vid, which won the first running, and for lifetime racetrackers it doesn't get much better than that.

Brubaker is one of those guys like my pal Eddie Rosen who went to law school, all the time wishing he could become a racetracker. That's just because the track is where their heart is. I met Warren the first year I was an agent, hanging on the paddock rail at Hialeah. He had graduated and passed the bar, but packed his bags and headed south to play the ponies for a living and did a pretty good job of it. Eventually he succumbed to respectability, taking on a lawyer's work, but when Warren and his wife

Debbie had three kids, they named their first offspring Aleah, so when folks would meet her they'd say "Hi, Aleah." The second got lucky to be called Anita for Santa Anita and their son they tabbed "Keene" for Keeneland.

Just fortunate for his kids that Warren's favorite track wasn't Ak-sar-ben.

One memorable character we called "Pockets" travelled the Jersey-Florida circuit in the 1970's. He slept in his car, eschewed the tack room living quarters that most grooms and hot walkers took for granted and made his living as what is referred to in track parlance as a "stooper."

Although modern racetracks would like to present themselves as perfect family entertainment, one thing that's never changed is the real reason people come to the track. Not to see the pretty ponies, but to gamble or try to eke out a living.

Stooping is almost a lost art these days since tickets are now printed on computer paper and bar-coded, but back when tickets were more substantial, the ones that didn't get ripped up all held potential.

Pockets would cruise the Grandstand Main Line all day, flipping tickets in the classic manner, with the toe of his shoe, looking for abandoned winners. Lots of stoopers preferred pointy shoes and could flip those cardboard tickets on their back with the alacrity of a ballet dancer.

He got the name "Pockets" from his custom of stuffing every one of his with anything available for free: condition books, matches, mutuel tickets...

Looking like a Michelin Man in green work clothes, he drove and virtually lived in a dented, weather-beaten car that was similarly stuffed, making it impossible to open the back doors. His enterprise could have been the basis for a racetrack version of the *Hoarders* shows that fascinate us these days on reality TV, following OCD ridden collectors of useless junk as they pile it up to the point of absurdity or insanity.

But Pockets showed up every day, walked his horses and made it to the windows for the daily double. Hard to say if he ever made anything on his bets and although we exchanged nods of recognition for a number of years, he avoided conversation and I never heard him utter a word and I never knew Pockets' real name, but it's not uncommon on the track to be acquainted with a person for decades and only refer to them by a nickname.

Trainer Herb Paley had a groom named Eddie Sherman that everyone called by his last name. Herb told me that in the three decades Sherman had worked for him, the man had never left the backstretch, other than to take a horse to the paddock or go make a bet or ride the van with the horses when they moved from track to track.

He might send someone out to the liquor store on Saturday night to bring him back a libation, but the track kitchen served three meals a day, and Sherman found everything he needed inside the stable gates. He passed away one night on his cot as he slept in his tack room, moving on to the "Great Race Track in the Sky."

It's easy to figure where Damon Runyon got a lot of the names for his characters, like Nicely Nicely, Big Jule and Harry the Horse, since many of his tales took place at the track.

"Peanut Butter" Brown worked for Jimmy Croll and rubbed some of the best horses ever in the barn that housed Mr. Prospector, Housebuster, Bet Twice and Holy Bull.

"Peaches" was a jock's agent known from coast to coast. "Goose" Heimer assisted trainer Dave Vance until he went out on his own and perennially topped the list of leading trainers at Philly Park.

Other guys with labels like "Rabbit" and "Stretch" and "Fats" and "Schnoz," "Spud," "Little Joe" and "Snake" made the racetrack work for a lifetime and followed the unwritten "Racetracker's Code," which would read somewhat like a combination of the Golden Rule and the Hippocratic Oath:

"Do unto others as you'd have them do unto you, and if you can't help, don't hurt..."

They'll all join Sherman someday in that Great Race Track in the Sky and root for a winner together...

VIII.

"You can't win them all."

--Connie Mack

Tropical Park owner Saul Silberman was often known to wander the grandstand to amuse himself, handing out envelopes containing twenty-dollar bills to unsuspecting patrons, just to get their reaction. Many thought he was a tout trying to give out picks, so the gag provided a lot of laughs when he'd practically have to force them to take the cash.

Unfortunately Saul passed away in 1971 as the track was having its last hurrah for the '72 meet before new owner James McKnight would finally close the classic oval forever and move the racing dates to Calder, his air-conditioned facility in North Miami.

What Calder lacked in beauty, charm and elegance, it made up for in utility. Patrons got used to the ugly box and came to appreciate it for the efficiency of its air-conditioning in the humid south Florida summers.

McKnight was a former Chairman of the Board of 3M and owner of Tartan Stables (which included my favorite Dr. Fager) and he had an idea that the safety of racing for both horse and rider could be improved with a synthetic track, also eliminating the variables of slow or muddy tracks and uneven surfaces. He brought a second generation of his "Tartan" track to Calder when it opened for racing in the summer of 1971. It was similar to the rubberized surfaces used for football fields that were becoming popular at the time and considering the excessive amount of rain that falls during the rainy season in Miami, it seemed a reasonable idea.

Horsemen had rejected the first synthetic track at Tropical for being too hard and Calder's was designed to have more "give." Nonetheless, it was too much of an unnatural footing and the horses' hoofs were unable to slide before making purchase and runners looked like they were bouncing up and down as they ran.

There was a popular bet at the time, usually on the co-feature and feature races, called the "Big P" which was essentially a wager on back-to-back perfectas. An unusual wrinkle with the bet required that if you selected the first winning perfecta, you needed to go back to the betting window and turn your ticket in exchange for a second one.

The pools were pretty healthy and a couple of long shots in the first end of the bet would create a market for "live" tickets. Exotic bets were just beginning to catch on and the big payoffs created both excitement and interest for casual fans and a big payoff opportunity for veteran players.

I got "live" in the Big P one afternoon of that first season with a pair of decent priced horses. There was a grey market in tickets that enabled you to take a quick profit by selling to a punter who was trying to get multiple chances and cover long shots in an attempt to win a big chunk of the pool, if not all of it. Offered a couple of hundred buyout, I passed on the flip and swapped my ticket for a cold perfecta of numbers 5 and 10 in the second half, a mile and forty-yard heat on the Tartan, with one of the best local jocks, Hector Viera, on my top pick.

As they ran to the first turn, the 10 horse went to the front and right behind him, Hector on the 5 made it tight for the horses inside him and one went down, causing a chain reaction that wiped out the whole field, eight of the ten starters. He passed the 10 on the backstretch and the 5-10 combination came home alone, pulling up just past the wire as to avoid the mess of horses and riders still on the ground.

Of course the stewards had no choice but to take him down and place him last for causing the chaos, declaring it to be "no-race" and turning my winning ticket into a wrapper for used chewing gum.

That was what we commonly refer to as "bad racing luck."

Nonetheless, the Calder track became an island unto itself, as none of the winter shippers trained there, preferring to station themselves at Hialeah or Gulfstream or one of the small training centers up the coast like Palm Beach Downs or Payson Park.

Calder trainers were permanent Miami fixtures, well stocked with horses that fit the "off-season" racing from May until December and they made very few starts at Hialeah or Gulfstream. Guys like Frank Gomez, Reed Combest, Manny Tortora, Happy Alter, Norman St. Leon and Gene Navarro never left Florida but developed top-class horses like Princess Rooney, Mecke and Halo's Image that could ship all over the country and beat the best. Most of the time they'd sell them to well-heeled owners from the North and get no credit since awards would go to the last trainer of record, but they toughed out the hot summers, valuing the benefit of raising their families in one place over the chance of higher purse money on the road.

Happy Alter was a wealthy guy in his own right, owning a company called "Bob's Barricades" and his racing silks had a pair of boxing gloves on the back, an homage to his career as an amateur pugilist. He loved to show snapshots of himself and Muhammad Ali training at a gym in South Miami Beach. Among trainers, Happy was an anomaly, arriving no earlier than nine a.m. in his Rolls Royce, explaining that his conditioning system required him to have his horses work as close to post time as possible and earlier training would take away from their rest time... and of course, his too.

Kenny Noe, Jr., the General Manager of Calder, was from a racetrack family. His father was a trainer and his son Jeff made a career as a Racing Secretary and later as steward on the South Florida circuit. Kenny ran a tight ship and made a productive operation out of what started as a barely second-rate track before moving on to run the NYRA tracks but while at Calder he ruled with an iron hand, discouraging "his" trainers from racing at other tracks.

For winter agents this was a good thing, since many mornings we would have to visit at least two of the tracks' stable areas to hunt down prospective mounts and Tropical was on the extreme south end of town. If you did have to drop in at Calder it was a rarity and there weren't many Calder shippers going to win at Hialeah or Gulfstream in any case.

Living near Hialeah, I concentrated on the horses there and got to know many of the finest trainers ever to tighten a girth, including Horatio Luro, who trained Northern Dancer and Secretariat's Lucien Laurin, as well as Moody and LeRoy Jolley, Everett King and Joe Nash and Harvey Vanier and Dave Sazer from Chicago, to name only a few of the great ones of that era.

When Hialeah finally closed, Woody Stephens' barn was still adorned with a sign commemorating his five consecutive Belmont wins, noting that all had wintered on that backstretch.

Of all the records in the annals of sporting history, I believe none compares with Woody's: taking one horse from a crop of over thirty thousand, getting that horse to the races, (only half the horses foaled any year do so), winning a maiden race with that same horse, (only half the horses that make it to the races ever win a race), winning the Grade I Belmont stakes, and finally, doing it five times. That's five times in-a-row...

The math is daunting.

In his later years, Woody was often working in the shadow of the titan D. Wayne Lukas, who revolutionized thoroughbred training and himself set records not likely to ever be broken. Lukas had been a high school basketball coach before he turned to training quarter horses, rising to the top at that game before switching to thoroughbreds in the 1970's.

Wayne was the first trainer to top $100 million in purse earnings. Through 2014 he'd won four Kentucky Derbys, five runnings of the Preakness and four Belmonts as well as twenty-one Breeders' Cup races. Tall, silver haired and handsome, Lukas became the articulate spokesman for the sport.

Wayne and Woody had a good natured rivalry, considering that most of Stephens' accomplishments pre-dated Wayne's, but whenever he was in earshot, Woody delighted in displaying a commemorative watch given him by New York Racing Association.

"Ask Mister Lukas if he's got one of these," he'd urge whoever was sitting nearest, tapping on the watch with five small horses on its dial.

IX.

"A MAN WHO CAN BEAT THE RACES CAN DO ABOUT ANYTHING HE MAKES UP HIS MIND TO
DO..."

-- CHARLES BUKOWSKI, FROM "ANOTHER HORSE STORY"

In my first season as an agent, that last December of Tropical Park's existence, I managed to pick up a mount for Frank on a horse named Spanish Riddle, by Ridan out of the Windy City mare Spanish Breeze. The big chestnut colt was trained by Canadian Lucien Laurin at Hialeah in the same barn that also housed the '72 Kentucky Derby winner Riva Ridge and the immortal Secretariat.

It was one of those rare rainy winters in south Florida, which turned out to be our good fortune. Before the Daily Racing Form became as sophisticated as it is now, horses that ran well in the mud carried an "X" next to their name in the past performances. Spanish Riddle had an "X" with a circle around it. That meant he was one of the elite, rated as a "superior mudder."

We rode that good son of Ridan in a race called the Dade-Metropolitan Handicap and I broke my maiden as an agent in style. Frank and I did our best "Indian Rain Dance" every time he hit the entries and were lucky enough to catch an off track a few times that made him about a cinch.

Years later, Spanish Riddle became somewhat of a curiosity when he went to stud, outfitted with an artificial foot after a paddock accident. Usually horses are unable to survive such an injury but he managed to cope and bred mares for five years with the prosthetic, and you could run to the betting window when one of his progeny raced on a muddy track.

When you're at the track watching race after race, you learn how to look for horses that are either flat-out better than their peers or ones that have a valid excuse for getting beat so you can "mark it down" for another day.

Every morning came another lesson from my street-smart counterparts, guys like Rocco Calabrese, Fats and Sonny Wiseman, Lenny Goodman, John Dale and Gene Fisher, all lifetime racetrackers who'd done it all and who'd perfected the "agenting" art. Vic Gilardi gave advice on stock market investment. "Little Joe" Verone was a songwriter of no small talent. His greatest line? *The trouble with our society/We're living in a lie/Everybody wants to go to heaven/Nobody wants to die...*

Life lessons come from everywhere.

Part of the wisdom imparted by my mentor-agents like Dave Hart and Delbert Clements was not to be a sucker and get caught up in the gambling, to pick your spots and make your bets count.

"You can beat a race, but you can't beat the races" has always been the sage gambler's wisdom, easy to understand but hard to heed for most occasional horseplayers who feel compelled to bet each and every race and can't figure out why they pick a bunch of winners and still lose money.

While horseracing is an esoteric enterprise by nature, about as simple as quantum physics for the uninitiated, there's a strong bias toward acceptance of mystery and imagination when first taking up the sport, understandable when you hear of folks who hit big payoffs by betting their house number or boxing their kids' birth-dates, but the truth is, given the huge amount of empirical evidence, handicapping is an enterprise you can succeed at if you learn the fundamentals.

On the other hand, gambling on horses is nearly impossible to succeed at on a casual basis. Fans who follow the horses and play every day will have a much better chance of turning a profit than those who drop in once or twice a year simply by the fact that they have a feel for what's happening around them. Trainers' and jockeys' win percentages are displayed prominently in handicapping material like the track program and *Daily Racing Form* and although they may fluctuate in the short term, "form" will prevail in the long term.

Statistical analysis of the long term indicates that the post time favorite will win roughly one-third of all races run at any track, but that percentage is for the entire meet, not necessarily any given day. This accounts for the streaks of long shots and mid-priced winners, which balance out the law of averages and make up the other two-thirds of the wins.

Most racetrackers of any duration possess access to information imagined to be unavailable to the general gambling public and many prefer to find a way to bet with "O.P.'s," short for "other people's money."

To regular fans, it seems that the jockeys, agents and mutuel clerks are vested with a particular mystique and that might be true as some go their entire careers cashing a multitude of bets while never having pulled so much as a nickel from their own pockets. The track may be the ultimate training ground for "thinking on your feet," since many there have proven you can make "something from nothing."

People to whom you give tips and who pay you off in cash for a good result are referred to in racetrack vernacular as "Eggs." With a little luck and a deep enough supply of excuses, some racetrackers could manage to eat, drink and keep their cars washed with a different set of Eggs at each stop on the circuit.

Of course, the same basic concept carries over to love and life in general and I guess you could say everybody's somebody's Egg. On the racetrack, you talk to anyone and everyone, never knowing where opportunity might dwell.

Hustling my jock's book at Hialeah one morning I met an old race-tracker from Kentucky named Rabbit Calvin. He walked hots, did catch-work anywhere he could find it and touted at the races in the afternoon with a twinkle in his eye and could charm a snake with his down-home twang. Everybody on the backstretch knew Rabbit, so when he asked me to borrow twenty until the end of the week, I said "sure."

The next Friday I asked the cashier in the track kitchen if she'd seen Rabbit and my double sawbuck and she told me, "Shit, honey, he left for New Orleans two days ago with a bunch of folk's money."

Call me Eggy...

Dave Hart had Craig Perret's book that winter and Delbert Clements, who represented Billy Phelps for many years, shipped in from Arlington with his new Latin sensation Manuel Cedeno.

Both riders drew respect from trainers on that Midwest circuit of Kentucky and Chicago as well as the East coasters and Dave and Delbert did their best to throw me second calls whenever they could, knowing well that they'd get them back next time out unless I got real lucky and won.

One of those back-up mounts at Hialeah paid off when Frank booted home an allowance winner named Seminole Joe for trainer Bill Sterling and we celebrated heartily until the next day when we learned the horse had come up positive in his post-race urine test.

Sterling was a class act and there was no possibility of him drugging the horse. The positive turned out to be for caffeine, which turned out to be directly traceable to the coincidence of his groom grazing him daily in the spot where they emptied the grounds from the barn's coffee pot.

Nonetheless, caffeine is a forbidden stimulant and the trainer ultimately responsible, so he lost the purse and we didn't get our ten percent.

Professional sports have had a couple of decades of black-eyes, mainly from the participants' use of performance enhancing drugs, and most of the controversy surrounding horseracing these days is related to the same topic.

Truth of the matter is, whenever competition involves money, either prize money or gambling winnings, competitors will do what they can to take an edge. In some cases it might be as minute as a baseball pitcher scuffing the ball with a piece of sandpaper to influence its flight, or more insidious like the steroids used by baseball and football players which became rampant during the '90's, finally exhausting the public's patience.

Horse racing is, as we know, a game of inches, with millions of dollars in purses and bets won and lost by a "nose." Until post race testing procedures became as sophisticated as they are today, it was not uncommon for trainers to attempt to get that "edge" in a huge range of ways.

It's a popular notion that racehorses ran on "hay, oats and water" before today's chemical enhancement began to give some trainers their huge advantage, allowing them to run at thirty-plus percent win-averages. Nothing could be further from the truth. Although not as sophisticated as modern methodology, individuals have always found a way to increase or decrease their chances and sometimes it's nearly as valuable to know who's not going to win as it is to know who will.

Simple tricks like feeding a horse or allowing him too much water right before racetime would often be enough to keep a favorite off the board and enable the barn to get more appealing odds the next time out. Or another easy fix was to skip the horse's exercise for a few days prior to the race and let them come up short. The race then became a workout and they'd be fit to go when the money was down.

During the '80's there was a rash of incidents when horses were found to have small round sponges up their noses and once the word was out, it became a popular trick, as horses are what is termed "obligate" breathers, unable to take in air through their mouths, so naturally, they ran out of gas every time.

Often the ploy wasn't found out unless a veterinarian was called to "scope" a losing horse suspected to have bled, but at smaller tracks with smaller purses, trainers would have to forego such an expense and those horses would run poorly until the perpetrator removed the sponge.

Prior to more advanced testing methods developed in the 1950's old time cheaters would use a "speedball," the combination of heroin and co-caine, rolling it in a ball and placing it down their throat as not to show in the saliva test and making sure a horse ran as fast as he could and feel no pain in the process. "Spit" tests were eventually replaced with the uri-nalysis which was more precise and the test barn's name changed from "spit-barn" to "piss-barn."

Charming...

Of course, such drugs picked up in the post-race urine test could get a trainer ruled off, sometimes for life, but the reward of the bet sometimes made the risk worth the reward. Any game played for money will tempt some to break the rules.

Previous to the turn of the millennium, you could say racing was played with a different attitude. Until the '60's, you could call it the "Wild West."

The easiest way to "beat the test" was to get to the person collecting the urine sample, commonly referred to as a "piss-catcher." It doesn't sound like a high paying job and it isn't and thus was logically the perfect spot to make a bribe. This doesn't work anymore since random blood-tests were introduced, but when there's money involved, where there's a will, there's a way, and the only true deterrent to such behavior will always be the effec-tiveness of those in charge of security. Racing officials now labor diligently to uncover cheaters and they are extremely effective, almost to the point that you could say the day of race-fixing is nearly a thing of the past.

Previous to the early 1980's when New York racing broke the model that had existed as long as anyone can remember, trainers were limited to the amount of stalls in the barn assigned to them. Many a trainer made a good living by training a dozen horses and cashing an occasional gamble.

Racing shaped up in 1946 when its internal private investigative agency, the Thoroughbred Racing Protective Bureau, or TRPB, was formed, headed by Spencer Drayton, Sr. Drayton was a former FBI agent and administrative assistant to J. Edgar Hoover, who was a racing fan himself.

The TRPB began the system of tattooing horses' lips to identify them conclusively as opposed to the previous method of color and hair description used by The Jockey Club since its inception in 1894. TRPB agents are plain-clothes cops, detectives who do a pretty good job of staying invisible around the track.

Still, any game worth playing must be worth trying to win, and some players will always rationalize their methodology as "if it's not exactly illegal, it's legal." Less insidious tactics can sometimes still get you an edge and sound good afterwards when you tell the story.

One Hall of Fame trainer used to boast of how he won the Young America Stakes at Meadowlands with a sore-footed horse by standing the colt in Amoco white unleaded gasoline for an hour before taking him to be saddled. He joked that the horse likely couldn't even feel his feet and it was fortunate that no one lit a match near him or the paddock might have gone up in flames.

As technology improves, so do testing procedures, and today it's increasingly difficult for anyone to use a performance-enhancing drug on a racehorse without detection.

Unfortunately, the litigious society we live in has enabled trainers like Rick Dutrow to mock the system, utilizing the civil courts to get around the penalties levied by Stewards.

In 2011 Dutrow was given a ten-year suspension for his repeated infractions, which included positive tests on winning horses for painkillers and possession of hypodermic needles in his desk drawer. Basically thumbing his nose at the authorities, Dutrow's lawyers began a lengthy appeal process, allowing him to continue training as if nothing had happened.

Indeed, if racing is a sporting event and they had conclusive evidence that he conspired to fix it, I don't understand why he didn't go to jail. I guess this makes him a modern version of Arnold Rothstein, who purportedly fixed the 1919 World Series and scammed the 1921 Travers but was never indicted for either.

This practice of "justice delayed is justice denied" began in the 1980's when jockeys first used lawyers to put off their suspensions in order to ride in big-money stakes races. Previous to that, the three Stewards, or presiding judges, were considered to have final say and had complete domain at their track over legal proceedings concerning trainers, jockeys and any other licensed employees.

In 1942 the legendary Eddie Arcaro unseated his rival Vince Nodarse in a race at the old Aqueduct track in Queens, New York and went before the Stewards for a hearing on the incident. Asked what he was trying to do, Arcaro glibly replied, "I was trying to kill the sonofabitch." For this the Stewards gave him an indefinite suspension, basically a life sentence. Were it not for the intercession of Helen Hay Whitney, mistress of the Greentree Stable and daughter of Abraham Lincoln's Assistant John Hay, Arcaro might never have ridden another horse. Her personal influence with the Jockey Club carried enough weight for her to have his punishment commuted after "The Maestro" sat out one full year.

Dutrow was eventually required to serve that ten-year suspension, essentially putting him out of the game.

There is little doubt that most of the problems that plague the sport are unsolvable simply due to the fact that the thirty-six states that allow horseracing pretty much have thirty-six different sets of rules and regulations.

No central board, no titular head or national commissioner, and widely different parameters for medication use as well as varying caveats and penalties, thus providing the proverbial uneven playing field. Imagine baseball with different length baselines or football with higher and lower goal posts.

I kept at it through the winter and by the time we got to Gulfstream in March we managed a few more wins and I was gradually increasing my clientele. With the help of Dave and Delbert, I managed to get involved with some of the better northern outfits heading to Jersey, taking second call to their riders and playing DH.

We shared information and I was able to supplement my limited income with enough winners to pay the rent and subscribed to the old racetracker's adage that "warm and broke is better than cold and broke."

After the Florida Derby, the winter horsemen would become anxious to return to their northern circuit, just as appalled by the coming summer heat in South Florida as they were by the autumnal frost that drove them there in the first place. Frank and I headed to Garden State Park outside Camden, New Jersey, where the plan was to gather business for the Monmouth Park meet that followed in June. We had our business with Jimmy Croll to start with and I managed to scout up some other decent horses to ride from the Jersey trainers who had put away their stock for the winter and were ready to bring them back for the new season.

One of the horses Croll pulled into Jersey with that year was a big bay colt named Mr. Prospector. The son of Raise A Native had been a $220,000 Keeneland sales topper as a yearling and was the fastest horse on four legs that year. His rider, Walter "Mousey" Blum, had the reputation as the best "gate-boy" in the business. Between the two they were unbeatable in sprint races and set the track record for six furlongs at Gulfstream, 1:07 4/5 and at Garden State, 1:08 3/5.

My friend Lou Raffetto was another Christian Brothers boy intoxicated with the backstretch. He had graduated from Georgetown with honors and was putting his college education to questionable use as a groom for trainer Jerry Caruso when I arrived with Iannelli from Florida. Jerry was a good, solid trainer who never had a huge stable but made a comfortable living all his life by hands-on work with lesser horses and he knew everything there was to know about getting one ready to run a big race and cash a bet.

Jimmy Croll's son Billy and I hung out a lot and he was with me when one morning when I stopped by Caruso's barn, looking for a mount. Lou asked me if I liked anything to bet on and Billy and I both laughed and told him Mr. Prospector could fall down and still win on Saturday.

A few days later I stopped by Caruso's barn and Lou confided in me that he had bet $2,000, a huge amount for a kid making $200 a week rubbing horses and after he cashed his tickets he declared himself retired from serious betting.

Lou has had a great careeer as a racing official, racing secretary and track official and made huge strides when he rose to the top echelon in track management, first resurrecting Boston's failing Suffolk Downs in the '80's and running Pimlico and Laurel for the Maryland Jockey Club after that. Years later he told me he'd never made another wager over two bucks since.

It's a rare man that's able to quit a winner...

X.

"Keep your friends close and your enemies closer."

--Michael Corleone (Al Pacino) from *Godfather Part II*

Garden State Park in the spring, there's nothing better. Apple blossoms, cherry blossoms, the Jersey beat, just warming up.

Frankie Valli and the Four Seasons croon from every radio – "Sherr-ee, Sherry baby, 'come, come, come out to-ni-ight, Sher-ee, can you come out tonight, 'come, come, come out to-ni-i-ight."

Grass so green and thick they have to cut it every other day, and hope springs eternal for better racing luck in the new meet, no matter how dismal it may have been at the last one.

At Cinelli's and Ponzios Diner, fresh faces beam at us over the counter... the Pagoda parking lot is stacked with shiny Cadillacs, Lincoln Town Cars and pricey sports cars. To us racetrackers, we imagine it's been the cold lifeless winter back home in Jersey since we left last November, fleeing at the first frost. Now it's finally summer a-coming, complete with blondes in red convertibles.

On the rail at the Garden State paddock, Sonia the white-haired madam looks like your grandma but when the horses depart the walking ring she posits in her Russian accent, "Gimme a vinna, I fix you up with my niece."

Sonia always has one of her good-looking "nieces" with her. She's on the road here but across the state on North Carolina Avenue in Atlantic City in a fashionable apartment on the first floor of her establishment she has a grand piano with an 8x10 picture of trainer Danny Perlsweig on it. Dandy Dan has obviously given her plenty of winners over the years.

Frank is winning his share, enough to get on the leading rider's list but not enough to seriously compete with local top guns like Walter Blum and Jimmy Mosley, and I am getting my next degree at agent's school thanks to lessons from seasoned veterans like the Block brothers, Carl and Henry, their pal Wally Pascal and the DelVecchio brothers, Jimmy and Domenic.

But it's Gene Fisher who might be the best jock's agent ever. He's a ringer for actor George Reeves, the guy who plays the TV Superman, dressed to perfection with the haberdasher's choice suit and tie, topped with a madras-banded straw hat. Always driving a new Cadillac Sedan de Ville, Fisher's been rolling hot with Donnie MacBeth since Hialeah and I'm fascinated by the terror he instills in the other agents, like he's able to snatch their best mounts away at will and they're powerless to defend themselves.

Gene grins through his black Steve Allen horn rims and other agents live in fear of his predatory skills, wishing he would fall prey to *demon rum, the Achilles Heel that periodically does take him down when he can't reconcile himself with his own success.*

He manages to run over fellow agents like a runaway Mack truck, stealing 6-to-5 mounts from everybody until one morning he goes missing at scratch time. Little Joe Verrone looks after Gene's business in a pinch and after the second day he's absent, Joe goes to the motel to check on him. The verdict's not good. Gene's locked himself in his room with a few fifths of Canadian Club, and his personal past performance chart predicts he won't surface for at least a week.

MacBeth puts up for it for about three days and finally hires Delbert Clements. Not that this is a bad thing for me, since having your mentor in the driver's seat would never be, but second calls behind a hot rider will only get you so far, like dating the boss's second favorite daughter.

Steve Vaonakis showed up from Maryland with Vincent Braccaile, Jr. and all of a sudden the rider colony gets almost as tough as Florida, shark-filled waters for a rookie facing the best agents on the "Mid-lantic" circuit.

Between Blum and Jimmy Mosley, MacBeth and Braccaile, they had a lock on all the best local customers so my only viable tactic is to hit as many barns as I can before dawn when trainers are getting their first sets out, in hopes that they might need a jockey to breeze one for an upcoming race. Frank's in his glory here in South Jersey, surrounded by mobsters and gamblers who've been awaiting the season's start for months and love to make a bet for a jockey in return for his opinion but he smells a chance at success, so he's not sleeping in.

Most trainers will put one of their regular exercise riders up for workouts until they get close to the actual race day. At that point they would like to have the jock familiarize himself with the horse and gain some confidence in the mount, so when a top gun would get stuck between the sheets, I'd jump on it and hustle Frank over there to fill in and once in a while we'd score the ride.

I got lucky that way one morning and picked up a nice mount from trainer Ralph McIlvane. McIlvane was tall and skinny, and with his tousled white hair and wire-rimmed glasses he resembled one of my college professors and the way he squinted when he talked, you couldn't see his eyes to guess what he was thinking. The horse in question was a big rangy colt called Smiling Jack and when his scheduled jockey overslept a workout we had the mount and a win in a nice allowance race.

Unfortunately, the one thing about "good" horses is that once they display their brilliance on the track, their potential becomes obvious to everyone. The Jersey Derby was coming up soon and Smiling Jack was eligible and ready for a $125,000 race that was almost as big a deal as the Kentucky Derby in those days.

McIlvane had a buddy, retired jockey Herb Fisher, whose claim to fame was his legacy as part of the "Fighting Finish" of the 1933 Kentucky Derby when he, on Head Play, and Don Meade aboard the eventual winner Broker's Tip literally fought on horseback, whipping and slashing, punching and beating on each other through the entire stretch.

The event was captured in a famous photograph and immortalized the participants in racing lore, clearly showing Fisher as he reached out to try and pull Meade's boot out of his stirrup.

By '72 though, Fisher was just another old guy hanging out at his buddy's barn and walking hots when he and Ralph realized they had a payoff horse in the barn. I stopped by Ralph's office early one morning to confirm the call on Smiling Jack and leaving the barn I had a bad feeling, a voice whispering something like "could this old reprobate be setting me up to get fucked?" Sure enough, McIlvane was evasive and out of sorts, and told me to go have a talk with my rider.

I went straight to the jock's room where Iannelli was pulling weight for the day's mounts and confronted him, and he hemmed and haw'd, finally doing his best to try and explain to me that it wasn't personal, "just business" and we'd have to part company or he would lose the mount.

I wasn't sure who I wanted to kill first, McIlvane or Fisher or Frank.

To this day, jockeys and agents work on a handshake contract, meaning that the only integrity attached to the agreement is that of the person attached to the hand. Usually the pursuit of the almighty dollar overrules conscience in many cases and agents can still be found dumping one jock for another to improve their chances, just as some jockeys will convince themselves that they can move up the ladder by "changing horses" in midstream.

Agents tend to stay with a good rider until he gets older, maybe in his late 40's and starts to show the wear and tear of injuries and ailments. That's when they look for a younger model and it's usually a good move since few riders are truly effective after fifty. Agents, on the other hand, have been known to rely on their personal relationships into their 80's and move whatever rider they have into the same barns they've always had.

After the initial shock of the backstabbing wore off, it finally dawned on me that I was in the real world, where loyalty may be fleeting, duplicity commonplace. Next day I found myself another jockey and moved on to Monmouth.

Marty Fromin might have lacked some of Frankie's riding skills, but he made up for it with a world-class positive attitude. He'd come out in the morning in a Superman t-shirt and talk the ear off any trainer who'd listen to him, charming his way into many a mount. We won more than our share of races that summer at Monmouth and went to the Atlantic City fall meet with plenty of business.

Unfortunately my plan for wintering in Florida had to be curtailed as most of our business went to Liberty Bell Park in Philadelphia and nearly none went to Florida, and I became a Jersey-Pennsylvania based agent for the next few years, living near Monmouth Park and commuting to the other tracks. Winter racing was fairly novel since tracks like Aqueduct were rare and when Liberty Bell closed for good, the new Keystone Park that replaced it was set up to accommodate indoor betting crowds.

The guys who do the Jersey/Florida circuit come back early in the spring, and one April morning I'm sitting in the back seat of Dave Hart's Olds 98 as he and trainer Joe Pierce are in the front, discussing where's the best place to go for Chinese food.

I'm working on the track for two years now and I've learned that when it comes to eateries, the Jewish guys always know which ones are the best, especially the Chinese and Italian places.

We're driving to Keystone Park in Philadelphia for a stake race, and Pierce has the favorite in the feature with Dave's jock Perret in the saddle.

My jock Fromin rides two claimers in the early races on the undercard, both of which have little or no chance, but I consider it part of my post-graduate education program to hang out with these guys whenever they let me.

Driving trainers to and from the track is a great way to get close with them and if the horse gets beat you have the whole way home to try and cool them out, blaming the track condition, the starting gate or sun-spots... just anything other than the rider.

I love the way they kibitz, doing kind of free-form shtick, partly theatre for the "kid" in the backseat. It's the kind of thing guys do when they get older and feel as if they have the upper hand in an empirical sense, which of course they do.

Like Benny Perkins, when he calls you "kid." Even though you're a grown man, maybe married and with a couple of kids yourself, he'd still call you "kid." I've always liked that, it goes a long way for your self-esteem when you're over fifty, and guys not that much older than you and certainly in no way condescending are still calling you "kid."

On this particular day, everybody's horse loses and we would have been driving all the way home in semi-silence except Dave remembers one of his hidden-gem Central Jersey Italian joints and offers to buy dinner. Dinner's great, we all have a couple of glasses of wine and head home to fight another day.

Another lesson from a great agent: "If you win, buy dinner. If you lose, buy dinner."

And my first experience with the winner/loser phenomenon: When your horse wins, everybody tells jokes and the ride home feels like it's about fifteen minutes even if it's fifty miles. If your horse loses, the ride is silent and fifty miles seems like six hours, so you'd better be prepared with some alternate form of entertainment to ease the mind. I've known agents who could have held their own with the best stand-up comics, like Barry Brown, who was often heard chirping to a trainer, "I'd rather ride a loser for you than a winner for somebody else."

What a guy...

Racetrackers love to have some fun at the expense of a rookie, and the old-timers get great pleasure from sending new hot walkers off to get a "bucket of steam" or to fetch "the key to the quarter pole," laughing themselves silly at how easy it is to recycle those gags.

On a warm August morning the day before the Haskell Handicap, I was across the tracks in the back stable area at Monmouth hunting for mounts when I walked through Tony Basile's barn and saw a guy in a porkpie hat grazing a monstrous bay.

A fellow agent, Nicky Pizzicillo, was there also admiring the horse from a respectful distance when a local owner, Teddy Frucht, strolled up and wanted to shoot the breeze. We all called him "Doc" since he was a small animal vet and you just knew in his heart he wished he were a horse vet, such a nice guy with a happy demeanor and only a touch gullible. On the track when you play a prank on someone, it's referred to as "putting him on the lead." Nicky points at the big bay and says, "Hey, Doc, take a look at the left ankle on that one, would'ya?"

Mensch that he is, Doc heads right toward the horse and says to the guy holding him, "Straighten him up, I'll have a look at that." The horse was Forego, and if Nicky and I didn't jump in, his trainer, Frank Whiteley, would most likely have given poor Doc a black eye.

Monmouth has a reputation for being the graveyard of favorites in big races and that year was no exception. Forego went off at 3 to 5 and finished third. The rest of the year he had no problem winning the Woodward and the Marlboro Cup on the way to being named Horse of the Year for the third straight season.

Fromin and I had a decent Monmouth meet, but by the following fall, he decided to move back home to the Chicago circuit and I began booking mounts for a maniac Hungarian jockey named Paul Kallai.

Kallai was known for his incredible strength and courage, fearlessness and limited mastery of the English language. I assumed he was at the back end of his career when we hooked up, something I got used to as the older, more established agents usually kept cycling in younger riders as everyone attempted to continuously improve their position.

Paul and I won a few dozen races and parted company that Fall. He was soon after implicated in a race-fixing scandal that occurred during the time I worked for him, although I never suspected a thing. It was the early days of the Trifecta bet, and Paul and some other riders had figured out that taking the favorite out of the money would make for huge payoffs, and they conspired to "tie-up" the last race several times a week.

When I mentioned the story to Bob Quigley, who was the GM of Atlantic City Race Course back then, he recounted the "inside story" on the scam. Apparently he had pulled in a ne'er-do-well jock's agent for cashing some bad checks and when threatened with prosecution the agent panicked and immediately rolled over, ratting on the jockeys in hopes it would make things easier for himself. Quigley brought in the Jersey State Police and they instructed the track stewards to do nothing while closely documenting the racing and betting patterns for a few weeks before springing their trap and arresting most of the riders. Kallai, Kevin Daly and a few others skipped bail and fled to avoid a sure prison sentence, Daly to Ireland and Kallai heading back to his native Hungary.

My oblivious naïveté worked to my advantage, since Paul was so clever at keeping the fixes quiet that I was totally unaware, even to the point that the State Police never even bothered to question me. Fortunately so, as it's likely I would have made more than a bet or two and ended up in the soup myself.

After Kallai high-tailed it back to Hungary, he kept riding there for another 30 years so I guess my assumption about "end of career" was way off. I ran into him at Gulfstream in the early '90's (the statute of limitations was up) on a busman's holiday, fit and looking good with a ponytail, diamond earring and a 30-year-old blonde at his side. Paul never won the Kentucky Derby but he won the Hungarian Derby twice, the second time in 2000, and he died in the winner's circle of an aneurysm at age 73 after riding his last winner.

A true racetracker!

At the Garden State fall meet, I began booking for a journeyman jock named Menotti Aristone, stable rider for Ben Perkins, Sr., who was as smart a horseman as I ever encountered and easily the best-dressed. Ben came from the Maryland circuit and was another "Old School" trainer. Menotti was from a wealthy family, and at best a capable rider, but like many jocks, he made up for ability by trying harder. It didn't hurt that his father owned most of the horses in Benny's barn.

Ben's horses always won the beauty prize for best turned out in the paddock and he specialized in getting his two-year-olds ready to crack first time out. He had learned over the years that most horses, no matter how good they look, are best sold off a win, and he made sure everyone knew he was always a seller.

Ben bought a filly named Brave Raj at a two-year-old sale for $24,000 and she looked good breaking her maiden. When Mel Stute, who was training Snow Chief, the best three-year-old colt in the country came from California looking for a filly, Ben priced his at $350,000 and they said yes. She went on to be a champion and well worth the money, but most sellers would have valued her more around $250,000. I asked Ben how he came up with the amount and he said, "I figure what they're worth and add on a bunch just in case they say 'yes.'" That might have been the one that got away, but there were plenty more he made up for it on, like Forest Wildcat.

Forest Wildcat was by Storm Cat, one of Kentucky's best stallions and when Ben spotted him in a sale in Maryland the colt had an "iffy" looking ankle. He ended up buying him anyway for his best client, New Farm's Ebby Novak, and ran off a string of wins in Jersey, putting the colt on every horse-trader's radar screen. Novak was a neighbor of Ben's in Marlton, New Jersey, and had quietly observed his training skill for years when one day he intercepted him at his mailbox and asked if Ben would get him a few horses.

Ebby had a company that produced two essential items for modern life: birthday candles and balloons. He also owned the rights to Batman, Cabbage Patch Kids, Teenage Mutant Ninja Turtles and Barney the purple dinasour. He had made a fortune in business and loved handicapping horses, and when he decided that he just wanted to have some fun, Ben provided him with all the fun he could handle.

Besides Forest Wildcat and plenty of his offspring, which they raced successfully, New Farm raced over 30 stakes winners including Conveyor, Meadow Monster and Appealing Skier.

Years later, after Due Process had folded, I had just gone on my own selling horses and breedings under the name of Star Stable/Star Bloodstock. Ben became my first customer when Fred Seitz of Brookdale Farm in Kentucky came looking for a Storm Cat colt that he could buy into as a racehorse for the rest of the year and retire to stud the following winter and Forest Wildcat was a perfect fit for the operation.

Fred and I had been high school schoolmates at C.B.A. and did plenty of business during the time when I ran Due Process Stable. I'd given him my syndicate votes to help him get Deputy Minister to his Kentucky farm when it became time to move his stallion duty from Windfields in Maryland and Fred knew he could trust me, so he flew up to Jersey with a check in his pocket. I met him at the track and we headed to the Perkins barn to see the colt and when we arrived Ben wasn't there but his assistant was, so I asked him to pull the horse out of his stall so we could have a look.

Forest was a flashy bay with a small star and looked every bit the part of a runner, until we asked the groom to jog him. Then he looked like he was going to fall down every other stride. Fred looked at me, shook his head and said, "Too bad, I'm heading to the airport."

I wanted to throw up on the spot, but something didn't ring true so I called Ben right away and he just laughed. "Always goes that way. He can't walk or jog worth a damn, but he just runs like the wind. Tell your man to stick around and we'll breeze him in the morning."

It took some fast talking, but in the end I successfully coerced Fred into waiting another day and at 6 a.m. the following day, Forest Wildcat hobbled out onto the track like an old man, breezed three furlongs in :34 flat and came back like he hadn't even taken a deep breath. Ben and Fred shook and the deal was struck.

Forest won a Grade III stake for their partnership next time out and went on to sire an English champion and a bunch of stakes horses, turning Ben's $52,000 purchase into millions and Fred's stallion pick into one of the best stud deals of the 1990's.

XI.

"I WANTED TO GET OUT OF THE STOCK MARKET AND INTO SOMETHING SENSIBLE..."

--DAN LASATER, WHEN ASKED WHY HE INVESTED IN RACEHORSES

Steak-house entrepreneur Dan Lasater was a close pal of soon-to-be governor Bill Clinton and Clinton's brother Roger in their home state of Arkansas and rumor had it that they'd partied together hard and often. From the demeanor Lasater brought to New Jersey, it wasn't hard to believe. He was the leading owner in the country from 1974 through 1977 and when he shipped a string of runners east with a Midwestern cowboy trainer named Dave Vance for the Monmouth meet, pretty soon they were winning races at will, claiming everything in sight.

Vance's entourage included his Robert Q. Lewis lookalike assistant "Goose" Heimer, a light-on-his-feet 300 lb. stable agent named "Tricky" Dick Fisher, as well as jock's agent "Harry the Hat" Hacek and half-a-dozen "turf advisors." Their barn was populated with hot walkers and grooms who answer to "Pop-eye," "Worm," "Rooster" and of course, "Snake." You can tell where this is going.

They brought their own rider, Darrell McHargue, but Vance ran so many horses they needed a back-up jock for entries or when McHargue was out of town to ride in a stakes race, and I was pitching Menotti Aristone for that spot.

Dinner with those guys was a financial disaster for me as the agent gets to pick up the tab most of the time and it wasn't unusual for Dave or Tricky to put away a 34 oz. steak at one of those joints where you pick out your own and they cut it to the size you desire, but that's the deal.

Due to the newness of the Keystone track in Philadelphia and healthy purses in the Northeast, there was an influx of excellent horsemen from the Midwest, chasing the money. Gordon Potter and his wife Marlene, Gary Thomas and Jimmy Garroutte all gravitated with the Lasater gang and forced the Eastern trainers to move their game up a notch. Lasater had horses all over the country and Potter also trained a string for him that included 1976 Santa Anita "Big 'Cap" winner Royal Glint.

They all had a dry sense of humor and enjoyed a good laugh, especially Gomer Evans who trained a few from time to time but mainly made his living as a bookmaker. Gomer was one of those "road gamblers," like Amarillo Slim or Doyle Brunson, known as a guy who'd bet anybody-anything-anytime.

One notable gamble of his involved a $10,000 wager he often made, challenging his mark that the guy couldn't eat a quail a day for a month. This is an old bet based on the Biblical references and a modern belief that wild quail become toxic from eating hemlock seeds. Usually the bettor would get sick and quit in a week or two, but in this case, they kept up the proposition until about three days before the end of the month when the guy suddenly dropped dead.

Gomer expressed sympathy to the widow at the man's passing and sent flowers, but had no one to kick but himself for not having a third party hold the cash, since it's a well known fact that you can't collect from a corpse.

When the Vance operation took stalls at Atlantic City, Menotti and I picked up second call behind their stable jock McHargue and basically doubled our earning capacity.

Between Benny Perkins and Vance, we campaigned through the fall and winter at Keystone until Menotti and I split the following spring when he went to Philadelphia and I opted to head to Jersey first with Timmy Jessup at Garden State, then move on home to Monmouth again with a second Kentucky rider named Billy Tichenor.

Same song, different tune, as Tichenor was another average rider who compensated for missing skills with a great work ethic, but he was a straight arrow, family guy with three little kids and when he finished riding for the day, he went right home, no Happy Hours or signing autographs for eager groupies. Most mornings when I hit the track kitchen for coffee at five, he was there waiting for me, ready to get on anything and everything.

Part of the checks and balances of the horseracing game is the system used to chronicle workouts. Most mornings they jog or gallop, but about every five to seven days, horses in competition require a full-out effort referred to as a "work" or a "breeze." Trainers judge how fit their horses are by these workouts as there's no greater sin than sending out a "short" horse – one who's unfit for the task.

Several individuals employed by the track or the *Racing Form* or both are stationed at fixed locations during the time the track is open for the horses' morning exercise. With their access to the Horse Identifier's office to scrutinize the foal registration certificates that contain a full description of the horse, including color, markings and any unusual characteristics, the clockers virtually know every horse on the grounds.

The clockers work together, divvying up the action as they anticipate horses' breaking off at the various poles indicating distance from the finish line.

One might say, "I've got Pletcher's pair at the half," while another replies, "Baffert, Game on Dude at the five-eighths."

There's more to the job than simply clicking a stopwatch and guys like Gary Young have made a living combining a horseman's eye with a gambler's nerve. Gary starts his day at 5:30 a.m., finishes when the mutuel windows close at the end of race day. We've known each other for many years and had a great friendly rivalry when Dehere was up against the horse he found for Albert Broccoli, producer of the James Bond films. Brocco beat Dehere in the Breeders' Cup Juvenile, but Dehere ended up champion nonethess on the basis of his incredible stakes triple at Saratoga and his dominating win in the Champagne. This all just served to provide Gary and I with a lifetime topic to disagree on.

Workout times are a significant part of the puzzle for handicappers, who otherwise have only past performance charts or in the case of first time starters, pedigree, jockey and trainer to go on.

Many a professional horserace gambler either clocks on his own or relies on a "private" clocker for information and opinions. Trainers who claim regularly either use their own clocker or pay for the information from free-lancers.

Part of the "taking an edge" at gambling is having superior information on which to base your wagering decisions, and therefore, trainers wishing to cash a bet on their horse need to find a way to confuse the clockers. The best way to do so is to work your horse as soon as the track opens in the morning, usually under cover of darkness during the last moments before dawn's light.

For the past dozen or so years trainers have been required to inform a track representative, stationed at the entrance to the track of the name of the horse and distance to be breezed when their horse enters the in-gap. Clockers enter their information on computers and the times are passed to the Racing Office and the Racing Form immediately.

Before the days of the sentinels at entry gaps, trainers could alter their horse's appearance by using a different saddle towel or changing from their usual exercise rider or putting bandages on to cover the horse's white socks in order to fool the clockers.

The mud or poultice used on horses' legs to draw out inflammation is white and a smudge of it applied carefully on the horse's forehead can look like a blaze through the clocker's binoculars. And many a gamble was cashed by trainers who covered up the white pastern of a bay horse with brown shoe polish.

Two-year-old horses don't necessarily have a name when they arrive at the track, and they might get by the clockers a few times before they figure out who they are. When the horse makes its first start, the Racing Form may only show the one or two works the trainer wants them to have and thus go off at a big price.

My first experience with a situation similar to this came at Monmouth when we were getting ready to run a nice two-year-old filly by Distinctive out of Eloquent Es. She was a lovely grey and easy to spot and already had the name Es's Distinctive when Brennan grabbed her out of a sale for a couple hundred thousand and the clockers were all over her. What they didn't know was that Bob had decided to change her name and honor a local Newark sportswriter, Wes Moon by calling her Distinctive Moon. Thus when she entered the starting gate at Monmouth that July afternoon, everyone was unaware that her lightning-fast "bullet" workouts were attributed to the non-existing Es's Distinctive and she sailed home by five lengths as a generous 7 to 1, and Brennan got his purchase price back in one swoop...

Back in the "wild west" days in Florida, trainers like Bryan Webb would ship in with horses from the farm and one year in particular he had a bunch. In fact, he had so many two-year-olds that he'd enter half a dozen in the same race under different trainer's names, just trying to get them out of each other's way. One day he gave my pal Woody a wad of cash and told him to put it on a first-time starter. Woody looked at the program and said, "But this isn't one of yours..." only to be told, "Don't worry about it kid. Lots of times it's better to know which ones can't run than it is to know which ones can."

Rarely, but nonetheless it does happen that "plain" horses with few markings can get mixed up at the farm at a young age as they are shuttled from the yearling barn to two-year-olds in training and the error doesn't come to light until many months later when they're getting tattooed and the identifier figures it out. Most of them don't even have names at that point, so the farm trainer will write it on a piece of tape and stick it on their halters and, as young horses will do, some manage to chew the tape off or rub it off on the wall of the van.

We had such an incident with the Due Process horses when a pair of plain bay colts got switched at shipping time. The one in Delaware with Eddie Colletti had made three starts before the New York identifier informed me that the colt Phil Gleaves was ready to enter wasn't who we thought he was and had the same pedigree. No betting coup, no ill intent, but nonetheless... Oops.

Some mistakes weren't quite so innocent. In the late 1970's, New York veterinarian Mark Gerard was shipping horses from South America to New York on a regular basis, so it was nothing unusual when he brought two colts up from Uruguay. The fancy one, Cinzano, was the champion three-year-old down there and the other colt, Lebon, was never destined to be anything but a claimer. When the horses arrived stateside, Cinzano got a case of colic and died, leaving Gerard a $150,000 insurance payoff. After Lebon won the last heat at Aqueduct one afternoon and paid 50-1, Gerard cashed a huge bet. Had not a disgruntled bettor from Uruquay tipped off the authorities – that the "Lebon" who won was actually Cinzano -- Gerard would likely have gotten away with the switch. Not exactly the kindly old vet who looks after puppies and kittens.

The racing game took a huge turn in the seventies, when veterinarians became as important to a horse's success as their trainers. Until that point, horsemanship was a trade learned through years of apprenticeship at the direction of a trainer who'd done the same. With litigation becoming so prevalent in American society, the "right to work" became more important that the requirement to acquire knowledge. Thus, many trainers and jockeys sidestepped the contract or apprenticing stage and were licensed as what we called "ninety-day wonders."

Previous to that, top horsemen like Jack Van Berg, Allen Jerkens, Charlie Whittingham and Gary Jones all learned every aspect of their trade. They could groom a horse, saddle a horse, ride a horse, and even shoe a horse. Other than one of their pupils, I'd bet you can't find one trainer in a hundred that could shoe a horse today (one who can is Billy Mott).

But skill was not the main problem for the "new" style trainer, since they had plenty of help from their vets. I have known many vets over the years, outstanding practitioners of the healing arts like Jim Kenney and Mark Ketner, Wayne McIlwraith, Ben Franklin and Tom Brokken, Pete Hall and Don Devine, and all were men of unquestionable integrity.

Unfortunately, some others preferred to use their knowledge to help less principled trainers win races, at any cost -- cost being the key word when what went from a previously nominal monthly bill for the horse owner became a four-figure charge. New "therapies" and the precise calculation of withdrawl times for those drugs became a science, and one south Florida circuit vet delighted in wearing a "Dr. Demento" license plate on the front of his truck as his clientelle enjoyed a spike in their win percentage.

We had a respectable summer and when Monmouth ran a rare fall meet, Tich' was leading rider. But his passion wasn't really in being a jockey and he had a young family, so Billy saved his money and eventually packed it in, moving back home to Kentucky and the family coal business.

During this burgeoning era of year-round racing, some trainers figured out how to place their horses at different tracks in order to take advantage of weak fields and were able to win a ton of races. Smaller tracks often had excellent trainers who were content to roll up impressive win statistics even though the purses didn't compare to the big time, and they usually were able to cash a decent bet now and then to supplement the difference.

Leading trainer at the new Penn National track near Harrisburg was a mountain of a man named Elmer Eugene Zeek.

All of six foot three and 300 lbs. and certainly no shrinking violet, "Gene" Zeek ran winners at Garden State, Liberty Bell and Delaware as well as Penn and claimed horses nearly every day, so it wasn't that unlikely that he would constantly be cashing checks at the track since the Horsemen's Bookkeepers didn't accept personal checks for claiming purposes. Plus he was reputed to be a high-roller at the windows, heavily backing horses he would claim for ten thousand and run back for five. This has always been the modus operandi of aggressive "claiming" trainers, unafraid to lose their horses since they make more than enough betting on horses running in races where it's nearly impossible to beat them.

Zeek became friendly with the managers of the New Jersey banks near Garden State Park where he kept his accounts and used to take them to night races at Penn National, for his version of wining and dining. Zeek would excuse himself from the table as the horses came on the track, saying he was going to get "information" and return to the table just as the race was ending to produce a winning ticket for the bank manager.

Of course, he was buying a ticket on every horse and pulling out the winning one as the horses reached the finish line, exclaiming, "We got it!" The banker fell into the trap, believing Zeek had "inside information" and they had struck oil.

Shortly before post for the first race one morning I was walking to the Racing Secretary's Office at Liberty Bell Park and ran into Carl Block, agent for leading rider Jimmy Mosley and brother to jockeys Henry and Johnny Block.

Carl called me over to his car and when I leaned in the passenger side window he said, "Hey kid, need any cash?" He laughed as he showed me a grocery bag that must have held at least a hundred grand in banded stacks of fifties and hundreds.

Trainers have agents do all sorts of favors for them, and cashing a big check to move funds for a claim or a bet wasn't illegal, unethical or even uncommon, since the rules required a cash or certified deposit to the track bookkeeper when claiming a horse, and actually the tracks like to have as much cash as possible in the hands of big players, since it usually finds its way back through the betting windows. Due to the "cash" nature of their business, tracks and casinos are some of the few places that checks don't clear immediately, rather get deposited once or twice a week, allowing for the time honored art of "kite-ing" wherein the client in question has the luxury of covering his scrip before it hits the bank.

The following morning at Garden State Park, the backstretch information mill was abuzz with the story of how Zeek and his stable rider Karl Korte had piled up a million in cash and split town, leaving the bank manager to explain why he'd been okaying checks for an overdrawn account. The big guy had done a synchronized cash-out at five tracks in 24 hours, knowing that the checks would take at least a couple of days to clear. That's about five mil' in 2014 dollars. You would have thought he was Robin Hood, spreading the wealth the way the story circulated, rather than an uncommon crook duping a lot of folks who thought he was their friend.

Sports Illustrated later ran a cover story, entitled "The Sting," recounting how Zeek and Korte had relocated to the Caribbean island of Grenada, purchased a sport fishing boat and were laying low in paradise, posing as the "Clancy" brothers.

The two sure things Zeek was counting on were the lack of any extradition policy between the island nation and the U.S. and the willingness of the country's Prime Minister to accept a payoff for protection. The Clancy brothers were good there until a sudden regime change ousted their protector and the sanctuary deal came to a halt.

Both were eventually returned to the U.S. and did the rest of their sport fishing behind bars.

XII.

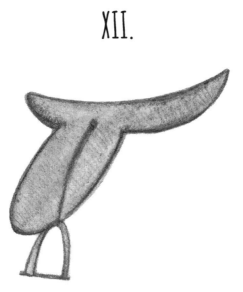

"THE ONLY PLACE SUCCESS COMES BEFORE WORK IS IN THE DICTIONARY."

--VINCE LOMBARDI

Garden State Park in Cherry Hill, New Jersey, near Camden was one of America's great racetracks, just across the "nickel bridge" from Philadelphia, and was built and opened in 1942 by contractor Eugene Mori, a son of Italian immigrants. This was a source of pride for my old man, whose own father had emigrated from southern Italy at the age of eleven before the turn of the century.

Experienced in the horse track business, Mori also purchased Hialeah in 1955 and ran both ovals himself until selling the Florida track to John Brunetti, Sr., whose family still runs it.

One of his era's great success stories, Mori had a hand in many industries, building theatres, restaurants and hotels and developing the city of Vineland, New Jersey.

Well-heeled horse owners would stay at the Cherry Hill Inn and trainers and agents preferred the gold-roofed Rickshaw Inn, whether they could afford it or not. Both hotels were within a stone's throw of Mori's track and plenty of horse business was done in those cocktail lounges. Trainers would steal each other's owners, agents would steal each other's mounts and everybody would try to steal the waitresses.

Dave Hart's girlfriend, a big blonde we referred to as "the Palomino," was the hostess at the high-end restaurant in the Cherry Hill Inn, so we made regular appearances there to take advantage of the "family discount."

Mori's friendship with another South Jersey Italian, Anthony Imbesi, would foster a friendly rivalry when Mori sold him the yearling filly Tosmah, out of his mare Cosmah, with the understanding that Imbesi would pay what she eventually proved to be worth. Imbesi owned the Seven-Up franchise for New Jersey, Pennsylvania, Delaware and Maryland, and soon developed a passion for racing.

Subsequently crowned the champion two-year-old filly of 1963, Tosmah would soon appear close-up in the female family of the legendary Northern Dancer. Imbesi paid off his debt in full and set out to apply the insight into bloodlines and pedigrees he had gained from years of breeding champion English Setters. The "Blue Hen" broodmare Tosmah became the basis for decades of breeding success for Imbesi's Briardale Farm. His son Joe passed on entering the family business and instead took to the horses, training the Imbesi home-breds with considerable success on the Jersey circuit.

The Garden State structure was built of wood due to a paucity of steel and concrete during the war years and the building predated modern fire codes. On April 14, 1977 -- Happy Birthday to me -- the entire structure burned to the ground when an electrical fire spread from the Clubhouse kitchen and ended racing at Garden State for eight years.

I heard the news when I went to work at my night job punching tickets as a mutuel clerk at the new Meadowlands racetrack.

Pushing long days with espresso coffee and a questionable diet, I'd developed a mild ulcer and decided to forego conventional medicine and cure myself with natural foods and better exercise habits. I used the autodidact's favorite refuge, the public library, and took night classes in nutrition. I was between jockeys and had wanted to know what it felt like to be on the other side of the window, and with a loan from the local bank we had opened a small health food store, figuring that if business was poor, we could eat the inventory, and when I eventually did find a jockey to represent, Bonnie could run the store. She was pregnant with our first child, so naturally a night job was the perfect thing to do with my spare time.

While it was in its prime, Garden State attracted great racehorses, many prepping for their seasonal debuts, including the two-year-old Secretariat and other household names like Whirlaway and Citation.

The nearby Latin Casino nightclub featured top acts like Frank Sinatra, Dean Martin and Liberace and overbooked nightly until the track burned down and casino gaming began forty-five minutes away in Atlantic City and the action moved east.

Big bettors at the horse races were easy prey for the casinos that gave them fast action, limo rides and free rooms and meals as well as liberal credit lines –- all things they couldn't get at the track.

By the time Garden State did reopen, all the track's high rollers were tapped-out and their money never made it back to Cherry Hill.

New Jersey Governor Christine Todd Whitman followed the lead of politicians who were either under the spell or in the pockets of the casinos when she vetoed a bill that would have allowed slot machines at racetracks.

On April 1, 1985, a new $120 million structure, built by Robert Brennan's public company, International Thoroughbred Breeders (ITB), attempted to resurrect flat racing in South Jersey and made a splash, attracting New York horses and flying New York jockeys in on Brennan's helicopter for the night races in an attempt to mimic the Meadowlands' success.

Bob Quigley, the dean of racetrack management, had operated Atlantic City at its zenith and opened the Meadowlands. Brennan hired him as Garden State's GM and Quigley brought not only class but cachet to the operation, since he'd worked on Jersey tracks since he was a kid and knew everyone who'd ever worked in any capacity in a Jersey track by their first name.

Bob grew up near Atlantic City and liked to re-tell stories he'd heard about the days when Enoch "Nuckie" Thompson and his cronies still ran the boardwalk, remnants of the free-wheeling Prohibition days portrayed in HBO's television series "*Boardwalk Empire*."

Garden State held on for sixteen years but finally threw up the white flag and ran their last horserace in May of 2001, done in by those same casinos at the other end of the Atlantic City Expressway.

Whereas tracks charge for parking and admission, casino lots are free and the doors always open. The essential difference between the tracks and casinos, however, is that within the "pari-mutuel" system that the tracks operate on, their profit comes from the "take-out" or skim, a percentage of every bet they are allowed to deduct before paying out the winners.

Thus, the losing bettors are paying the winning ones and the track merely acts as an intermediary or middleman.

Casinos, on the other hand, operate with their "win" as primary motivation. If they can clean you out, so be it, it's you against them.

Seven years is an eternity for gamblers to wait for a track to be rebuilt, and in the meantime a new group had erected a track outside Philadelphia to replace Liberty Bell Park, a venue that was always problematic as it was designed principally for harness racing, converting surfaces to accommodate thoroughbreds.

The new Keystone Racetrack was located on the north side of town, convenient to the Pennsylvania and New Jersey Turnpikes, and although it reportedly cost $20 million to build, most observers speculated that someone might have swung with more than a few bucks. But since it was a basic as possible, "The Key" was set up for cold weather racing and made a perfect fit with the Jersey tracks that weren't winterized and could only run spring, summer and fall meets.

I got a tip that some big outfits from other parts of the country were interested in trying a new venue, so I approached Racing Secretary Frank Gabriel, Sr. and got him to agree to pick up my expenses for a campaign to bring in new blood. One of the outfits I'd heard wind of was the Joseph P. Dorignac Stable from Louisiana. Joe D III was an up-and-coming trainer with a big string of his father's runners that had been dominating the Fair Grounds track, which was also owned by his father.

I head to New Orleans and meet with "Mister Joe" at his office, which turns out to be a table near the front window of his supermarket. Not just any supermarket -- Dorignac's was the busiest in the Big Easy and also the town's biggest wholesale meat vendor.

Scrubbed and polished in my best suit and tie, I introduce myself to Mister Joe and told to "have a seat, boy." Only when I notice the pistol tucked in his belt did I realize I wasn't in Kansas anymore.

The Fair Grounds track weighs heavily in the history of American racing, credited with originating both the post parade of horses and the pari-mutuel system of betting used by all tracks today. There's a strong connection between New Orleans racing and the Kentucky crowd, including Churchill promoter Matt Winn, Col. E.R. Bradley and Calumet Farm, which consistently triumphs there during the winter meet.

Louisiana is known for skilled jockeys, especially those of the Cajun variety. Eddie Delahoussaye, Ray Broussard, Randy Romero, and Craig Perret, and later Kent Desormeaux and Joe Talamo, distinguish themselves with brilliant careers.

New Orleans also has a reputation for slick politicians like the Long brothers, Hughie and Earl, and likewise New Orleans horsemen are tenacious and cagey, able to compete anywhere. You might be able to attribute this partly to the fact that a lot of them are descended from pirates, retaining the gene for ruthlessness.

Mister Joe and I make a deal and he agrees to send Joey to Keystone with a string of forty runners. I would be his stable agent, in charge of business affairs and, in addition to a nominal salary, I get to handle the book of our contract jockey Angelo Trosclair, Jr. at the usual agent's rate of twenty-five percent.

It makes a jockey agent's job a lot easier if you have a big outfit to count on for "first call," providing a base for daily business, but the drawback is that other trainers can be reluctant to ride that jock if the outfit does a lot of claiming. Angelo can certainly horseback and we win plenty of races, but I had to push hard on my good customers to get outside mounts and eventually we break into the top three on the leading rider's list.

All goes well until a spark from an exposed wire sets fire to the Dorignac barn. We lose half a dozen horses and the survivors are damaged goods from smoke inhalation. Horses that formerly ran in stakes company suddenly can't make it a half-mile and the mighty Dorignac Stable is done, packed up and headed home to Louisiana.

Racing was becoming a game of information and as I learned more about thoroughbred bloodlines, I became interested in the breeding industry as a possible next move, starting a bloodstock agency with my friend Tim Raymond. We called it Eastern Bloodstock, and fashioned our logo after that of the most popular airline of the day.

Timmy was the son of W.T. Raymond, who trained a stakes horse named Freetex among other notables for the Stavola Stable and we began proffering breeding nominations to trainers in hopes of getting our bloodstock agency off the ground. We sold a few shares and seasons right away to, guess what, Easterners.

When Tim's dad suddenly passed away from a heart attack, Tim suggested I approach the Stavolas to manage their racing interests, which included hundreds of horses on farms in New Jersey and Ocala, Florida. It seemed to be an excellent fit as I had gone to high school with the Stavola sons. I sent the resume they requested and never heard back, which eventually turned out to be a good thing.

With a young child and another on the way, I was seeking some stability and began to give considerable thought to the concept of business management applied to racing stables on a more comprehensive scale. Just before our second daughter Liza was born, Bonnie and I had an offer on the health food store, so we sold it and decided to spend the winter in Florida again where I had the possibility of an office job at Gulfstream if nothing else worked out.

Gulfstream Park is located in Hallandale, wedged between North Miami and Hollywood in what used to be nondescript paradise in the days when there was still space between Miami, Fort Lauderdale and Palm Beach. Now you can't tell where one town ends and the other begins.

Reminiscent of the sentiment that inspired Joni Mitchell's "pave paradise, put up a parking lot."

Gulfstream opened in 1939, and was owned and run by the Donn family since 1944. They were originally florists so the place was lush with landscaping, including orchids everywhere, inspiring a purple color theme.

Gulfstream had turf racing since '59, and its Florida Derby became the first $100,000 race in Florida during an era when racing dates were regulated by a state board. Hialeah always had the prime dates from January until March, and when Gulfstream opened it was relegated to finish off the winter season.

Inside the turf course was a great infield lake with good looking girls piloting small sailboats, and occasionally a huge tarpon made its way through underground channels and could be seen leaping from the water.

Gamblers liked to speculate that since the lake was linked to the Intercoastal waterway, the tides might influence the speed of the track. Low tide, forget the speed, the track would be dead, high tide, speed would carry. Unless speed held up at low tide, then they'd go to another theory.

Horsemen tolerated the harder, speed-favoring track whose composition contained micro-bits of coral that migrated to the surface and precipitated foot problems in many horses, causing them to shed the sole, or frog, of ther foot.

In the mid-1980's Doug Donn, grandson of the founder, engineered one of the great moves in American racing when he outmaneuvered Hialeah's John Brunetti for the "middle dates." It was the beginning of the end for what is arguably the most beautiful track ever built.

Gulfstream PR man Joe Tannenbaum began a masterful campaign against the Miami track that worked so well that people couldn't finish saying "Hialeah" without saying "but it's in a bad neighborhood."

Hialeah's owner, John Brunetti, was a construction magnate who'd built major highways in northern Florida and was well connected politically and loved the game. He bred and raised his own thoroughbreds at his Red Oak Farm in Ocala, running them mainly in New Jersey and Florida. Unfortunately John's penchant for playing hardball when it came to negotiating worked against him on the track dates issue, and when offered a permanent deal of forty-four of the most desirable "middle" dates in January and February, he refused and held out for half a dozen more.

Racing Board members finally had enough dickering and succumbed to Gulfstream's campaign, awarding the next season's middle dates to that track, virtually turning the tide against Hialeah and ringing its death knell.

Trainers loved the track surface at Hialeah, as it was much more forgiving on horses' legs. They were shocked when the racing board assigned Gulfstream the prime dates for 1985, but they jumped like rats leaving a sinking ship and never looked back as Hialeah became a memory. Brunetti made a few attempts to get the middle dates back but finally had to close shop in 2001.

The advent of slots at Gulfstream Park made it worth resurrecting Hialeah, the "Grande Dame" of racing, in 2009. Brunetti was denied Thoroughbred dates, but he was clever enough to bring in quarter horse racing. Hopefully sentiments go in his favor at some point and horoughbreds will run there again, but in the meantime he'll get to build a major league casino and laugh all the way to the bank.

Gulfstream changed hands a few times after Doug Donn's dates victory, going first to horseman Bert Firestone, the owner of Kentucky Derby winner Genuine Risk, then to a Japanese group before landing in the hands of Austro-Canadian car-parts billionaire Frank Stronach and his public company Magna Entertainment Company, (MEC). Gulfstream is now the premier track in Florida, prepping grounds for many a Kentucky Derby winner.

But in the 1970's and early '80's, the Gulfstream meet merely signaled the end of the winter season and the smaller outfits began to run more as cheaper races became available.

The big boys from New York had finished their southern campaign. Other than stakes races, they were saving allowance conditions for Belmont Park in May when purses were higher.

By April's end the Gulfstream races got cheaper, purses dipped and the fields were filled by Calder-based trainers wishing to get a conditioning race in to their horses before they settled in across town for the summer meet.

XIII.

For me the next winter in Florida is tough, between riders again and picking few winners. I had been late in making the decision to head south, and with no jockey to represent, I'd run out my string and was faced with the ugly prospect of taking a legitimate job until one of the all-time great racetrackers, trainer Stanley Rieser, changes my direction.

The best way to seek opportunity at the track is to show up early, get there before five, and you never know what might happen, which is why I stop by Stanley's barn each morning. He's a great handicapper and he and his best pal Sam are always busy working on the Racing Form *as soon as the ink dries.*

It was the early days of today's Pick-Six bet, then known as the Super Six, and we begin to play it in earnest until it goes un-hit for a couple of days and the large pool carries over. Stanley forms a betting syndicate of his cronies, but I'm short to even put up the seventy-five bucks for my one-seventh share. Stanley, who treats me like a son, insists on staking me. He's another "Old School" racetracker, having been a jock's agent before embarking on a successful training career, and subscribes to the philosophy that it's better to own part of a good horse than to own a whole bad one by yourself. This notion he applies to his betting tactics as well.

That particular rainy February day at Gulfstream, our daughter Gina comes down with an ear infection necessitating that Bonnie and I find a pediatrician, and quick. Doctors don't accept racetrack IOUs, so I do the next best thing and write a check that has no chance to clear.

(We refer to such faulty financial instruments as "Okechobee-readers," not "bad" checks, since the intent is not to stiff anyone, but rather to try to cash a bet and cover them before they make it to the bank.)

When I stop back at Gulfstream on the way home from the doctor to grab an overnight and check other unforeseen possibilities, Stanley informs me we have already won the first two legs of the Six with a nice maiden of Woody Stephens's named Saratoga Fleet in the first and that another tepid favorite, Antino, ridden by Eddie Maple, came home for us in the second, and that I should maybe "stick around."

The next heat goes to another favorite but we're "alive" after the fourth leg when Jerry Bailey boots in a $12 winner for Bert Sonnier on a horse named Sandbagger and Donnie MacBeth comes right back with the T.J.Kelly 6-to-1 shot Raj Kapoor to make us the possessors of one of only a couple of dozen tickets left with a chance to win the whole thing.

My reality becomes a series of trips from the agent's parking lot where wife and baby await in the car, back to the Rieser syndicate on the Clubhouse apron.

In the final leg of the bet we have the favorite, Wistful, and so do a dozen other players, but typical of Stanley's gambles, we're also holding two long shots on our ticket that nobody else has on theirs.

As J.P. Souter boots home a four-year-old filly named Sober Jig in the Shirley Jones Handicap, she lights the board with a $37 payoff and knocks out all the other players. We have the only ticket with all six winners and take down the whole pool.

I'm suddenly solvent again.

As the member of the crew most in need of funds, Stanley appoints me the designated ticket-casher. When the mutuels manager sends me out with a check for $100,000 and nearly forty grand in cash, Stanley shakes his head and does the math, then sends me back for seven envelopes, all cash, making my share double to cover the taxes.

The next day Miami Herald sportswriter Luther Evans recounts the story and immortalizes me as the "fan that didn't want to be identified."

Around the track that's referred to as "shipping money," which means we are headed back home to Monmouth with full pockets.

We had managed to beat the winter weather and in the meantime I was conversing with John Forbes, a New Jersey/Maryland circuit trainer, about the idea of my becoming his Stable/Racing Manager. John and I hammered the idea to death on the phone and finally decided to give it a shot at the next Monmouth meet. I spent the next two and a half years working with John, acting as his business manager, tending to details with owners and enabling him to be hands-on as much as possible with over a hundred horses in training. This was way before the advent of the huge outfits of today like the ones Todd Pletcher and Steve Asmussen have, spread out over several tracks and training centers.

John was a protégé of John Tammaro, Sr., a horse training genius and innovator, and Forbes himself was a second-generation trainer with incredible intuitive skills. I would dissect the "Mid-lantic" tracks' condition books, using my agent-skills to look for spots to run, and John would have them ready to fire.

Without any high-priced yearlings or expensive purchases, the Forbes stable ranked in the top three nationally for several years, mainly running low to mid-level claimers and a few stakes runners, putting them on the van to ship to the most advantageous spot. One day we won races at five different tracks: Aqueduct, Monmouth, Laurel, Philadelphia Park and Penn National.

John had never wintered in Florida, but listening to me relate stories of warm days and nights and hot business opportunities there convinced him to give it a try. We took a limited string of the horses that might fit and left the bulk of the stable up north at Belmont with one of John's assistants, Steve Brown. John would commute home to Jersey every other week for the four-month trial period and his main assistant, Pat McBurney, would cover the Florida duties in his absence. I'd do the paperwork and hunt for spots to run, enter and scratch as he pleased.

It's a different ballgame in Florida as compared to what we did back in Jersey, since you can't enter your horses at different tracks when your race doesn't fill. It's more like being on an island, or in California. Nonetheless, John became quickly addicted to Tark's chicken wings and Joe's stone crabs that season, and for many years to follow he became another "snow bird."

Although common in other parts of the world, few U.S. outfits had a racing manager and our financial arrangement was that I would work for expenses and act as the stable jockey's agent, thus giving me first call with a deep bench.

Per the Tammaro school, we wanted a bug-rider under contract, in order to take advantage of the weight allowance given to novice riders. Most riders in those days started out under contract and the contract holder was further rewarded by a three-pound allowance after the jockey lost his bug-status. Plus, a contract gave you some control over the kid's behavior. If he misbehaved and you decided to sit him, he couldn't ride for anyone else.

Usually the young riders would have a few years before they reached physical maturity and had to deal with weight problems. Horses are weighted differently, kind of on the same principle used in golf whereby players receive strokes from each other in an attempt to even-up their chances and make the contest more interesting.

The "scale of weights" for horses has been revised in recent years, but for many years some would receive allowances that required the jockey to weigh as little as 100 lbs. or less. This stipulation had a dire effect on many riders who couldn't get within the five-pound "overweight" limit and had to resort to extreme tactics.

Most common was the practice of "flipping" or "heaving" whereby they would eat and head for the bathroom to purge themselves like bulemic super-models. All the jock's rooms around the country still have one toilet reserved for this and many riders over the years have had to suffer the effects for the rest of their lives, including chronic stomach and kidney inflammation and ruined dental work.

Laffit Pincay's story of dining on a single peanut – half now, half later -- is often quoted for humor, but to those riders fighting weight the subject is deadly serious. Some careers have been ruined when jocks resort to drugs like cocaine or speed that have the effect of killing their appetite. Unfortunately the drug habit that comes along with it makes the cure a short-term fix.

Most riders immediately gain weight after retiring and some encounter heart or kidney problems. The forced reducing for many years has definitely shortened the life of many.

In the search for our stable jock we went through quite a few riders before finally coming up with a Puerto Rican bug-boy named Chuck C. Lopez. Son of the respected journeyman Carlos Lopez, C.C. had all the potential necessary for a top rider and didn't disappoint us. Carlos had a dozen kids that he admitted to and at least six of them made pretty decent riders over the years, but "Chuckie" was easily the best. He was small, light, athletic and willing -- the perfect "contract" jock -- and his aggressive style made him leading bug, then leading or second leading rider at every meet for the next year and a half, with one unfortunate side effect... his propensity for getting disqualified.

When riders have their horse taken down, they are required to visit the stewards office the next day and receive an official ruling on the matter. If the judges decide that the infraction was not the rider's fault, they rule so, but if they find reckless or carelessness the cause, the jockey gets "set down," usually for a minimum of five racing days. Chuckie's record for the most days suspended, (thirty at a ninety day meet) still stands at Monmouth.

Even so, C.C. began making good money right away and were it not for his habit of buying a new car about once a month he could have been a rich jockey early on. He learned his lesson, though, and eventually became a good quality New York rider.

A good percentage of our Forbes winners came from the New York "sheet" stables of Ragozin and Esposito, the Tresvant Stable of Arthur Berg, and the Dennis Heard Stable, long before their methodology became widely known and accessible to the general population of horseplayers. For the average horseplayer, the introduction of Andy Beyer's "numbers" to The Daily Racing Form was the great facilitator. For a select few, the Ragozin "sheet" numbers proved to be an even more insurmountable edge when it came to gambling.

To only say the "sheet" players had an edge would be gross understatement. They placed their own chart-callers at major tracks and calculated ground-loss, track depth, wind velocity and actual running time for each horse, assigning a numerical value to its performance. The "sheets" had refined handicapping well past the speed rating and track variant that were the horseplayer's standard tool since the Form had been in existence.

Up to that time, horseplayers had a plethora of advice available in the form of books like *Beat The Races* by Jack Kavanaugh, *Playing the Races* by Dowst and Craig and Ken Kling's *How I Pick Winners*, which were mainly anecdotal and their authors' personal opinions rather than analytical treatment of the process.

In 1968, author and journalist Richard Carter published the pivotal tome, *Ainslie's Complete Guide to Thoroughbred Racing* under his pen name, Tom Anslie. He was the first to treat the subject seriously, giving technical insight to horseplayers and showing the way for other handicappers like Andy Beyer, Jim Quinn and Steve Davidowitz to publish later works.

Beyer, whose *Beyer On Speed* became the best-selling handicapping book of all time in 1975, divided handicapping literature into two eras: "Before Tom Ainslie and after Tom Anslie."

Beyer refined the process to a strict methodology that assigned a "speed number" to each horse's performance, based on the times of all the horses running on a given day, in order to enable bettors to compare those performances. As his calculations became recognized as valid criteria for gambling, the Daily Racing Form incorporated them into the past performance lines, and they became simply referred to as "Beyer Numbers."

While the Racing Form contained a track rating and variant for each race, the advent of Beyer Numbers stepped them up a level, but players with sheet numbers were using Howitzers against peashooters.

There are still two companies competing in the production of "sheets," the original Ragozin organization, whose numbers are referred to as "Rags," and the Thorograph sheets published by Jerry Brown, a former Ragozin employee who took the art a step forward with improved graphics, bar charts and commentary included. Both systems are effective, and it's a matter of personal preference for horseplayers which one they use.

In a simple illustration of how "sheet" players are a important element in the daily ebb and flow of odds, one need only watch the tote board in races with older horses which have run a significant number of times although not against each other. When one of those horses has sheet numbers superior to the field, even though his previous races may not show it, the odds will reflect the flow of money to the win pool.

Several times a week we would get a call from one or more of the sheet stables, identifying a potential claim. Most of the time the horses were not favorites and it was always worth a bet if they wanted to reach in for one and I'm not alone in saying that they revolutionized the claiming game, identifying "sleepers" with great potential.

When Chuckie Lopez finally lost his bug it was time to look for another apprentice. Timmy Raymond told me a story about a sixteen-year-old kid he'd just met who could shoot pool with either hand and juggle three balls standing on one foot.

And he had already been riding at bush tracks for four or five years. Kenny Black weighed about eighty-five pounds, had the Ricky Schroder-like blonde Midwestern look from the movie *Champ* and a personality to match, and was chafing at the bit to get on with a riding career. I introduced him to Forbes and we had our new bug boy.

Another Old School method for training your contract jockey included riding him on a lot of slow horses during the learning process. Most kids of sixteen with Kenny's talent and enthusiasm wanted instant gratification, and he was no different, driving us crazy to put him on a live one.

John put him on horses that needed experience and let him get a lot of dirt in his face for months before he finally decided Kenny was ready to win one.

On a cold day in late January, Kenny got his chance when we put him on a claimer named Balmy Beau at Keystone (later Philadelphia Park, now called Parx) for one of the sheet players named Dennis Heard. The winner's circle photo shows six empty panels behind him finishing up in 1:10 4/5.

He won by so far, it might as well have been a walkover and when Kenny got off the horse he was so exhausted that he needed his valet to help him carry his tack to the scale for the weigh in. Kenny weighed eighty-seven pounds and Balmy Beau carried one-twelve with his ten-pound, three-bug allowance, meaning the horse toted an extra twenty-five pounds of lead pads in his saddle.

John decided to ship to Pimlico for the spring meet as Maryland was home and he had a couple of owners from there who wanted to see their horses run.

I shipped down with him and hustled Kenny's book for a couple of weeks but decided to wave the white flag when my pal Chickie Lang and his dad Chick Sr. realized Kenny was the golden goose and engineered an agent change.

It made perfect sense in most respects as the Langs nearly ran Maryland racing and could do a lot more with a rider there than I could have, so I abdicated without a fight since Maryland held no interest for me anyway.

Although claimers were his bread and butter, John Forbes later organized a syndicate of horse investors, raising capital to go to the Keeneland September Yearling Sale and purchase a group of young horses with either stallion or broodmare potential, the intent being to race them and sell out when they were done at the track.

It's a common method of prospecting for gold in the horse game, since many successful and wealthy people would like to participate in the excitement of a big league sport but either don't have the assets or the nerve to buy a baseball, basketball, football or hockey team.

Thoroughbred racing gives them an opportunity to be on TV on Saturday afternoon without spending $250 million and there are few things that stimulate as much adrenalin as having a racehorse on the Derby trail or heading to the Breeders' Cup. Ownership of a team is the ultimate vicarious thrill in any sport and racing a horse carrying your silks is as good as it gets for those obsessed with competition.

An old saw repeated consistently around the track goes: "He got to be a millionaire in the horse business. Started out with ten mil and worked his way down..."

This venture might have been another of those, except for the confluence of experience, skill and luck that blessed it.

One of the members of the team John assembled to seek a stallion prospect for his Phantom House partnership was a close friend of mine, Ed Rosen. Eddie followed in his parents' footsteps and became a lawyer, but was stricken at a young age with an incurable ailment. Bitten by the bug, he wanted to be a racetracker.

Ed spent his years at Cornell with a *Daily Racing Form* tucked between his law books, gazing out Ivy League windows imagining stretch runs, head bobs and photo finishes.

He toiled at real estate law in the practice bequeathed him by his attorney-parents and put his two daughters and his son through college but longed for nothing more than to be hanging around a racing barn, inhaling essence of horse.

Introduced to the game by his father, who owned a few good runners himself, Eddie studied bloodstock journals and gradually acquired a superior knowledge of and, more importantly, an understanding of that essential Thoroughbred element, the pedigree. John Tammarro was one of their trainers.

So it was that when John Forbes formed a syndicate to go the the Keeneland sales in quest of yearlings with stud and broodmare potential, he chose Eddie as a pedigree expert, allowing him to sift through thousands of horses in the catalogs.

A good-looking colt Eddie identified for the team to consider was a dark bay son of Storm Cat, out of the Mr. Prospector mare Yarn. Storm Cat was universally recognized as a "sire of sires" and although the bidding went to $375,000, John became fearless and stepped up to make the winning one for his syndicate. They named him Tale of the Cat.

He didn't win the Haskell at Monmouth, which I think was John's original intent, but he did win the King's Bishop at Saratoga, blazing incredible fractions against a strong field and impressing the hell out of Kentucky breeders in attendance.

The group John put together sold Tale of the Cat for $10 million, and Eddie's expertise was finally recognized, his dream realized... to shuck the law game and become a pedigree consultant.

As success often does, it begat success for Ed, as both prominent breeders and new players in the racing game sought him out. Consulting for Jimmy Scatuorchio, one of the Tale of the Cat partners and working with the team of physical appraisers and vets, he picked out other stars like More Than Ready and English Channel for short list consideration based on their pedigrees.

It was a cold February morning and I was in my office at Due Process Stable in New Jersey when Eddie called from the Florida Fasig-Tipton Two-Year-Olds in Training sale, bubbling with excitement. He had a new client, David Moore, a Wall Street guy determined to make some noise in the game.

"We bought him a Carson City colt, he's gorgeous!" he exclaimed. "Seventy-five thousand, he's big, good looking."

"Sounds like a steal," I said, "I love Carson City."

A moment's silence, then he says, "Only problem, he's got one eye."

I waited a beat, containing myself.

"Okay, let me get this right," I said, "New client, wants a good horse, money's no problem."

"Right," says Eddie.

"And this is his very first one," says I.

"Yep."

"So there's only about three hundred horses in the sale and you had to buy him the one with one eye?"

We laughed for five minutes.

"Are you fucking crazy?" I said.

More laughter, we're choking and snorting now.

"Probably," says Eddie.

The movie *Seabiscuit* had been released the previous summer and refreshed America's memory of that tenacious little colt and the courage of his half-blind jockey Red Pollard. Owner David Moore collected those sentiments and paid respect to his new colt's impairment by naming him Pollard's Vision.

Moore was determined to do everything right in the horse game including hiring Todd Pletcher to train for him. After breaking his maiden at Saratoga by 12 ½ lengths Pollard's Vision got stakes placed, and of course thoughts immediately drifted to the first Saturday in May. They took him to Churchill for a swing at the Derby, and Eddie called from Louisville.

"We're thinking we have a chance if it rains. He loves the mud."

I couldn't resist.

"Twenty horse field, no chance he'll get mud in his eye?"

Five more minutes to stop laughing.

The one-eyed colt didn't run any good in the Derby but went on to win $1.4 million in purses before retiring to stud and siring a champion filly, Blind Luck.

XIV.

"THE FIRST QUESTION I WAS ALWAYS ASKED — INVARIABLY, ANYWHERE — WAS
HOW I FOUND HORSERACING COMPARED TO BASEBALL. MY ANSWER — INVARIABLY,
ANYWHERE — WAS THAT, FANS EXCLUDED, YOU MET A NICER BRAND OF HUMAN BEING IN
RACING."

--BILL VEECK FROM *THIRTY TONS A DAY*

The opening of the Meadowlands Racetrack in north Jersey for thoroughbred night racing in the fall of 1977 was a game-changer for a lot of racetrackers.

The New Jersey Sports and Exposition Authority used the track as the backbone of the Sports Complex that included the new football Giants Stadium and would eventually add an arena for hockey and basketball.

Brain-child of David "Sonny" Werblin, the former head of the New York Jets, the track was predicted to be successful, but from the day it opened for night flat or harness racing, the track was not merely a success, it made enough money to carry the whole complex.

Minutes from the Lincoln Tunnel and George Washington Bridge, the facility had two top-floor dining rooms that looked like something out of Las Vegas and booked full every evening. Crowds of 30-35,000 were common, even at the onset of the declining days of the sport.

There were plenty of opportunities to run horses that couldn't win in New York and the money was almost as good, but the truth is, the thoroughbred game was never meant for night racing. Training at daybreak is in some sense traditional to thoroughbreds and a difficult mold to break, and good help can work overtime but day and night gets to everyone eventually.

Forbes had a barnfull of horses there and we had good success, but everyone from the hotwalkers to the trainers hated it, especially the grooms. When your horse ran in the last race, even if he was off the board, it was likely you were giving him a bath at midnight. That meant it would be 1 or 2 a.m. before you had him bedded down and got to bed, and dawn was four or five hours away.

Grooms rub at least three horses, so there was no sleeping in unless a swingman could let you catch up, and in a busy barn the process was chaotic. Sleep loss leads to fatigue, fatigue to short tempers and soon there's a help shortage.

As Forbes used to say, "horses are all maintenance," and it takes bodies to do the maintaining –- even more so in a stable that's actively claiming, constantly bringing in new horses.

One of the most difficult things to explain to novices about thoroughbred racing is the claiming process. People understand auctions, so that's the closest they usually get to the concept.

You put your horse in a claiming race so he can have a chance to win against ones of similar class and ability, and anyone who's eligible with an owner's license can put up the money and buy him out of the race, similar to an auction, except the price is fixed and if two or more try to claim him, they draw lots or "shake" to see who gets him. In most races, no one gets claimed, but when a really desirable one comes up, I've seen ten-way "shakes" to determine who gets the horse.

Generally speaking, horse ownership is personal, part of the game you play trying to win races. Although putting something you own up for sale may be an objective decision, allowing someone to buy it if you don't really want to sell can be taken many different ways.

Stan Hough and I played golf for years when he reached in and claimed one of our Due Process maidens as she won by ten at Saratoga for $50,000. I felt like he'd caught me stealing and didn't talk to him for a year, until I realized she was running in cheap claimers and he'd done me a favor, so I apologized.

The way thoroughbred racing is structured, claiming races are the great equalizer. A horse, when he or she has gone through their "conditions," defeating the competition in maiden and allowance races, is compelled to step up to the stakes level in order to have any opportunity to win.

Unable to make this "class leap," most horses will be entered the claiming races and keep dropping in price until they reach the level at which they are competitive. At the bigger venues, claiming prices may sometimes be as high as $100,000, whereas the bread and butter of the industry will be races in the range between $5,000 and $25,000.

Most familiar to most fans, Seabiscuit is the often referred to former claimer who achieved moderate success at the $2,500 level for legendary trainer "Sunny Jim" Fitzsimmons in the 1930's before being sold privately for a modest price to California auto dealer Charles Howard. Laura Hillenbrand's account of the Seabiscuit story is as good a read on the topic of racing as one could find, and filmmakers did justice to it with Hall of Fame jockeys Gary Stevens and Chris McCarron playing the roles of

George "Iceman" Wolfe and Charlie Kurtsinger. Tobey Maguire, later of *Spiderman* fame, played as Seabiscuit's regular rider, Red Pollard.

Seabiscuit won the Santa Anita Handicap and the Hollywood Gold Cup, but was best remembered for his performances in "match" races, where only two horses compete head-to-head. His defeat of War Admiral on November 1, 1938 at Pimlico Race Track in Baltimore, Maryland, before a crowd of over 40,000 fans has been referred to as "The Race of the Century."

From 2005 to 2007 a horse named Lava Man who had previously been claimed for $50,000 shocked racefans when he won the "Big Cap" at Santa Anita twice, the Hollywood Gold Cup three times and earned over five million dollars in purses. Being a gelding, at the end of his racing career Lava Man was retired to become the stable pony for his trainer, Doug O'Neill.

Trainers consider horses in their barns to be personal property, no matter who owns them. Usually when someone claims one they figure it's part of the game and stew over it for a day or so, then let it go.

John Forbes had a practice of making a bet on any horse that got claimed from him the next time it ran for the new trainer. That way, he knew he'd feel bad if it won for the new guy but at least he'd feel good about the extra cash.

Occasionally a trainer will claim one and realize he got a peach. Then he goes back to the well and claims another one. Then another. Soon the guy he's picking on strikes back and gets himself a good one back. Next thing you know, it's what is referred to on the track as a "claiming war."

The best claiming war I ever witnessed was in the mid-1970's between Charlie Robbins and Billy Prickett, two of the leading trainers in the New Jersey-Pennsylvania region who each won tons of races, mainly with cheaper horses.

Horsemen in those days came from all regions for the Atlantic City fall meet, commencing immediately after Monmouth closed toward the end of August and running for the eight weeks that took you to the end of October and into the Garden State fall meet.

Robbins had Hollywood good looks, wavy silver hair and was a dapper dresser with the suavity to match. Billy Prickett resembled comedian Buddy Hackett and had to deal with a stammer and an Elmer Fudd-like speech impediment, but he too could charm the owners and had a barn full of runners.

Prickett had taken a few from Robbins at Liberty Bell in Philadelphia and Delaware Park and done pretty well with them, taking Charlie right to his boiling point, at which time he went on a tear, claiming everything Billy ran. They'd just about spit at each other if they had a chance encounter and the whole racetrack community watched the daily drama as it were a live soap opera, the two men avoiding any chance of crossing paths, and the rest of the backstretch population needling each of them at every opportunity, hoping for an explosion.

It was break time one morning at Atlantic City when the two realized they were standing next to each other in line for breakfast in the track kitchen and Charlie, probably half-a-foot taller, began to needle Billy.

Nobody noticed until Billy's "whuh-whuh-whuh" stammer drew their attention and he slammed his tray into Charlie's, decorating a good-looking sport jacket with eggs, grits and orange juice. There were a couple of deflected swings from Billy before Charlie's right cross knocked him flat on the floor and drew management to intervene.

That track kitchen was another run by Richard Anderson, "The Frenchman," who took great pride in keeping his dining rooms to a high standard, so he personally collared the pair and escorted them to the door and banished the two trainers from his establishment for the rest of the meet.

Their claiming war went on, eventually dying out when Charlie and Billy moved on to other venues.

XV.

"IF YOU AIN'T BEEN TO THAT KENTUCKY DERBY, WHY YOU AIN'T NEVER BEEN NOWHERE, AND YOU AIN'T DONE NOTHING."

--COL. MATT WINN, ORIGINAL PROMOTER OF CHURCHILL DOWNS

We were fortunate to have a ready buyer for the health food business, so Bonnie and I decided that it might be good timing for our new daughter Liza to spend her first winter in the Florida sunshine.

Forbes had decided to forego the southern trip, instead trying to go in another direction with his business and transition from "claiming trainer" to "stakes trainer," which made plenty of sense since he had raised his profile with a few stakes winners gleaned from the ordinary stock he had to deal with and looked to be ready to make the move.

At Hialeah I picked up the book for a jock from Chicago named Rene Riera. He was a capable journeyman with a good reputation, had some customers from home, and we won a few races for Lou Goldfine and Harvey Vanier. Rene was known as a class act and later went on to a long career as steward in the Midwest.

All winter I'd been seeing grooms leading horses into the paddock wearing green t-shirts and caps emblazoned, "I believe in Due Process."

On the racetrack, t-shirts or caps with stable logos are like the flavor of the week at Baskin Robbins, so I think nothing of it, but when a trainer who has labored for years in obscurity suddenly wins the Gulfstream Park Handicap, it piques everyone's interest and I start to pay attention.

By the time we get to Gulfstream, I've got a second jock, another veteran named Buck Thornburg who's riding a pretty decent grey horse called Double Sonic that has a chance to make the Kentucky Derby if all things fall right.

Double Sonic has won the first "derby" of the year at Calder in January and if he makes a good showing in the Blue Grass, it's a sure thing his trainer George Krnjac will be on the road to Louisville with him.

Aside from hot prospects at the yearing sales, there is no time in its life when a horse is worth more than as a promising three-year-old in the early part of the year, since everyone has Kentucky clearly in their sights and at that point the only way to get a horse in the Derby is to buy one.

The old saw of horsemen goes, "If you don't know which one is your Derby horse by January, you don't have one."

Years later, in 2002, my neighbor in Sierra Madre was a white-haired guy named Bob Baffert. He'd already won the Derby with Real Quiet and Silver Charm and one evening he invited me in and we talked horses for a while as I admired his trophies, especially those from the Derby. He had a couple of decent three-year-olds that season, but nothing spectacular.

As I was leaving I asked, "Who's your Derby horse this year?" He replied with a good measure of resignation, "I guess I don't have one."

Saudi Prince Ahmed bin Salman called his stable The Thoroughbred Corporation. He'd won the Epsom Derby in 1999 with a horse named Oath, but he was set on winning the Kentucky Derby, and when a War Emblem romped in the Illinois Derby that April, Salman shelled out a million dollars for ninety percent of him and turned the colt over to Baffert to train.

War Emblem won the 2002 Kentucky Derby and the Preakness, and if he didn't stumble coming out of the gate in the Belmont, the record crowd of 103,000 might have witnessed the Triple Crown they were hoping for. That's how quickly things can change if you're lucky.

So it was in '81, and as I head to New Jersey with the family before heading to Kentucky, I hear that the guy who owns the Due Process Stable I've been seeing all over the t-shirts is looking for a racing manager of sorts.

It just happens I have an extra resume from my unsuccessful inquiry to the Stavolas and I stick it in an envelope and send it to the offices of one Robert E. Brennan at 40 Broadway in Manhattan. Right away I get a call from his secretary to make an appointment for an interview.

Up to that point I'm pretty ambivalent about the whole thing, since after ten years of agenting I'm finally heading to the Kentucky Derby and usually trainers control the owners, opposing the concept of racing managers. But I figure I should check it out.

It's about ten-thirty in the morning on the fourteenth floor at 40 Broadway and I've been waiting for about an hour when Brennan's secretary Nora finally shows me into his office.

The room is designed to test your attention span, with his glass topped desk set before a picture window that frames an unobstructed view of the Hudson River over his shoulder and behind it, New Jersey, after which his company was named, First Jersey Securities.

Careful compliance has enabled Brennan to win every case brought against him to date by the SEC, and the silver framed photo on the cover of Forbes Magazine shows him standing before his trademark helicopter under the caption "Golden Boy."

From 8x10 glossies on chrome-tipped shelves, he smiles, arm-in-arm with anyone of influence from the President to the Pope. But among all the prized trophies of the rich and powerful man who's across the desk from me, one thing stands out about the way his trappings of wealth are displayed, just by the way they're positioned. The horse trophies are the most important to him.

Sometimes you can be standing by the paddock and watch the horses walk by and one will just jump out at you as if it's yelling "Get to the window, now!" This was one of those epiphanies you might have once or twice in your life. As I left, I had no doubt that positive action was in order before he had a chance to consider too many other candidates.

The following day I sent him a two page Western Union Telegram, that era's version of a ten-page letter in a FedEx box. It cost me about thirty bucks, but it got his attention and I was called back for another meeting to make a deal.

My only condition was that I finish up with Buck through the Derby and we agreed on June 1 as my starting day as Executive Director of Due Process Stables. Bob wished me luck and I headed off to Kentucky.

The first time in Louisville for the Kentucky Derby can be an overwhelming experience.

Kentucky is a peculiar state, weather-wise. They have the wicked hot, humid summers of the East and the brutally frigid cold winters of the North, but fall lingers late and spring usually arrives early, accounting for a lot of spring storms and sloppy tracks.

Louisvillians grow up imbued with a passion for horseracing, and the Derby is simply an annual culmination of the emotional event that they anticipate like the birth of a child, ready to rent their front lawns to cars with out-of-state license plates and peddle bottles of cold water to the horde of frenzied invaders intent on the annual bacchanal.

Churchill Downs, as racetracks go, is not the prettiest or classiest, but simply by virtue of the race they run on the first Saturday of each May it is the most well known. And on that one day, it hosts the largest gathering of racing fans in America. Every year.

First run in 1875, twelve years after Saratoga, Churchill's premier race has captured the imagination of sports fans in general. Many who never attend another live race will make a point of watching the Derby on television, making a bet and singing along to "My Old Kentucky Home," as their eyes well with tears.

One hundred-fifty thousand racing fans (read party-goers) will amble into the facility and wager over twenty million dollars, a good portion of them walking out of the building well over the legal limit for alcohol consumption. The tradition of ladies donning hats for the Derby turns into a fashion contest itself, although many "fashionistas" exit looking like wilted roses at the end of a day spent slamming mint juleps.

The Derby is the only race in America run with a field of twenty horses, and it's sometimes like watching equine Demolition Derby or the the chariot scene from *Ben Hur* as the horses round the first turn, riders taking up to avoid clipping heels.

Since few horses get a good "trip," and the truly best horse might not often win, industry leaders and fans have debated the wisdom or necessity for having such a large number of horses squeezed on to an 80-foot wide track.

It would make more sense to put the best fourteen three-year-olds in one starting gate, if for no other reason than to increase the safety factor for horses and riders. Unfortunately field size is one the most essential contributors to betting handle, and since the public company that owns Churchill makes no bones about being slave to the bottom line it's likely there will continue to be twenty in the gate for years to come.

For as long as I can remember, it has been racetrack lore set in stone that the betting favorite is the least likely horse to win the Derby, a notion attributed to the fact that bookmakers stand to clean up if any long shot wins. Logically, to make huge profits, one would only have to eliminate the favorite and the statistics do support such a theory.

Beginning in 1980 and for the next two decades, only one post time favorite won the Derby, that being Fusaichi Pegasus in 2000. There was a string of favorites in the 1970's beginning with Secretariat's stablemate Riva Ridge through Cannonade and Foolish Pleasure, and including Seattle Slew, but for the most part they were vastly superior horses, all going off at odds of less than 2/1, three of which won the Triple Crown (Secretariat, Seattle Slew and Affirmed.)

In 1994, Holy Bull went off the Derby favorite at 2/1 and ran an uncharacteristic tenth, never getting into the race. He would finish the season as three-year-old champion and Horse of the Year, head and shoulders above the rest of his class, and trainer Jimmy Croll was convinced his horse had been "gotten to" by the bookmakers.

One morning in the Monmouth Park track kitchen he told me how Holy Bull had arrived at Churchill on the top of his game and been on the bit all Derby week, only to turn dull and listless the day of the race.

A Hall of Fame trainer and a man who was intimately in tune with his horses, Jimmy was neither a bad loser nor a redboard player. I believe he had good reason to suspect foul play, as until very recently the security at Churchill was almost laughable.

We ran a Due Process horse in the '86 Derby, a nice homebred colt named Fobby Forbes, by Bold Forbes out of the mare Plum Happy.

The Derby winner that year was a long shot trained by seventy-two year old Charlie Whittingham and ridden by a fifty-two year old jockey named Willie Shoemaker.

It was a strong crop of three year-olds, including Broad Brush, Snow Chief, Mogambo and Groovy, and I was at barn 43 every morning before dawn and hung around most of the day. If anyone had wanted to come in the barn all they had to do was wait until the rent-a-cop stationed there went for a coffee break. No one would have stopped them.

But for my first trip to Louisville with Thornburg, I had flown in a few days early and partaken of a sufficient sampling of the insanity, cruising the backstretch mornings, maintaining a low profile for traditional dinner circuit nonsense, but hitting all the traditional spots like Wagner's for breakfast and Pat's Steak House for dinner.

My jock was on a long shot and we were hanging out with Donnie MacBeth who's there to ride Well Decorated for Gene Jacobs. Since it's between him and us for whose mount will be the longest price on the board for the Derby, and even if it is the "Big Show," nobody is feeling a lot of pressure.

Top Canadian rider Jeffrey Fell is on the favorite, Proud Appeal, and with twenty-one of the top jocks in the country here, it's a wonder they can find anyone to ride at the other tracks that day. We have Jorge Velasquez, Cash Asmussen, Laffit Pincay, Jr., Eddie Delahoussaye, John Lively, Willie Shoemaker, Ruben Hernandez, Angel Cordero, Jr., Sandy Hawley, Benny Feliciano, Tommy Chapman, Tony Black, Larry Snyder, Phil Rubbicco, and David Whited, each dying to leave with their own Derby trophy.

Our mount Double Sonic would be double digits, save the fact there's an overflow field due to a court order that's forced Churchill to waive the twenty-horse limit and allow a twenty-first horse in the gates for the biggest field since they started limiting the entries after Cannonade's twenty-three horse debacle in 1974 that looked more like a NASCAR event than a horse race.

In those days, when there were more horses in a race than the tote board has numbers for, the track odds-maker would select several longshots and couple them in the betting in what is called the "mutuel field." By the fact that you get two, three or more horses on the same ticket and if any of them wins you get paid, plenty of gamblers bet on the field, and it usually goes off with significantly lower odds than would any of the horses were they in the race individually.

That year, 1981, the tote board only showed odds for twelve betting interests. There were nine horses lumped under one betting interest in the in the "field. The morning line favorite was an entry of Proud Appeal and Golden Derby, neither of which hit the board.

I stood on a folding chair in the first row just before the wire with Buck's wife, Rita, and Donnie's wife, JoAnne, and watched the cavalry charge pass us as they came out of the gate. Double Sonic ended up going off at 7-to-1 and splitting the field by finishing eleventh behind winner Pleasant Colony.

To this day, I couldn't drink one of those mint juleps if you gave me a hundred bucks.

XVI.

"RACING, WHATEVER ELSE IT INSPIRES, CERTAINLY PRODUCES NO INDIFFERENCE. THIS IS PRESUMABLY BECAUSE OF THE BETTING, FOR THERE IS A POLITE FICTION THAT THERE IS SOMETHING IGNOBLE ABOUT SUPERVISED BETTING AS COMPARED WITH BETTING OVER WHICH NO ONE EXERCISES CONTROL."

--JOE PALMER, FROM *THIS WAS RACING*

Considering the paucity of fans in the stands at even the major tracks these days, it usually shocks most observers to learn that thoroughbred racing was once the number one spectator sport in America.

The first season I worked at Monmouth Park, the Saturday crowds always exceeded twenty-five thousand fans, and Belmont would regularly hit forty thousand.

As in other sports, there are distinct differences between the top level and the rest. In baseball, the top is the Major League, the bottom, Double AA ball and the rest of the minors. Football has the NFL and players who can't cut it there might go to play in the Arena Football League, while NBA hoopsters have the Continental League as an alternative.

On any given day, Thoroughbred racing doesn't make a distinction between the top tier and the rest, but the difference is palpable. I worked mainly at the top two tiers when I became a jockey's agent, but I would occasionally day-trip with my rider to a smaller track like Charles Town in West Virginia or Rockingham in New Hampshire chasing a stakes race with a generous purse.

One significant difference at the smaller tracks is the amount of multi-tasking required of everyone who works there. Exercise riders ride in the morning and sell tickets in the afternoon. Hot walkers and grooms spend their afternoons pushing hotdogs at the concession stands or maybe taking pictures in the winner's circle.

The meets at New York's Belmont, Aqueduct and Saratoga tracks and California's Santa Anita, Hollywood and Del Mar comprised the very top class of racing, as well as Gulfstream in Florida and Keeneland and Churchill Downs in Kentucky.

Following in class of competition are Baltimore's Pimlico (primarily because it is involved with the Triple Crown via the Preakness), Fair Grounds with its position on the Derby trail, and Arlington Park in Chicago, home of the Arlington Million, an internationally significant grass race which draws the best turf specialists from all over the world.

Monmouth still remains in the hunt with its million-dollar Haskell Invitational, while and Tampa Bay, Lone Star, Laurel and Golden Gate all run a few notable stakes races, but their day-to-day cards rely on mostly lower class claimers and regional restricted races for state-breds to stay in business.

The advent of casino gambling changed racing in a bizarre way. Small tracks in less populated areas used to be referred to as "bullrings" or "half-milers" in reference to their circumference of six furlongs or less compared to the top tier tracks which were at least one mile.

Where purses are minimal, crowds insignificant and horses slow and unsound, trainers, jockeys and management are called "Gyps," an expression meant to evoke the corner-cutting they need to do in order to eke out a living.

Charles Town and Mountaineer Park in West Virginia were two of the places that those slow and unsound horses ended up when they could no longer compete or pass muster at the better ovals, and New Mexico and Arizona provided similar refuge well before they hit the *New York Times* as poster boys for horse abuse, cheating and drug money laundering.

Slot casinos at Penn National, Sunland Park and Ruidoso in New Mexico, Prairie Meadows in Iowa, and Hoosier Park in Indiana allowed them to offer huge purses and stakes races they never previously dream about.

Woodbine in Toronto and Fair Grounds in New Orleans were always at the top of the second-tier tracks, and when they were allowed to install slot machines, purses tripled to the detriment of similar tracks as the horses "followed the money."

Installed in places like Gulfstream, Aqueduct and Woodbine, the one-armed bandits have boosted purses and to a degree have rejuvenated attendance, although most of the new patrons are there to put their betting dollars in the slots, not on the ponies.

Combined with the diminishing interest in racing as a sport, an aging patron demographic and America's fascination with gambling, slot machines have been both the key to resurrection and a death knell for horse tracks, depending on whether they have them or not.

Plants like Belmont, Santa Anita, and Monmouth, built to hold crowds of forty thousand or more, are now lucky to get a few thousand patrons during the week and only fill the stands for two or three big events each season.

Belmont wishes for a hundred thousand patrons on Belmont Day but in reality they only have a chance to get them if one of the starters is going for a Triple Crown.

Santa Anita attendance tops twenty-five thousand for Big 'Cap Day and the Santa Anita Derby. The rest of the time it feels like a quiet city park.

Churchill gets their 150,000 attendees on Derby Day, but on a Thursday in June they might be lucky to have a couple of thousand fans scattered under the Twin Spires and both Santa Anita and Churchill pack the place when they get the Breeders' Cup, but that's a moveable feast.

Monmouth fills the house on Haskell Day, but barely breaks four figure attendance other days and had to cut back to weekends-only in 2012 when New Jersey's governor decided there was more future in playing ball with Atlantic City and New York casino interests than the horse breeders and farm owners in the Garden State.

Until the mid 1970's, more fans attended racing than they did baseball, football or basketball for simply one reason: before that time, the only other legal way to gamble in the U.S. was either go to Las Vegas or buy a smuggled Irish Sweepstakes ticket. There were no state lotteries, no Indian casinos, no poker halls and no Internet bookies.

Horseracing was a part of American life, attended by movie stars and politicians, featured in the fiction of the day as an element of glamorous and exciting lifestyles. Eddie Arcaro and Willie Shoemaker were household names evoked in everyday conversation as much as Babe Ruth, Sam Snead and Crazy Legs Hirsch.

Racing was consistently featured in movies and the most popular stars of the era, like Mickey Rooney, Judy Garland and William Holden, were frequent visitors to the track.

The Marx Brothers *A Day At the Races*, shot in 1937, is one of a dozen films set at Santa Anita. Stanley Kubrick's early work included *The Killing*, filmed at Bay Meadows Race Track in San Francisco. William Holden did a brilliant job playing a jockey's agent in *Boots Malone* in 1952, as did Walter Matthau portraying a gyp-trainer in the 1978 *Casey's Shadow*, a film inspired by the family of Hall of Fame jockey Randy Romero.

Bing Crosby and Pat O'Brien were the 1930's equivalent of Tom Cruise and Brad Pitt. Crosby and his cronies got together and started a racing "Club" at the beach near San Diego when August heat in L.A. became unbearable.

Today, Crosby's Del Mar is one of the fashionable "boutique" meets like Saratoga or Keeneland that still draw huge crowds, more because it's the "in" place at a summer resort area than for the quality of its horses.

Opening day is a gawk-fest, packing in forty-five thousand fans including every exotic dancer within a hundred mile radius doing their version of a Victoria's Secret runway show. Beginnining in 2014, Del Mar added a fall meet to shore up the Southern California circuit, which was devastated by the closing of Hollywood Park at the end of 2013.

The sport began its precipitous descent beginning in the early 1970's after a number of unfortunate decisions by racing's controlling elite, beginning when they refused to promote racing on television, succumbing to their fear that if fans could watch races on TV, they'd stay home and bet with a bookie, cutting out the live handle at the track.

Meanwhile, golf became a made-for-TV sport and thrived. Arnold Palmer's fans were proud to be called "Arnie's Army" as everyone in America learned to swing a club at the driving ranges that popped up in every town.

Today, ironically, simulcast broadcast and internet betting on racing handles the majority of money wagered on horses.

The deleterious effect of that initial blunder was further compounded by the advent of state lotteries, principally the one in New Jersey that refined previous unprofitable attempts in New Hampshire and New York and spawned the multi-state jackpots.

It wasn't until years later when the gaming industry became more organized and began referring to "discretionary income" and the fan's use of "gaming dollars." Simply put, given a choice of ways to gamble, patrons will pick the most attractive game, namely the one they think is easiest to win.

Since horse racing involves complicated handicapping methodology and uses its own jargon, for the uninitiated it can be like learning a new language.

Coinciding with competitive lottery gaming in the 1970's was the legalization of the Seminole Indian bingo parlors in South Florida, opening the door for eventual full Native American casinos in more than twenty-five states. Racing was still a viable sport, although badly wounded.

Apathy and elitism among racing people also deserves its share of the blame for contributing to the slide. In the summer of 1980 I went to Monmouth to see Spectacular Bid whip champion Glorious Song in the Haskell, toting 132 pounds. The crowd was over twenty-five thousand strong, giddy with excitement at seeing history, and when I ran into the head of the track's publicity crew, I commented on their enthusiasm. He replied, "Yeah, what a pain in the ass... You have to get in line to make a bet."

In the early 1980's, the chronic problem of short fields in daily and stakes races inspired the New York Racing Association to make some changes, bringing in new management determined to toughen up and induce the horsemen to support their racing program at the entry box.

Until that time, trainers were restricted in how many horses they were allowed to have on the grounds, with top outfits allowed the maximum of what one barn would hold. Usually this was forty stalls or less depending on the track. If the barn had thirty stalls, that was your limit. If it had forty-two, you could have forty-two horses and not one more.

A few trainers were able to accommodate owners with more horses by platooning them to training centers, like Arnold Winick in Florida with his Delray training center. You could see it from the Turnpike and Winick flew to the track in his helicopter. But other than a handful of entrepeneurs, most trainers were content to handle the number of horses they could put their hands and eyes on every day.

When NYRA began to allow stabling at Saratoga, it opened the door to the modern "super-trainers" like Todd Pletcher, Steve Asmussen and Bob Baffert who were eventually given multiple barns, housing in excess of a hundred horses. Their statistics and achievements as leading trainers are undeniable and it's no wonder the wealthiest owners in the racing world want to have their valuable horses in those stables.

New NYRA management allowed trainers to have as many horses as they could acquire, moving out smaller stables which didn't keep up on their entries, and housing the overflow of the big outfits at Saratoga, in facilities which to that point had been closed from October to June. Amazingly, at one point legislators even considered closing and dismantling Saratoga as an economy move.

A testament to their great training abilities was the fact that Hall of Fame trainers like Woody Stephens and Allen Jerkens never had more horses than the stalls in their barn could accommodate, usually thirty, and rarely did they ever get a yearling or two-year-old from the sales. True, they had progeny from the best bloodlines but they had to work with the home-breds, whether they were correct, crooked or otherwise.

Jerkens, who got the nickname "Giant Killer" by the press after he beat the great Kelso three times and knocked off Secretariat twice, preferred to be called"Chief," which is what he was known as by fellow racetrackers. In his 80's, he still accompanied his horses to the track every morning astride his pony.

Todd Pletcher and Kiaran McLaughlin direct racing stables whose organizations mirror those of major league baseball and football with their deep "benches" and "farm systems." Both learned their trade well from the living legend D. Wayne Lukas, a former basketball coach who brought training horses into the 20th century and made it a respectable profession rather than just a job working with animals.

Lukas stressed consistency, uniformity and obsessive attention to detail in his stables. Wherever they were stabled or shipped, all Lukas horses received the very same feed they were accustomed to, drank the same water every day, slept in stalls knee-deep in the finest straw.

He dressed the barn with flowers, himself in Brioni suits and finished his office at the barn with Wall Street décor, including extra-large winner's circle photos of the champions he trained.

To sum up Wayne's approach, it would be, "Go first class or stay home."

Obviously, a trainer can't give personal attention to 150 or 200 horses domiciled at various locations, or even the 60 or 80 lodged at one track, and the process becomes that of skillful management by the head trainer, indoctrinating numerous assistants to his methodology and freeing him up to focus on looking after the owners. Wayne's "Svengali" charm overcame many an owner in the '80's when he signed for sales-toppers at the yearling sales then turned them into champions like Winning Colors, Life's Magic, Landaluce and Open Mind.

One major problem created by huge stables is the reverse of the ailment it was intended to remedy, that of field size. By allowing high profile trainers unlimited stall space, it also enables them to accommodate more owners, and thus creates a "logjam" effect with entries.

If a "super-trainer" has ten or twenty maiden colts in his barn, he has to be careful not to allow them to beat each other and discourage the owners who have paid huge amounts for those horses at yearling and two-year-olds in training sales and whose monthly board charges fuel the cash flow for the organization.

During the '70's and '80's, maiden races in Florida would overflow, necessitating the "star" system for preference based on the number of times horses were entered and excluded. Most of the time you would need at least two "stars" to get in a race, meaning your horse had been entered three times before actually drawing into a race. This process for the most part ensured that horses were fit and ready when they finally drew into an extremely competitive twelve-horse field, and provided great betting opportunities for fans.

When only a few trainers have most of the horses in any category, maiden or otherwise, it becomes in their own best interest to determine which ones are best and parcel out their runs in order to keep the faster ones out of each other's way.

Were those horses in a smaller stable, they would be in the entries more often and the fields would be larger. Thus, NYRA management's well intended tactic ended up being a self-inflicted restraint of trade for the racing industry overall and weakened the sport in general by putting a lot of small-barn trainers out of business.

Other remedies such as cutting back schedules to race three or four days a week helps the tracks to reduce overhead but doesn't do much for the employees or the horsemen looking to run as often as possible. In places like New Jersey this efficiency move has kept the game going but destroyed the state's breeding industry, ultimately turning productive farmland into housing developments and forcing horsemen to move elsewhere to seek work.

Cheaper races don't attract betting handle like the higher quality ones, but it's a racing fact of life that there are more cheap horses than quality ones and running for purses is the only way to make money with thoroughbreds unless they have intrinsic value for breeding purposes --which excludes all geldings, more than half the male population.

The adage to keep in mind is that the horses will always follow the money. The highest purses will attract the fastest horses and force the slower ones to seek another venue or become weekly cannon-fodder. Since it can cost up to $50,000 a year to keep a thoroughbred, return on investment becomes a necessity if one is to stay in business.

Smaller outfits have difficulty surviving when cash flow is disrupted, since the grooms, exercise riders and hotwalkers all have to be paid whether or not the horses compete, a *Catch 22* for racing.

Some trainers will encourage their owners to keep a horse in the barn even though it is going to need some R&R to recover from an injury, simply because the number of horses must always balance with the number of grooms, or you are overpaying for labor.

Generally a groom will "rub" or attend to three horses in most parts of the country. At some smaller tracks with cheaper horses, they'll take care of four, but that's pretty much the limit for doing a decent job. The groom receives a salary and gets part of the "barn stake" which is a percentage of the purse earned by the horse for finishing in the money.

Plenty of "Old School" trainers like LeRoy Jolley, a Hall of Famer who won the Kentucky Derby with the filly Genuine Risk, or Billy Turner, who won the Triple Crown with Seattle Slew, or Jack Van Berg, another Hall of Famer and the first trainer to win 5,000 races, eschewed the concept of training huge numbers of horses.

They kept their barn size to a number of horses they felt comfortable with, an amount that they could put their hands on daily and thus have become irrelevant in today's version of the game.

As their income/cash flow diminished, so too did their ability to afford pricey veterinary "technological advances" and their win percentages dropped, a deadly blow when so many owners rely solely on statistics to select a trainer.

This, of course, was a conscious decision on their part not to deviate from the art they practice and thus they have gone the way of the two-dollar window and Harry M. Stevens clam chowder. They didn't lose their ability to train, just their opportunities.

XVII.

"THE LESS YOU BET, THE MORE YOU LOSE WHEN YOU WIN."

--W.E. "BILLY" CROLL

I met Sonny Hine on the Monmouth apron one morning near the finish line, as he was clocking one of his horses. I figured I'd charm a mount out of him with a compliment on the winner he'd had the day before.

His real name was Hubert, but "Crying Sonny" was the full backstretch nickname for Sonny.

"Nice win, Mister Hine," I said as he grimaced, squirmed uncomfortably and responded.

"Only paid seven-sixty, I thought she'd pay at least twelve bucks," he said, shaking his head in sincere regret.

Although Sonny had worked for the CIA and spoke about six languages including Mandarin Chinese he wasn't secretive at all if he liked you. He would tell you right up front if he thought one could win, and I was fortunate to be sitting with him in the Racing Office lobby at Monmouth one rainy Saturday in August. He was running Skip Trial in the Haskell later in the day and told me he was shocked to see he was twenty to one in the program and that his colt would love the going.

He went off at 35 to 1 and paid $73. Another case of being in the right place at the right time.

A pair of true racetrackers, Sonny and his wife Carolyn travelled from track to track, living in hotels wherever their horses were stabled and didn't own a home until they finally decided to commit to going south every winter and bought a place near Gulfstream Park in the '90's.

The penchant for hotel living is definitely a bygone style, a throwback to the glory days when racetrackers enjoyed a minor celebrity status and you had to move at least twice a year before the advent winter racing.

Trainers, jockeys and agents customarily took a room at a trackside hotel for several months at a time, using room service and laundry to compensate for foregoing the actual comforts of home. Horses campaigning in the north would either go to Florida, California, New Orleans, or a farm in Virginia or South Carolina to take the winter off altogether so they would be fresh for spring.

It's no wonder horses stayed sounder, raced longer and didn't need medication. One of my favorite horses was a mare named Arctic Aria that Tom Harraway would only bring out for the Monmouth meet. She was a New Jersey bred and a bleeder so she had only a limited amount of starts in her, since it was before the introduction of Lasix, but he would train her gently, making sure she could peak in June and maybe have three well-spaced runs before going back to pasture for the rest of the year. She might have run for four or five seasons that way, winning the majority of her starts and retiring a happy horse.

Sonny Hine might have lived the ultimate racetracker's life, fulfilled when he bought Skip Away for Carolyn because she was having vision problems and wanted a grey horse so she'd have less difficulty spotting him. Not only did Skip Away become a champion and win more than $9 million in purses, but when a post-sale vetting discovered a chip in Skippy's ankle (which turned out to be of no consequence) Sonny got a rebate on the purchase price of $27,000.

Sonny won the "big race" at all the tracks on his circuit, including the Haskell twice and the Gulfstream Park and Donn Handicaps, but unfortunately passed away before he could enjoy his induction to the Hall of Fame.

That good relationship I had with Sonny paid off for me at Due Process when he agreed to sell us a nice grey Icecapade filly named Icy Dial for $125,000. He'd won some good money with her and wasn't interested in breeding as it took too long to get a trainable horse, and that was a fair price at the time. She won some small stakes races for us and improved her pedigree enough to make a productive broodmare for many years after.

Being a large multi-faceted stable, with up to a hundred horses suitable for all levels of competition, Due Process required multiple trainers to operate efficiently.

Our main trainer, Reynaldo Nobles, would domicile the horses in his care principally at Monmouth, Hialeah/Gulfstream, and Saratoga since that was where the boss preferred to go racing. A few times Rey tried Hollywood or Belmont but we were limited on how many stalls we could get, so I farmed out the other horses based on where they were bred or what trainer I thought most suitable.

We had a little Maryland-bred filly by Exceller out of Foreign Missile that we purchased as a weanling through the noted British bloodstock agent Joss Collins, but she was given to flighty behavior at the gate which immediately gave Reynaldo a bad opinion of her. You never want to have a horse with a trainer who doesn't like the horse and since she was eligible for the restricted state-bred program in Maryland, I sent her to Carlos Garcia at Laurel. He was an Argentine who trained much in the style of Horatio Luro or Angel Penna and made Maryland his home year-round.

Carlos loved her and Squan Song went on to be the Maryland Horse of the Year and Maryland champion four times in the next five years, even venturing out to New York and Pennsylvania, winning the Rare Treat and Affectionately stakes at Aqueduct and the Cotillion at Philadelphia Park among her fourteen stakes wins.

Brennan had named her with a play on words for Manasquan, a town near his home on the Jersey shore. She set track records for a mile and a sixteenth at Meadowlands and Garden State. During her career, Squan Song had chips in both knees and came back both times from arthroscopic surgery to win multiple races before retiring as a successful broodmare. She was one of the eary successes of Dr. Scott Palmer, who would later become the New York Equine Medical Director, responsible for overseeing the health and safety of the horses at the state's racetracks.

Carlos put the Due Process silks in the winner's circle many times, and in 1986 he took us on our first trip to the Kentucky Derby with colt called Fobby Forbes.

Fobby's name was Brennan's way of poking fun at *Forbes Magazine*, which had been harassing him for as long as I can remember. They would print a brutal attack on him, put his name on the cover, and he'd turn it around and treat it like an advertisement.

In one article, they said he was "fobbing" his customers, using a fairly obscure word to intimate he was ripping them off, but the cover picture of him standing by his helicopter was so flattering that Bob not only named his horse using the word but had a few thousand reprints made. I assume *Forbes* editors had a "tickle" file that reminded them to do an anti-Brennan article every couple of months, but he usually got the better of them.

Bob made the best of that Derby opportunity, flying about fifty friends in for a huge party at the Due Process Farm on Newtown Pike in

Lexington, delighting the crowd with his imagined call of the race as he put Fobby in front by a nose at the wire.

I was real foggy the next morning, heading over to Louisville in a helicopter, but I was at barn 43 at five sharp, hanging with Carlos as we shared the anticipation of our big day. There was no parade from the barn in those days and the forty-five minutes we waited for Fobby to arrive in the saddling area seemed like 24 hours. He broke from the fifteen stall in the auxillary starting gate and never got comfortable in the race, running seventh under Randy Romero, splitting the field as another longshot, Ferdinand, won for trainer Charlie Whittingham and Willie Shoemaker.

These days, casual fans and the uninitiated are often quick to point fingers and allege malfeasance whenever a longshot wins and it becomes known that someone cashed a big bet.

This is a huge mistake, confusing cheating with the age-old practice in sports of "taking an edge," which is the correct term for a situation in which one takes a chance in the belief that they have more information or insight into the particular contest being wagered on than the person or persons they are betting against.

Most races are won by the best horse only when everything goes right, and rough trips, equipment malfunctions and just plain bad racing luck account for the outcome of many contests.

I used to think they should just give the riders a check-list for excuses like the menu in a Chinese restaurant: one from column A ("He didn't get a hold of the track"), one from column B ("That idiot jock on the five horse didn't know what he was doing and slammed me"), and one from column C (" A seagull flew in front of us"). After all, there is only one winner in every race.

Bob Connors is operating on the Pennsylvania circuit and takes our Due Process horses that can't cut it in tougher competition but still have value as solid runners. He is a veteran polo player and a solid horseman, and he knows how to use bad luck to make good luck.

One winter at Gulfstream, he enters a big grey called Dusty Roads in the first race on a Friday afternoon. Al Goldberg is staying at my condo for the weekend and he's got a first time starter that he likes in the second race that day. Al was schooled in the trainer's trade by Walter Kelley in New York, one of those Old School guys who never crack with one until it has a few races under its belt, but this was an exception. The colt has worked a few bullets in the morning and hopefully the clockers haven't tuned in on him.

We compare notes and I know Connors is always trying with our horses, but winter racing is as competetive as it gets since everybody there is trying all the time and Dusty looks to be in tough. So we handicap the first and decide he's got a chance, but we pick a few other likely ones to play as well in the Daily Double with Al's horse.

Besides, Al's owner is a big player from Philly, and if he knows Al likes one they rarely go off at big price, so we figure we need to make a Daily Double to get any value. I tell Al I'd check with Bobby in the paddock and we could adjust accordingly if he thinks he has a shot, since my horse would be at least 10 to 1. He was well beaten in his last start up north and is dropping to the bottom claiming level at ten thousand.

Bobby gives the rider a leg up and turns to me. He always talks behind the back of his hand when being confidential, as if he had a thing about lip-readers figuring out what he is saying.

It's about five minutes to post time, and Bobby says, sotto voce, "Last time he ran at Philly the saddle slipped. Bet what you want, he won't lose."

The grey horse stalks the pace and draws off handily, paying $27 to win. Al, Bobby and I each have a couple hundred on him plus $200 Daily Doubles alive to Al's horse in the second race. Since Goldie's not a trainer who's supposed to win first out, his horse gets some play but gets overlooked in the Double. When he wins it comes back two-hundred fifty plus as the three of us take down most of the pool.

That Connors is a guy who knows how to take an edge.

XVIII.

"BE NOT AFRAID OF GREATNESS, SOME ARE BORN GREAT, SOME ACHIEVE GREATNESS AND SOME HAVE GREATNESS THRUST UPON THEM."

--WILLIAM SHAKESPEARE FROM *TWELFTH NIGHT*, ACT II, SC.5

Manhattan on the first of June. Since my compulsion to be on time borders on OCD, I drive to Jersey City take the PATH train to the World Trade Center, make the walk down Broadway and wonder at the number of guys sleeping in doorways, if I'll end up one of them. I usually have to wait for one of the executive secretaries to unlock the office door.

Right away I find myself sequestered in an office full of loaded file cabinets and presented with a stack of folders the boss's secretary has been stuffing with every invoice, receipt and newspaper clipping relating to Due Process Stable for the past nine months

It takes me a couple of weeks just to figure out where half of the horses are located and who's training them and the whole thing is further complicated by Brennan's public company, International Thoroughbred Breeders, which is an entirely independent enterprise that I have nothing to do with, but nonetheless gets constantly confused with his private holdings for which I am solely responsible. No board of directors, no nothing, just me. Call the man.

I came with sterling recommendations from the track people Bob had checked me out with, but probably the best thumbs-up I got was from his trainer Reynaldo Nobles. Rey was a Havana-born son of a Key West Cuban horseman known universally around the track as "Papa Chico," who could have doubled for jazzman Louis Armstrong. He worked for many years as an assistant to trainer Tommy Heard and he was a gifted horseman who passed his talents on to his son. In his later years Papa just hung around the barn, raking up with a big cigar in his mouth, wearing a straw hat and spinning yarns.

Limited in education but savvy to racetrack life, Reynaldo had ridden my jockeys from time to time over the years but he never had much to work with in the way of horses. He caught a break when Kerry Fitzpatrick recognized his talent and recommended him as trainer to a couple of Jersey lawyers named Don Robinson and Andy Zazzalli, interested in finding a horse for their Sui Generis Stable since they'd just gotten paid on an insurance claim for the loss of their only horse, Tip Top Tony.

They went to the two-year-old sale at Hialeah and got a bargain on a snotty-nosed colt by Naskra out of Nursey, mainly because he was a Jersey-bred and Reynaldo didn't mind the fact that the horse was sick. He knew the cold was curable and wouldn't have anything to do with how fast he was when he finally got to run. Plus, the price was right, exactly the amount they had received from the insurance company.

They named him Thanks to Tony, respecting the lost predecessor from whence the purchase money came, and the lanky colt went on to finish first or second in eighteen starts for Sui Generis, including a win in the Grade I Monmouth Invitational, now called the Haskell.

Robinson was the leader of Brennan's plethora of lawyers and the excitement of his friend's success was enough to put Bob over the top. He bought in for a piece and made the deal extend to stud duty when Thanks to Tony would retire to the new Due Process farm we were building in Colts Neck.

Bob had walked up to Reynaldo in the paddock one day and announced, "You're working for me." He bought horses by the bunch and one of the first transactions he made was to purchase a package deal from Chicago horseman Russell Reinemann that included several slow horses and one very fast one.

Hurry Up Blue won both the Donn Handicap and the Gulfstream Park Handicap in 1981 and accelerated both Brennan's enthusiasm and his horse-related activities. Bob liked to wheel his bets, like the one for $2,000 he made with "Blue" on top in the Gulfstream Park 'Cap, after which a longshot no-chancer named Yosi Boy plodded in second, returning an exacta payoff of a whopping $650.

The mutuels department wanted to give him a check for the $650,000, but Bob reminded them that the race track policy stands, "cash in, cash out" and they sure didn't want to offend a guy who pounded the betting windows like he did.

Mister B left Gulfstream in his helicopter with a brown paper grocery sack full of hundreds.

Bob Brennan was the essential Jersey guy and almost the quintessential American success story. One of nine children, he grew up in an apartment in Newark and became a CPA upon graduation from Seton Hall University. Quickly learning the brokerage business with Mayflower Securities, he stepped out on his own, establishing First Jersey Securities in the late 1970's to specialize in the sale of "penny" stocks and start-up companies, what are referred to as "emerging growth companies." When I went to work for Bob, he had dozens of offices across the U.S. and Puerto Rico and hundreds of young, energetic brokers working for him.

As soon as I announced to my contemporaries that I was going to work for Brennan, I received multiple sets of the same advice: "Don't do it, the guy's a crook."

I chose to ignore the track mavens, and although they were eventually right about him heading for the grey-bar hotel, I don't believe he went to jail for anything but his attitude. He often referred to himself as a "nose-tweaker" and couldn't resist rubbing his court victories in the faces of his adversaries. Playful as he meant to be, it just came across as arrogance in the long run and the prosecutors at the SEC had him in their sights, aiming to get even sooner or later.

As Roy M. Cohn said, "You can't beat anyone who can hire more lawyers than you can." That would be the Federal Government.

Bob spent most of twenty years going to court with the Securities and Exchange Commission for alleged stock trading violations, always choosing to stand his ground since he would have been untrue to himself if he didn't defend his principles.

Brennan named his racing operation Due Process Stable as a statement of personal belief in the rights guaranteed to every citizen by the U.S. Constitution, that procedure and proof of guilt have to be demonstrated in court.

When I went to work for Bob in June of 1981, he had about $300 million in the bank and no pending litigation. As far as I know, he never was convicted of any securities violation. Rather, he was sent away for ten years for bankruptcy fraud in what appeared to be a fairly stacked case brought by those SEC prosecutors who were sick of having their noses tweaked. They found a sympathetic federal judge willing to place a $100 million-dollar judgment against Bob, and when he resorted to a Chapter 11 bankruptcy filing to reorganize they had him cornered.

Brennan liked to use his horse names to poke fun at the prosecutors and judges in his SEC trials, ridiculing them and theirs as in So Called

Judge, Sarah Lee Dork, Dork's Peter and Sprizzo. He was at one point en-joined from naming horses after federal judges when one of them got mad, not because the judge disliked the name, but because he missed getting to bet on his namesake when it won.

Bob was a firm believer in the Bill of Rights and named his racing stable Due Process to point out just how strongly he felt. Over the years I worked for him and for many before, he was continually in court, defend-ing himself much of the time against allegations made by the Securities and Exchange Comission. The SEC oversees activity in the stocks and bonds game, and they are used to having brokerage houses bow their heads and pay the fine when accused. Bob was different then most, preferring to go to court and fight it out when he thought he was right, and for all the time I worked for him, I don't think he lost a single case.

Brennan may have tread closely on that fine line between staying with-in and breaking the rules, but he was never afraid to defend himself, and when CBS's Mike Wallace called, wanting to feature him on *60 Minutes*, Bob agreed but made one condition: the interview had to be done live. Bob was accustomed to seeing statements misconstrued and comments cleverly edited, and he knew they could paint him as a crook if they want-ed. He wasn't about to give them a chance to do so.

Unfortunately, because of his penchant for nose-tweaking he antago-nized the sleeping giant for too many years. Prosecutors failed to share in his sense of humor and just marked it down as another reason to stay on his tail, finally putting him in jail for nearly ten years. Many compared his situation to the Al Capone case, where when they could't get him for what they said he did, so they got him for something else, whether or not it was true.

The sentence of nine years, three months for bankruptcy fraud evolved from claims that he had a half-million in Vegas casino chips that he hadn't declared. Their contention was that no one could win that much in the few months since he went Chapter 11.

That was truly a joke as I saw him win hundreds of thousands many times. The house judge particularly disliked Bob's refusal to kowtow and tagged him with an extra three-year sentence for contempt of court. And he did nearly ten years of the sentence in the Maximum security facility at Ft. Dix, NJ, not a country club atmosphere by any means. Whenever given an option to switch, he declined, knowing that they might send him to Wisconsin or Michigan where he'd never have any visitors and would lose touch.

Talk about pissing off the wrong guys.

Any of us who knew Bob in the gambling ring could have testified to having seen him run a thousand up to fifty grand many times at the track and twenty thousand to two hundred grand plenty of times at the craps table.

He once landed his helicopter at a heliport on the boardwalk in Atlantic City and played craps at the Resorts Casino for a couple of hours. They wanted him to take a check for the winnings, but he insisted they pay him in cash, so they piled the bills on the counter and told him they didn't have any bags, just to bust his chops for having beaten them. He dumped a trash can, took the plastic bag out, stuffed it with his winnings and flew home with a million in greenbacks.

The man simply possessed the best gambling instincts of any person I've ever seen. He was absolutely fearless when it came to "pressing" a bet, which means putting up all your profit from a win for the next bet, sometimes more than once.

We ran a couple of Due Process horses at Aqueduct one spring afternoon -- a decent stakes horse named Vittorioso in the eighth and a New York-bred maiden, Count Advocate, in the last heat -- and Bob popped in with his helicopter for the last few races. He had a guest with him and was talking business, so he dispatched me to the window to bet two grand on a horse he picked in the seventh and when that one came in at around 3½ to 1 he told me to parlay it to Vittorioso in the next at 5 to 2, and he romped, winning by open lengths.

I waited until two minutes to post to finish his parlay to Count Advocate at 6 to 1. When he galloped home five in front, Bob had turned two thousand into a hundred-fifty grand.

Most owners of large stables, and I suppose most smaller ones too for that matter, prefer to have "Saturday" horses. Those would be horses capable of competing on the weekend card, either running in races a cut above the ones during the week, or stakes horses in the feature.

The Due Process barn consisted of high quality bloodlines and expensive stock, and I reckoned it might be a good practice with regard to my job security to try and run as many horses on those weekends when the boss liked to show up with his friends.

There are plenty of things you can do to improve your chances of winning a race, but the best practice has always been to run with slower horses. Horatio Luro, the trainer of Northern Dancer, was often quoted: "I like to keep myself in the best company, and my horses in the worst."

Keeping in mind that allowance or non-claiming horses are the toughest to find spots for, since they are usually in situations based on how many races they have won. For example, a "non-winner's of a race other than maiden or claiming" field would be comprised mainly of horses that had only broken their maiden, or won a single race.

In order to have the best chance on the Saturday cards, I would often place horses "out of conditions" on a weekday card since I knew Bob wouldn't be joining us.

We would run a horse that had won one race in a spot with others who had won several and thus would have less of a chance of winning. Sometime they were good enough to win anyway, but mostly they'd just get a good workout, tuning up for when it counted. Then, on a Saturday card a couple of weeks later, we could run in the correct spot and have a better chance as well as get higher odds, while the horse would feel like he was in easier competition.

Bob and his guests would get a trip to the winner's circle and cash a ticket. We did this successfully several times a meet in Florida and New Jersey, his favorite spots, even scoring a "three-bagger" once at Gulfstream. Members of the entourage that day started asking me what the horses were going to pay and how far they would win by. I wanted to tell them that if I knew that, Bob would be working for me.

It seems to be a fairly common occurrence, when a wealthy individual decides to dive into the thoroughbred racing game, that they start slowly and pretty soon get to warp speed, buying horses from sources that nearly didn't exist a month before.

Lots of trainers make the mistake of thinking the horses are theirs, forgetting that without the owner paying for the horse and paying the bills there would be nothing in their barn but empty stalls.

They show up early and like to keep their owners uninformed, quoting the great Charlie Whittingham: "Owners are like mushrooms, you need to keep them in the dark and throw shit on them." Charlie was one of the greatest conditioners of all time and could get away with a crack like that, even if he was half joking. Other trainers who try that tactic can end up losing their horses to another more attentive trainer when the owner gets tired of not having his calls returned or, worse, having his horse entered and not hearing about it until after the race.

Busy owners may not be able to get to the races all the time, but that doesn't mean they're not interested. I realized over the years that the goodness of the news is directly proportional to the time it takes to be delivered. If the horse wins, you can expect a call as soon as he crosses the finish line. If it finishes up the track, maybe you'll hear sometime later that evening, or you might get the post mortem the following day, if you're lucky.

Occasionally I would go to the barn first thing in the morning and Reynaldo would show me some horse that arrived during the night, neither of us having any idea who it was or where it came from. I soon realized that there was a "ghost" committee that forms around every high profile horse owner, willing to proffer "expert" advice on trainer, jockey and race selection whether their opinion is invited or not. New owners sometimes take a while to learn not to grab up everything that's offered, no matter how good a story they come with. And for many horses, the story is the only thing that's good.

Part of the romance of the racetrack that attracts successful business-men is the assortment of colorful characters populating the backstretch or the Turf Club, and it's amazing how many of them know where there's a horse for sale when someone with big money shows up.

My office during the formative stage of Due Process was at Bob's headquarters on the fourteenth floor at 40 Broadway in Manhattan, and Brennan's other equine operation, International Thoroughbred Breeders (ITB), was a public company set up in Heightstown, New Jersey, in the office complex where the Daily Racing Form was published. Although Bob owned both companies, the difference was that in Due Process he had no partners but with ITB he had shareholders.

ITB was run by Kerry Fitzpatrick, a clever guy who knew the name of the unknown soldier. He could be smart as a whip at buying top-class broodmares, but when it came to racehorses, he was strictly a breeding guy and Anglophile to boot, and not a bettor. He loved the Brits and Irish for their accents and lifestyle and realized that when it came to horsemanship they had few peers.

Folks who never make a bet always have a different perspective on horses, somewhat simplistic and tending to usually only focus on the small percentage of runners that are at the top of the ladder. They see racing as a sport rather than a game. Horse breeding is a fascinating endeavor and to some it has the same esoteric appeal to be found on a chessboard or in higher mathematics scrawled on a blackboard.

Kerry was constantly hopping to England and Ireland for horse sales, buying and bringing his purchases stateside, which is okay, but the trainers there love high profile buyers and many of them have perfected the art of making their runners look good in handicap races, since the purses there are not that great and it's more profitable to sell.

Referred to over there as "market gardeners," they will sometimes run two or three horses in the same race, simply to produce an impressive win chart, and it's not that hard to do if you match horses of less than total fitness against ones ready to roll.

European horses in those days ran only on the turf as there were no dirt or "all-weather" tracks at the time and their breeding reflected the affinity to grass. That can be a drawback in America, where grass races are moved to the main track if it rains too much. Since most Euro-turfers can't run at all in the mud and many of them don't run well on the firm grass courses, they never getting an opportunity to compete on the same soft or yielding turf they excelled over at home. Most of the time it's a fool's errand to try and convert a turf horse to the dirt track and the only thing I can tell you for sure is that the Euro horses will run a bit farther on American tracks. Otherwise the best handicapping move is to bet on the ones with a *Racing Post/Timeform* number around 100 the first time they get Lasix.

We never got a good racehorse from Kerry, but when he offered a mare named Stage Luck for lease I loved her pedigree to cross with our new stallion Deputy Minister. The resulting foal was the champion filly Open Mind, from just the second crop of Deputy Minister. We were trying to prime the pump by selling some of the dozen or so offspring we had bred in order to get some nice runners in the hands of other stables, a common practice of breeders attempting to enhance public opinion of their stallions.

Open Mind was smallish and kind of plain, and when Wayne Lukas bought her, more than one wiseacre cracked that she was a Jersey-bred, meaning that to be a knock. Wayne's comment back was, "You've got to keep an open mind," giving owner Gene Klein a name for a filly destined to the Hall of Fame.

Open Mind broke her maiden at Monmouth, trained by one of Wayne's assistants, Kiaran McLaughlin, who went on to be a pretty good conditioner in his own right and a good bet for a future spot in the Hall of Fame himself. Open Mind won the Breeders' Cup Juvenile Fillies race and the next year at three took New York's Filly Triple Crown, earning a championship for two years running.

I always considered myself lucky that Brennan was so in touch with his ego that he could forgive my staff and me for selling one of the best horses he would ever breed.

XIX.

"Dying is no big deal. Living is the trick."

--Red Smith

On my first trip to Lexington, accompanying Brennan in his Lear jet to the Keeneland Yearling Sales, I was shocked at his acceptance of the many hustlers who have him squarely in their sights, and no matter how transparent their motives, how he lets them pitch.

It doesn't take an FBI agent to figure out that there's plenty of wheeling and dealing going on there, and plenty of cash to do it with. When you landed at Bluegrass Airport, the first thing you noticed was a white Boeing 747 parked to the side of the runway, with Sheikh Mohammed's name painted on the side in the colors of the United Arab Emirites, and there's little question if it's located there to intimidate since it belongs to the head of the ruling family of Dubai and owner of many of the best horses on the globe. Sheikh Mohammed's Darley Stud stands some of the finest stallions in Europe, and his Godolphin Stable has won every major race outside of the U.S., even though they have yet to come close in the Kentucky Derby or the other American classics.

As you exit the airport, you will pass the old Bluegrass Farm, formerly owned by Nelson Bunker Hunt. In 1979 and 1980 Bunker and his brother William Herbert Hunt nearly cornered the world market in siver, taking down a few billion dollars before the U.S. government decided they had bent a few too many laws in the process and drove them straight into bankruptcy.

Bunker was a truly international horseman, racing great ones like Vaguely Noble and Dahlia. He won the Epsom Derby in 1976 when Lester Piggott booted home his colt Empery three lengths in front. Even after his empire crashed and burned, Bunker could still occasionally be seen at the horse auctions in Kentucky and Ocala, doing his own bidding.

When Brennan and I pulled up to the front door of the sales arena, there was nearly a queue around the block of old "quality" bluebloods tripping over one another to introduce the most eligible of their daughters to a Yankee they'd likely not look at twice if he weren't spending five million at every sale.

When it comes to racetracks, Keeneland ranks at the top of the list with the most elegant. Another of the ovals that came into being around the Second World War, Keeeneland was founded in 1935 by a group of well-heeled horse-breeders that included J.O. "Jack" Keene, Hal Price Headley and Louis Lee Haggin II, who were succeeded in later years by others who shared the tradition of multiple names followed by Roman numerals: James E. "Ted" Bassett III, W.S. Farish III, and W.B. Rogers Beasley.

There was an interesting absence of Jews, Irish or Italians on the board, but that's probably just a coincidence.

Keeneland is the ultimate in boutique tracks, opening only twice a year, in April and October, for three-week meets, but it draws capacity crowds principally due to its location in the heart of the "bluegrass" and its proximity to Lexington and the surrounding breeding farms.

So attached was Keeneland to tradition, management prided itself on not having a track announcer until they succumbed to modernity in 1997 and finally let their fans know when the horses were "off." Until then, a race could be running in silence and the majority of the folks in the stands might not be aware of it taking place.

The entire operation is run as a non-profit, so a lot of the huge revenues it reaps are poured back into the property. Keeneland has been the main source of thoroughbred bloodstock since its inception as an auction sales company, and since then it's been responsible for trading the finest pedigrees in the world. You can buy yearlings, two-year-olds in training or mares and foals there. Just bring money...

To this day, horsemen generally agree that the two best places to breed and raise a good horse are Kentucky and Ireland. I would concur. Both places possess an abundance of rich grass full of minerals from the limestone soil, and the benefit to young horses is immeasurable.

In the late 1970's into the early '80's, a consortium of Irish racing men including Europe's greatest trainer, Vincent O'Brien, British soccer pool magnate Robert Sangster and O'Brien's son-in-law, John Magnier, began to compete with the Arabs in an effort to acquire the offspring of Kentucky Derby and Preakness winner Northern Dancer. This rivalry helped drive the price of Northern Dancer yearlings into the millions and raised his stud fee at one point to $1 million for a breeding, with no guarantee of pregnancy.

O'Brien, known simply as "M.V." to his inner circle, began his horse training career as a steeplechase trainer, winning the Grand National, the Cheltenham Gold Cup and the Champion Hurdle, each of them for *three consecutive* years. He switched to thoroughbreds, and soon won the Epsom Derby with Ballymoss, but it was when he teamed with Sangster that together they changed the world of horse-trading.

O'Brien possessed that rare insight that seemingly allowed him into the mind of his horses. He envisioned Northern Dancer as the ultimate stallion and trained Northern Dancer's son Nijinsky to win the British Triple Crown in 1970.

Northern Dancer himself was a smallish horse with a bit of a dip in his back, broad of chest and forehead and possessed of a wide jaw and intelligent eye, those things that horsemen love. His short cannon bones and thick shoulder and hip muscles gave him a look of powerful athleticism, but it was his tenacity that made him the world's greatest stallion.

When his breeder, E.P. Taylor, offered the diminutive son of Neartic at auction, he ended up having to keep Northern Dancer, likely since his size caused him to be passed over by prospective buyers. Even his trainer, Horatio Luro, underestimated what he had, suggesting that the colt be gelded.

There's no doubt that might have been the most significant blunder ever made in racing history as Northern Dancer became an incomparable sire of sires. Besides the great Nijinsky, he fathered Be My Guest, Lyphard, Danzig, El Gran Senor, Sadler's Wells, Danehill and Nuryev, to name only a few. He appears in the paternal line of dozens of champions, including the unbeaten wonder horses Frankel and Black Caviar, and is arguably the most influential sire in modern thoroughbred history.

O'Brien, Sangster and Magnier treated the Keeneland Yearling Sale like a private wine cellar, plucking the best of the Northern Dancer colts as well as valuable fillies with bloodlines that would eventually cross well when bred to those stallions.

I met Magnier through his main operatives in the States, becoming good friends with Paul Shanahan, Clem Murphy and veterinarian Demi O'Byrne, joining them in the ritual consumption of endless bottles of wine necessary to overcome international jet lag.

Due Process owned controlling interest in Deputy Minister and "the lads" from Ireland recognized the distinct possibility that the grandson of Northern Dancer might become a significant stallion.

Coolmore bought Deputy Minister breedings by the bunch for their Kentucky domiciled mares, and when they syndicated their top prospects, we jumped on the opportunity. Brennan didn't hesitate to pay a million dollars for a package deal of a share in El Gran Senor and Sadler's Wells, which included extra bonus breedings to both young stallions for the first few years.

We shipped some of our better mares to Ireland and kept them at the newly constructed Coolmore facilities, thus cementing the relationship, and two years later I sold one of our first Sadler's Wells yearlings for a sales-topping $500,000 at the Goffs Sale in Kildare, Ireland, another at Keeneland for $350,000.

Eventually Sangster's involvement diminished and Magnier introduced another former British bookmaker to the team to replace him.

Michael Tabor broke onto the U.S. thoroughbred scene in 1995 when he won the Kentucky Derby and Belmont Stakes with Thunder Gulch, a colt purchased privately on his behalf by Magnier's Coolmore agents. The owner of a chain of betting shops, Tabor was another "bitten by the bug" of racing and became their partner at the U.S. and European yearling auctions as they continued to add to their inventory of the finest bloodlines on the planet.

I met Michael at the Keeneland yearling sale in 1994 as he and I followed John Magnier, Paul Shanahan and Demi O'Byrne from barn to barn while they examined prospective purchases. Although he was "the money" in most of their subsequent purchases, his unassuming demeanor belied his importance, and we often spent more time discussing golf than horses.

The blue and orange Tabor colors have since been carried by the winners of every significant stakes race in Europe and most in the U.S., including the rare Kentucky Derby/Epsom Derby double, a combination only achieved by three other owners.

Although not a horseman himself, Tabor recognized the expertise of Magnier's team and set them loose to gather all the best horses they could buy, basically in an attempt to corner the market on the best blood.

Competition with Sheik Mohammed al Maktoum's Darley/Godolphin Stables served to escalate yearling prices and push all but a few others out of the running for top young horses for most of the 1990's and early 2000's as both filled their stud barns, although the Irish clearly had an upper hand due to M.V.'s insight in the '80's.

When it comes to skillful manipulation, no one has ever come close to the Irish. The Coolmore "machine" is the closest anyone has ever come to beating the game, and for good reason. John Magnier, son-in-law of Vincent O'Brien, is the man who solved the Rubik's Cube that comprises the racing, breeding, buying and selling of Thoroughbreds.

As a member of the Irish Senate in the '80's, Magnier used his persuasive powers to convince others of the long-term value to be had from foregoing tax revenues from stud fees, thus allowing stallion stations to grow and create jobs. He used influence and social stature to raise the funds for the Coolmore complex in County Tipperary, then filled the stallion barns with the best stallions and the broodmare barns with the finest mares.

M.V.'s brother Fonsie gave me a tour of the farm the year they began to put it together and Magnier's insight was truly remarkable. He had a plan to domicile the mares in smaller barns in order to limit exposure to disease and put his stallions on the other side of the road, each in individual barns of their own.

Next step was the modern phase of development of the nearby Ballydoyle training center where M.V. prepared his many classic winners. When Vincent O'Brien decided to retire, Magnier didn't hesitate to install young Aidan O'Brien (no relation to M.V.) at that facility and turn him loose with the best young horses money could buy or breeders could breed. Magnier and partners began to reap the rewards as the successor to M.V. proved more than up to the task. Aidan, writing his own history, began winning races across Europe at an astonishing clip, shattering records previously thought unbreakable.

The Coolmore machine ran stallion-grade colts in every maiden race in Ireland, winning over forty per cent of their starts and discouraging competition so badly that many times they would have half the starters in any given spot, racing under a variation of their colors, either as Tabor, Magnier or another combination of their partnerships.

Virtually ruthless in their business dealings, the Coolmore empire blossomed and grew as Magnier's team followed their marching orders: "If there's a lot, take most of it. If there's a little, take it all."

Aidan O'Brien's adept management of the finest stock in the racing world resulted in unparalled dominance of Europe's top events, among them victories in eleven Irish Derbys, four Epsom Derbys and the Arc de Triomphe.

Before he became exclusive to Coolmore/Tabor, et al, I was lucky enough to have Aidan train a Quiet American colt for me. His name was Mercaldo and I bought him for thirty thousand at the Keeneland yearling sale. He was perfectly conformed but big and growthy and never would have made a 2 year old runner in the states, so I shipped him to Ballydoyle with the understanding that he'd get some experience there and come back to the states for the Triple Crown races if he was good enough. I made a September trip to Ireland and Aidan told me Mercaldo had enough talent and he'd win "if you like." Of course I said I'd "like" and he made a maiden start on a seven and a half straightaway at Tralee, a second tier track, where although matched with one for the Aga Khan, a Darley homebred colt and two other high priced yearlings, he whistled in a winner.

We shipped Mercaldo home to John Forbes and although he didn't make the Derby, he won a few races and didn't disgrace us in the Haskell, but I have to believe it might have been a different story had he not his first US experience been so bad when an assistant starter at Aqueduct wrapped his tail around the gate and forgot to let go. He broke last by half a dozen lengths, leaving half a lovely tail in the starting stall and was only beaten two lengths and quite understandibly never behaved well at the gate after that. C'est la guerre...

The Coolmore brand today encircles the horseracing globe, having won every major race in Europe and with their stallion stations in Ireland, Kentucky and Australia standing the best studs that money can buy.

XX.

"LEAVE THE GUN, TAKE THE CANNOLIS."

--PETER CLEMENZA (RICHARD CASTELLANO) FROM *THE GODFATHER*

Since Brennan's approach to everything in life was always been to charge forward and take command, we became fixtures at the Keeneland auctions for the next ten years, regularly buying sales-toppers and million-dollar broodmares, yearlings and racehorses as Due Process Stables remained prominent among the leading stables in North America.

At its peak, our enterprise employed nearly 250 people, most of them in the care of horses at three farms under the DPS banner.

Due Process South was comprised of more than 800 rolling acres in Reddick, Florida, north of Ocala, with a racetrack and starting gate, and turf gallops through the woods, styled on the ones I'd seen at Ballydoyle. We had a lake where horses could swim for therapy and barns for every category of racehorse, including a separate complex for stallions and mares when their racing careers were over.

While in Lexington for the 1984 Keeneland November Mixed Sale, I got lost driving Bob to his hotel and ended up on a back country road. He noticed an "absolute auction" sign on a farm on Newtown Pike, just down the road from the Fasig-Tipton sales grounds, and made note of its convenient location.

Bob sent an agent and made the winning bid without ever setting foot on the property. Thus we had our own Kentucky nursery, the White Horse Acres farm where Seattle Slew had been born. It was in the same foaling stall that our best racer, Dehere, would be born in 1991, and we kept our best mares and foals there to breed to Kentucky's best stallions.

The original farm in Colts Neck, New Jersey, eventually totaled more than 400 acres, and also had both training and breeding facilities to rival the finest in Kentucky. The property combined the contiguous Bernadotte Farm and Tinton Falls Farm, and when finished it was bordered by twenty miles of four-board fence and contained two forty stall barns, a five-furlong training track and accommodations for eighty broodmares as well as the five stall stud barn.

Bob was a masterful judge of market timing, never averse to taking a profit, and during that strong market of 1984 we launched our sales program with John Sikura's new Hill 'n' Dale Sales Agency. John topped all consignors at the Keeneland November breeding sale when he sold three of our mares for over $8 million, including It's in the Air, the former two-year-old filly champion who was in foal to Seattle Slew. She alone went for $4.6 million.

It's in the Air was a $1 million private purchase by Brennan from Lou Wolfson's Harbor View Farm in 1981, which made the daughter of Mr. Prospector one of the best bloodstock deals we ever made.

Most of the time, though, between the pirates with Mayflower blood who lived there and the others trailing us from Jersey, I figure we are lucky to get out of Lexington town at all.

Foreign bloodstock agents were all the rage, with British, French and Irish at the top of the hill and Americans taking feverish notes to refine their technique. The mailbox at 40 Broadway was stuffed daily with offerings of every sort of racehorse, stallion and broodmare deal, most proffered by agents playing both sides, hoping to get a bite on something so they could run to the horse owner and make an offer.

It's a common horse trader's ploy -- they call and ask,

"Would you take $200,000 for that filly that won yesterday?" If you continue the conversation a deal starts to form. They then go to a prospective buyer and say,

"I have an exclusive to sell that filly that won yesterday..."

It's known as prospecting, and occasionally you strike gold.

We get out of the rental car at the valet parking entrance to the Keeneland Sales pavilion and there's a kind of paunchy little bald Italian guy waiting for us, his swarthy, black-suited "chauffeur" two steps removed.

From the foyer of the auction arena to barn twenty-seven at the top of the hill, he never stops talking long enough to take a deep breath.

From what I can gather, Brennan has been lucky enough to run into one of the smartest guys ever to look at a racehorse, and we're going to buy a yearling he's picked out just for us. The guy's name is Bob LiButti, and as mom used to say, "He could charm a snake."

For some reason I'm not immediately able to ascertain, this individual prefers not to put his name on any transactions. Instead, he wishes to receive his commissions through regular mail to a post office box.

We end up with about ten yearlings, averaging about four hundred thousand each. One of them makes a decent broodmare but the rest were unremarkable as I recall, but we certainly felt good about the purchases at the time as each came with a great story.

A few weeks later Brennan shows me a gold horseshoe he's received from LiButti and tells me to make out another commission check and to let Reynaldo know that a filly named Sugar Gold would be arriving from Calder.

Bob quotes LiButti as saying "she's the fastest thing in south Florida and will be the fastest in Jersey," and that's probably true. But he also hasn't mentioned that she's only slightly larger than a Great Dane.

It's not until years later that I got the real inside information on Mister LiButti, about the same time as the rest of the racing world. In the early 1990's, his daughter Edie was the owner of record of a good horse named Devil His Due, a handsome black son of Devil's Bag, trained by Allen Jerkens to win almost four million dollars. But LiButti's involvement with racing went back to the top racehorse Jim French, in one of those *Confederacy of Dunces* kind of stories.

Johnny Campo, who later won the 1981 Kentucky Derby with Pleasant Colony, was early in his training career when he ended up with Jim French, a son of Graustark bred by Buffalo Bills owner Ralph Wilson. Campo trains "the livin' shit" out of him, running the little brown colt in sixteen stakes races from six furlongs to a mile and a half at ten different tracks. The diminutive colt obviously loves the drilling, since he finishes second to Canonero II in the Kentucky Derby, third in the Preakness and second in the Belmont along the way.

The athletic performance of such a horse was remarkable enough, but when Campo shipped him to Saratoga for the 1971 Travers, the stewards discovered that Jim French had been impounded by the Saratoga County sheriff's office. They refused his entry for the race since none of the horse's previous owners had a valid title to him and some had never even held an owner's license.

The New York Racing Commission began an investigation, tracing Jim French's ownership through several transactions in which a 70 percent interest appeared to be owned by two individuals, although in fact no money changed hands, and finally revealing the true owner to be one R. Robert Libutti. Doing business as Robert Presti, he had been barred from racing since 1968 for undisclosed and unlicensed ownership.

An obvious misunderstanding.

A decade later, according to the New Jersey State Attorney General, it seems Robert LiButti is a "known associate" of Mafia family boss John Gotti and has embarked on a wicked losing streak at Atlantic City casinos, gambling about twenty million dollars between September of '84 and October of 1990, losing over $12 million and at the same time getting barred from the gaming floor for verbal abuse of the dealers.

I guess he should have stuck with horses.

As it turns out, Due Process has had purchased on our behalf quite a few broodmares in Ireland. Bob tells me to go check them out, and while I was there to look over a three-year-old for sale that Kerry Fitzpatrick smoked out with trainer Dermot Weld.

The best way to get to the Curragh is to fly to Dublin and take an hour drive west to the yellow-flowered gorse covered hills where hundreds of horses train every day, the place where the Irish Derby runs at the end of each June.

I grab a red-eye flight on Aer Lingus out of Kennedy and get no more than fifteen minutes of sleep on the six-hour flight. There's a driver waiting when I stagger through Irish customs at five-thirty in the morning.

Of course, it's raining in Dublin and the traffic is backed up, making the forty mile trip endless and exacerbating my jet lag. We arrive at Dermot Weld's yard on the edge of the Curragh about 9 a.m. and I'm about as useless as if I'd been on a three-day bender. So I doze in the car as we wait for ages by the farm gate for someone to finally let us in.

A pretty good percentage of Irish horse stories somehow involve the Curragh, the gently rolling plain of about 5,000 acres of what we'd consider public land, located about fifty miles west of Dublin.

It's rich with the history of pre-Christian kings, fairies, and ancient Celtic battles, and it houses most of the Irish Army in rustic barracks surrounded by a sheep-trodden golf course. The Curragh was the site of the first international motor race in 1903 when Ireland was still referred to as part of the United Kingdom.

Since then, the Curragh has been home to the five classic races of Ireland: the Derby, the Oaks, the Irish 1,000 and 2,000 Guineas and the Irish St. Leger, and I'd consider it one of the most significant racecourses in the world, simply by virtue of it's being the great test of a horse. All races there finish with an up-hill grade for nearly half a mile. When you see a horse charging past the wire there, you've seen a racehorse.

In 1981, a three-year-old chestnut colt with a brilliant blaze won the Epsom Derby by ten lengths. Four weeks later he joined an exclusive club by winning the Irish Derby in a gallop.

His name was Shergar and his trainer, Michael Stoute, was the son of a Bajan police chief, later to become Sir Michael when knighted by the Queen, and having trained winners of every British Classic as well as five Breeders' Cup races in the U.S. as well as the Dubai World Cup.

Shergar was bred and owned by the Aga Khan and retired to stallion duty at the Aga's Ballymany Stud at the edge of the Curragh, being in great demand for what was equivalent to well over a $100,000 stud fee. His syndication for over $10 million was the record for any stallion.

Until that time, horse farms found little need for security, simply employing night watchmen to make sure horses didn't get cast in their stalls or run through a fence at night.

Thus, the entire thoroughbred world changed on February 8, 1983, when half a dozen masked men entered Ballymany and kidnapped Shergar, simply packing him off in a two-horse trailer.

In a case that took over the headlines for nearly a year, yet remained unsolved with the horse never found, Irish police theorized that the perpetrators were IRA members with a poorly constructed scheme to raise funds.

They surmised the colt had been killed when the kidnappers panicked after realizing how uncontrollable a force a riled up thoroughbred could be in civilian hands, which is very likely what happened. Non-horse people could easily underestimate the power and fearsomeness of a high-strung stallion, and if they were guys with guns, the eventual outcome could easily have left Shergar in an unmarked country grave.

Suddenly guarded gates and video surveillance became the norm on farms around the world -- like Dermot Weld's yard. When we were eventually admitted we discovered a state-of-the art training center, in sight of the Curragh racecourse stands. Dermot holds a veterinary degree as well as his title that season as leading trainer in Ireland. Whenever Vincent O'Brien isn't winning, Dermot is.

The colt I'm there to see is a named Stramaar. He's a flashy black rascal with a big blaze that trickles down his forehead and a couple of white socks, and he just so happens to still be in the indoor ring, circling with about a dozen others, cooling down when we arrive.

This may or may not be some mean coincidence, since he's already been out and done his morning work. Everybody who walks by and looks at him says "brilliant" and "grand, grand," so we watch him walk for a bit more before Dermot welcomes me into his parlor for tea and biscuits.

Out comes the Timeform *book, the Euro-version of our* Daily Racing Form, *along with race charts and a video of Stramaar at Naas or Tramore or Tipperary, crushing his four or five hapless competitors with ease in each instance. Obviously he's a candidate for the American classics, no?*

I'm not sure if the television's out of focus or it's just my eyes, but Dermot's so polite I don't dare bring it up.

Poker players have an old expression, "If you look around the table for the sucker and you can't see one, it's you." I'm alone in the room with Ireland's sharpest trainer, and my stomach hurts.

Two cups of tea and some biscuits later, after interminable polite conversation, finally we have a handshake to seal my first Irish horse-trading lesson. It's not until much later I hear the Irish guys use the expression, "Never tell the truth when a lie will do."

A week later, four hundred grand is wired to Ireland and Stramaar arrives at Reynaldo's barn at the training center in Colt's Neck. It seems the flashy black colt possesses a mean streak, and he promptly sends his first groom to the emergency room with a broken leg as the result of a well-aimed kick.

We get him ready and run in the Cherry Hill Mile, mainly as a race-filler for Spend A Buck, who's prepping for the Kentucky Derby and getting eligible for the $2 million bonus scheme Brennan has hatched to put his new Garden State Park back on the map.

To win the bonus, Spend a Buck needs to win the Cherry Hill Mile and the Garden State Stakes, then win the Kentucky Derby and return to Brennan's new track to win the Jersey Derby.

Spend a Buck wins while Stramaar finishes up the track, and by now the Irish colt has either kicked, bitten or stepped on virtually everyone in the barns. For his sins he is gelded, which as it turns out has little or no effect but at least makes the rest of us feel better, since cutting his throat is pretty much out of the question.

XXI.

"You want a friend on Wall Street, go get a dog..."

-- Stockbroker's advice

When Spend A Buck bounces out of the gate in front, he never looks back and posts the third fastest time ever in winning the 1985 Kentucky Derby. Later that evening his owner Dennis Diaz rattles the patrician Thoroughbred world by announcing that he will be skipping the Preakness with its $750,000 purse to go instead for the million-dollar Jersey Derby and Brennan's additional $2 million bonus for which Spend A Buck is eligible by virtue of winning both the Cherry Hill Mile and Garden State Stakes, along with the Kentucky Derby.

Chick Lang, Sr., the general manager of Pimlico, aka "Mister Preakness," promptly denounces Brennan as a "snake oil salesman" on the front page of the *Racing Form* and once again, Bob gets exactly what he wants, maximum publicity.

As one of Brennan's great delights was poking fun at those who messed with him, he immediately named one of our best prospects, a high-priced two-year-old colt by Raise a Native out of Mrs. Peterkin, "Snake Oil Man" to commemorate Chick's attack.

Diaz also continues to thumb his nose at convention and Brennan is reviled by the "quality" for messing with their game, but two million is two million and when someone says "it's not about the money'" you usually can figure it's about the money. Patter is exchanged daily on the front pages of the Racing Form about the ethics of having denied the racing public a potential Triple Crown candidate, but the Jersey Derby is nonetheless an historic race in its own right, having numbered Citation, Iron Liege, Jaipur and Candy Spots among its winners. In fact, the notion of a Triple Crown didn't even exist until 1930, when writer Charles Hatton used it to describe Gallant Fox's sweep of the Derby, the Preakness and the Belmont Stakes, so perhaps he and his predecessors shouldn't be on that list. How do you aspire to something that doesn't exist?

Spend A Buck ends up three-year-old champion and Horse of the Year, proving that horse racing is more than just the Triple Crown.

Bob's inclination toward taunting his opponents was no doubt one of the main factors in his undoing, but you had to admire his style, and one of his favorite ways of poking fun at critics was our annual naming procedure.

Because all thoroughbreds share the common birthday of January first for the sake of orderly categorizing when it comes to racing, The Jockey Club requires they be named by February first of their two-year-old season.

You can wait until they're ready to run, but there's an additional fee and naming fifty or so horses can add up, so I would start prodding the boss for names in about October, hoping to get a list by January.

The Jockey Club is the presiding body that oversees pedigree and registration of all thoroughbreds and enforces the naming guidelines. Names are restricted to eighteen characters, including spaces, and must be submitted to The Jockey Club for approval, where they're on the lookout for trademark infringement and double entendres.

Conventional horse naming sometimes combines components of names or notions found in the animal's pedigree, such as Spend a Buck, by Buckaroo, Funny Cide, by Distorted Humor, or War Admiral, by Gun Boat.

All time king of the horse-naming game was Caesar Kimmel, the mastermind of Warner Communications, who raced a successful stable of horses in the '50's, '60's and '70's, and whose son, John, became so enamored of the game that he went to vet school and took up training horses as his life's work.

Caesar first drove the track race-callers crazy when he named a filly Cunning Stunt. He joked that his dream was to have her run at Belmont, coupled with another of his horses, Cunning Linguist, and imagined how the great track announcer Freddy Caposella would likely call, "They're off... and on the lead that's... One and One-A..."

Other classics among Caesar's naming handiwork were I Found Gold ("ah-fongool") and Crack Doctor Jack, named for his wife's gynecologist.

Caesar's father Manny was a legend among gamblers, having taken MIT math professor Edward O. Thorp to Las Vegas and revolutionized the blackjack world by perfecting the science of card-counting, thus beating the casinos at one of their most profitable games.

Thorp's book *Beat the Dealer* made the *New York Times* bestseller list and still is the definitive work on how to count cards. Thorp and Manny eventually were barred from the casinos, and henceforth Vegas went to counter-measures like multiple decks and frequent shuffles in an attempt to thwart skilled practitioners of the technique.

His names may not have quite measured up to Caesar's double-entendres, but Brennan definitely came up with a bunch of great ones and often used them to honor those to whom he was closest.

One gem was the $900,000 Keeneland sales-topping Deputy Minister colt he named Jack Livingston after the caddy-master at his golf club.

He named a Deputy Minister home-bred filly Noraquillon after his secretary, and after she won two races we sold her to Sheikh Mohammed for $2 million. The filly, not his secretary.

Bob loved to name horses after his alma mater's mascot, the Seton Hall Pirates, and he hit the mark squarely with a Deputy Minister colt he called Dehere. Terry Dehere was a record-setting point guard on the Big East Conference Championship teams Bob followed all over the country in the early '90's, and it seemed appropriate that the colt Dehere was a freakishly fast two-year-old of 1993.

In a rare year when we had more horses than names, Bob told me to come up with a few. I had a cousin, Margie Lang, who was formerly a nun of the Sisters of Mercy variety, and she and her fellow sisters liked to play the ponies just as much as the priests did. Bob regularly monikered high priced colts with references to the monks at St. Benedict's where he attended high school, like "Aggot" (for the abbot).

Since cousin Margie would regularly call me for passes to the track, I had named a horse of my own "Tell Margie" for her, and every year around horse-naming time her best friend Sister Mary Dora made a pitch, saying, "What am I, chopped liver?" She got her wish when I named my pick of that year's crop "Sister Dot."

Brennan's rise to wealth and power was undeniably one of the great American success stories and he was rightfully proud of his Irish roots. One of nine children born to Agnes and Henry Brennan in Newark, New Jersey, he started a career in accounting at the local Catholic schools, St. Benedict's and Seton Hall, before receiving his CPA and eventually establishing himself as a shrewd force to be reckoned with in the stock-trading game.

When Bob's mother died suddenly of a heart attack -- or more likely a broken heart when her youngest son was shot to death before her eyes in a case of mistaken identity -- Brennan's father made a dramatic late-life career change from salesman to Dominican monk. Bob kept his connection with his alma maters and many of the priests at St. Benedicts and Seton Hall remained close friends, and were often among the guests at his dinners and parties.

He liked to reminisce of the days when his family was poor and his mother would take the kids to an annual Christmas display in Newark, and in her memory, every December he would decorate the street where he lived in Brielle with thousands of tiny lights and holiday scenes, inviting local parents to bring their kids.

Years later, when we finished creating Due Process Farm in Colts Neck, the first thing Bob did was design his own lavish display, winding through the barns and pastures. We lit up County Road 537 for a half a mile outside the farm and hired two dozen local cops to monitor the traffic. It was a great way to give back to the community in a lot of ways, boosting paychecks with overtime and treating folks to a free show. The display included a crèche with live sheep, goats, ducks and chickens hovering around the baby Jesus, and as cars passed by an antique calliope spouted holiday tunes. We ran the spectacle starting two weeks before Christmas and kept it going through the first week of the New Year for a dozen years. Our farm manager tallied the crowd, counting over 74,000 cars one year, most with four to a car.

When it comes to holiday movies, some people are *It's a Wonderful Life* people and some are *Christmas Story* folks. Bob was in the former camp, and the display was his way of showing his appreciation for all the good fortune he'd enjoyed.

When the horse market took a wicked downturn in the late '80's, Bob decided it was time to clean house. We put the entire stable in a dispersal sale in Kentucky. Racehorses, mares, foals, yearlings and all went on the block as we closed up shop at the Jersey farm. He told me to pick out a dozen of the racehorses just so he could keep Reynaldo employed and have some action at the track and let the rest go. We sold about two hundred horses for $8.8 million, including some between $500,000 and a million, which meant a lot went for peanuts.

Included in that dozen we kept was that home-bred filly by Secretariat out of the Damascus mare Sword Game, the one that I had tagged Sister Dot, figuring every time she ran we'd get the benefit of novenas and extra rosaries pulling for a win. 'Can't hurt.

Sister Dot was a moderately good race-mare, placing in a few stakes, and we always had a crew of out-of-uniform nuns in the paddock whenever she ran. But she was big and beautiful, and I knew her best chance for success in the future was going to be as a mommy.

Every fall I'd do the matings for the upcoming breeding season, and when Sister Dot retired to become a broodmare I thought Deputy Minister was a logical mate for her. What a pedigree -- Deputy Minister and Northern Dancer on top and Secretariat and Damascus on the bottom!

The resultant foal was a blocky, Northern Dancer-looking colt, the one Bob called Dehere. He broke his maiden at Monmouth in July of '93, walking out of the gate under Joe Bravo and blowing past a nice field to win for fun.

Dehere swept the two-year-old stakes at Saratoga, winning the Sanford, Saratoga Special and Hopeful, the first horse to do so in seventy-six years.

The colt had a habit of breaking a beat slow. When he got boxed in two races in a row only to wheel out at the sixteenth pole and fly to the front, Eddie Maple took the heat and we swapped riders for Chris McCarron, who flew in from California and rode him to a romp in the Hopeful. *"Dehere is moving like a rocket!"* exclaimed Tom Durkin.

I've always thought that Chris was one of the two best jocks I ever saw atop a horse, the other being Angel Cordero, Jr. I made a deal with Chris to commit all the way to the first Saturday in May for the Derby, should we be lucky enough to get that far.

On a sloppy track, on footing that he hated, Dehere lost the Futurity at Belmont to Holy Bull by a long neck, but he romped again in the Champagne, which used to seal the deal for two-year-old champ before the advent of The Breeder's Cup. Many candles were lit on his behalf and rumor was that rosaries rattled as he crossed the finish line as the nuns rooted for Sister Dot's little boy.

There were brush fires in the nearby San Gabriel Mountains the week before we took Dehere to Santa Anita for the '93 Breeders' Cup, and the air was filled with soot. You'd go to your car in the morning and it would be covered with ashes. I was coughing and sneezing and taking all sorts of over-the-counter allergy remedies thinking they might help, but to no avail. As it turns out, the air was toxic for both horses and people.

Dehere didn't run on Lasix and went off at 4 to 5, as the shortest priced favorite of the day. He bled about a "3-plus" on the scale of 5 and finished up the track, well beaten by Brocco, who was a nice colt himself. I can only blame that defeat on the irritating air since he had a great throat and never bled before or after.

We put on a full-court press with Eclipse voters when Brocco went to the well one time too many and managed to get beat in the Hollywood Futurity. Dehere was named two-year-old male champion of '93, marking him as the early favorite for the 1994 Kentucky Derby.

Dehere was one of the best betting horses I've ever known, simply because he never failed to fire when he was supposed to win. That doesn't mean he won every time, but he gave his all and if he lost there was a good reason for him doing so. Of his two second place finishes, the one to Holy Bull was palatable. I knew Dehere was vulnerable in the Futurity because a muddy track might his Achilles Heel, and there was already little doubt that Holy Bull was destined to be a great horse himself.

The defeat by Ride the Rails was also an "iffy" spot since we were using it to set him up for the Fountain of Youth and the Florida Derby. As an odds-on favorite coming off a lay-off, it wasn't a betting situation anyway. You can try to win every time but unless a horse is undefeated or on an incredibly long win streak, it's better to point ahead to a significant prize than worry about losing any one race.

Old-timers will tell you the toughest race for a top class horse is the second time off his layoff, stretching from short to long, and we wanted to take away the risk of that bounce.

Gulfstream Racing Secretary Bobby Umphrey did me a favor by writing an open allowance race and getting it to fill, knowing that we needed to get around two turns, not having raced since Breeders' Cup, and it is better to lose when it doesn't matter than when it does.

Every other time Dehere ran I bet him like he'd already won, making for cold exactas and several times cold trifectas.

I'm a firm believer in superstition, especially if there's any fact at all to back it up. The so-called two-year-old champion's curse hit us in March after Dehere won the Fountain of Youth at Gulfstream, on a muddy track no less. Chris McCarron was on a suspension, so Craig Perret replaced him, and when we walked back from the winner's circle Craig told me Dehere hated the track and won on sheer class.

"Nobody in that bunch beats him, ever," said Craig.

And note that eventual Kentucky Derby winner Go for Gin was a well beaten second in that race.

Dehere was going to be a huge favorite for the Florida Derby and was working an easy half-mile one morning at Palm Beach Downs when he must have hit the ground wrong.

Reynaldo and I both clocked him working a dull half in :48 4/5, very out of character for a colt who'd usually break your watch with a bullet every time. Fast horses always work fast, they say.

Dehere came back to the barn okay but began walking short as he cooled out, and I could tell by the look on Reynaldo's face that we were in trouble. X-rays revealed a non-displaced condylar fracture of his right hind leg, ending all hopes for any Derby -- Florida, Kentucky or otherwise -- and putting his career in jeopardy.

I mark it as one of my worst days ever when I had to call Bob Brennan and tell him his Kentucky Derby dream was over. Incredibly, he took his time to console me and called Reynaldo right away to do the same with him.

My very next call was to Dr. Alex Harthill in Kentucky. Doc Harthill was the best veterinarian in America at the time and a good friend since our Louisiana Derby days. He informed me that he wasn't licensed to operate in Florida but that he would put me on to Wayne McIlwraith at Colorado State, a surgeon he considered the best in the business.

Wayne wasn't well known then, but since has become the pre-eminent equine surgeon in the world. He flew in and did the job, placing three stainless steel screws in Dehere's hind leg. The colt would need six months to recover and lost the remainder of his three-year-old year, just like his old man, Deputy Minister.

Swamped with offers from stud farms, I told Bob that our best shot was with the Irish. He agreed. We made a deal with Coolmore to stand Dehere at Ashford Stud in Kentucky in the event he didn't make it back to the races, and if he did we would be partners until the next season.

Our farm manager Bob Prater did an incredible job getting Dehere fit at Due Process South in Ocala, galloping him and swimming him in the lake, but when Reynaldo got him to the track and began to tighten the screws, it became apparent the colt wasn't quite the same.

I had reserved the decision as to when Dehere would be finally retired. Coolmore was okay with whatever the call, but there's a big difference between just getting a horse back to the races and doing it at the level where he'd performed so well.

Top class racehorses can easily make over a million dollars a year but the higher class the company, the harder they have to run. Stallions get paid every time the mare has a baby, and at $25,000 times a hundred, it's rarely worth it to make a comeback unless everything is perfect. That is why it didn't seem right to pass on a full book of mares for Dehere at the stud farm on a chance he might return to his Grade I form.

Besides, we had a two-year-old full sibling, cleverly monikered Defrere, a play on the French for "brother."

Hope springs eternal...

XXII.

"I'M NOT ALWAYS RIGHT, BUT I'M NEVER IN DOUBT."

--TOM DOOLEY, NFL REFEREE

There might have been a few other racetrackers with the self-confidence of Woodrow Cefis Stephens, but they were surely few and far-between. Woody had his own barn at Belmont and one at Hialeah, and for twenty years it seemed as if nothing walked out of his stalls that couldn't fly.

We stabled the main Due Process Stable string with Reynaldo at Hollywood Park for the winter of '85 and kept a handful of horses at Hialeah with Billy Burch for the Bob's entertainment when he'd helicopter down from his home near Palm Beach for a Saturday at the races.

There was an English trainer there named Adrian Nicholl, trading off horses for the Arabs, mostly ones they'd purchased at sales with U.S. style pedigrees and later found they didn't want to run on the soft European grass courses or be capable of winning graded stakes races. He had a nice colt by Ack Ack out of the good mare Dogtooth Violet that Stanley Rieser used to train, which alone was enough to grab my interest.

The colt was called Violado, and when he won an allowance race pretty easily one Saturday, Adrian told Billy that they would take a hundred and quarter. I called Brennan and got the go, and as we made the deal I realized that nominations to the Louisiana Derby closed that weekend, so I nominated him on pure spec.

Billy was a third generation trainer, son of Hall of Famer Elliott Burch and the grandson of another Hall of Famer, Preston Burch, who literally wrote the book on training thoroughbreds. It was called *Training Thoroughbred Horses*. Billy had a great personality and knew everyone from the Turf Club to the track kitchen. He had a lighthearted approach to training and nothing bothered him. As a kid who just about grew up in a barn, he'd basically seen it all.

We decided to ship Violado to New Orleans early for the race and Billy made arrangements for us to go into Doc Harthill's private barn. Harthill had a reputation as a great surgeon, genius diagnostician, and the best pre-race vet in America. He had taken care of a dozen Derby winners and seemingly had the ability to make most minor ailments disappear. His girlfriend trained a big string between New Orleans and Kentucky, and the barn had a chain-link fence around it that I don't think James Bond could have gotten through without an invitation.

Jacinto Vasquez, on his way to the Hall of Fame, flew in for the ride and we got the job done in a photo finish. Brennan was too busy to make the trip so when they took the winner's circle photo in the infield, it was me, Billy and his wife Trish, along with two guys who looked like Mutt and Jeff. I figured they were Billy's friends and he thought they were with me. Turns out they crashed about twenty years worth of Louisiana Derby pictures.

I had never been around Woody Stephens much, other than to exchange pleasantries. When we went to the Trustees Room at the Fair Grounds for a post-Derby champagne toast to celebrate our win with Violado, I congratulated him on his game second-place finish with Betty Moran's gelding Crème Fraiche, halfway expecting a patronizing, "Thanks, nice win, congratulations."

Instead from Woody I got a big smile and --

"You got lucky there. One more work I'da beat you easy."

Coming up in a classic generation of horsemen such as John Nerud, Mack Miller, Frank Whitely and Allen Jerkens, Stephens was a Kentucky "hardboot" and as good a horseman as ever was. Although sometimes wrong, he was never in doubt.

He delighted in telling folks that Vincent O'Brien was known as the Woody Stephens of Europe and Charlie Whittingham the Woody Stephens of California.

It's probably worthy of note that Crème Fraice did go on to take the Derby Trial and later become Woody's fourth Belmont Stakes winner in a row, so he was probably right about me being lucky to win that day in Louisiana.

I later got to know Woody better when we hired one of his former assistants, Phil Gleaves, to train a string of horses for Due Process. Phil had worked his way up from exercise rider to protégé. When he went on his own at age twenty-four, he hit the mark early, winning the Travers with Wise Times that first season.

Phil's proud of his English roots and often boasted of his aspiration to be the fifth most famous person from Liverpool –- right behind John, Paul, George and Ringo. He clicked well as part of our team and won the Grade

I Jerome Stakes at Belmont with Evening Kris, a nice colt I bought in a private deal from a sea captain who dabbled in breeding horses.

Evening Kris went to stud in New Jersey and did a credible job as the runner-up leading sire for a number of years. He was bookended by our other studs Papa Riccio and Defrere, either of whom were leading sires eight times between 1994 and 2011.

Phil handled the New York string, Reynaldo the Jersey horses, and we farmed out a few to Carlos Garcia in Maryland, Dr. J.R.S. Fisher (his track nickname was "Alphabet"), and some went to Pennsylvania with Bobby Connors. This gave us plenty of ammo for Monmouth and Saratoga, so we could go easy on the ones we were planning to take to Florida for Gulfstream, the boss's favorite spot.

Our inside joke was the annual push for the "birthday horse" that we tried to have primed and ready to win for Brennan each February 6. Usually we won one around that date and a couple of times managed to pull it off on the exact day, once with a double by Reynaldo when he got Disquieting and Hot Words home in '84. Phil lit up the birthday candles with Yucca in '90 and Jack Livingston in '93.

After Brennan discovered the Spa, he adopted it as his personal respite from city summers and started renting a house there, first on Union Avenue only a few blocks from the track's entrance. He'd bring a household staff from New Jersey for the month of August, handicap races in the mornings between calls to Wall Street, and stroll over for the Daily Double. When the landlord realized he had a tycoon on his hands, he tried to double the rent, so Bob bolted and did the next best thing -- he bought the nicest house for sale in Saratoga, an old stone mansion with eight bedrooms and a carriage house at the top of Broadway near the entrance to Skidmore College.

He called me at horse-naming time and said, "I've got a good one for you... pick out a runner and name him 'Bye Union Ave'." The homebred gelding by Vittorioso won over $400,000 for us including the Grade II MacKnight Handicap at Calder.

The Saratoga summers proved to be a source of frustration. Although we placed second or third in plenty of stakes, like the Saratoga Special and the Travers, we went winless for the first *seven* years we raced there, 1983-1989. That served as a great topic for dinner table conversation, and I came to dread the "'Think we might win a race this year, John?" that came with each new season. Every year I gave the same reply,

"Absolutely, positively."

Running a stable as large as Due Process, you'd think it would be easy to win a few races at any meet. But running in hot maiden races and stakes against the best in America isn't the way to do it.

Phil Gleaves got to be the hero in '89, at last getting a select group of Bob's friends in the Saratoga winner's circle with a big grey horse named Yucca, ridden by Angel Cordero, Jr. Phil did it again the next summer with the same horse and jockey combination, only the '90 version had a packed winner's circle. They'd finally gotten faith.

To show how fickle the "Racing Gods" can be, when we had at last opened the door to success at Saratoga the curse seemed broken for good.

In the summer of 1992, our homebred colt Dehere was referred to by racecaller Tom Durkin as "the Saratoga Sensation," as he won the Sanford, Saratoga Special and Hopeful. We ruled Saratoga, winning almost half our starts that season.

XXIII.

"Breed the best to the best, and hope for the best."

--Old Kentucky Breeder's adage

From the outset of my time with Due Process Stable, I was fascinated with the possibility of prolonging our horses' careers.

Since so many foals are not conformationally correct, which is to say they have offset knees or ankles or other physical defects, they are naturally inclined to eventually break down or become unfit for racing from the rigors of serious race-training.

There have always been several dramatically different schools of thought on this topic, the most popular that horses put in to training as yearlings and raced at two are forced to undergo too much strain on young joints and bones and thus are be unable to enjoy long careers. The opposite side of the coin proposes that the early training establishes good bone and joint structure and it is an advantage to start horses young.

Both sides have always had plenty of research and data to support their contentions and I think they are each right about some points, wrong about others.

I noticed early in my travels that European horses seemed to hold up well although having the same conformation faults and enjoyed longer careers, the main difference being the surfaces they were trained on, which are naturally softer and more forgiving.

The Irish trainers utilized wood-chip tracks for long gallops and warm-ups, then breezed their horses on open fields that rarely dry out in the rainy climate. They are extremely sensitive to their horses' ability relative to the "hardness" of the ground and will often scratch from a race when they think the going is not what they need.

Many decisions are based on the pedigree, knowing how the sire or dam liked the going and assuming (often correctly) that the preference is passed on. This makes sense in that the horses' "way of going," or stride, is similar to that of their parents in some way, and the locomotion is either favored or at a disadvantage due to the hardness or softness of the ground. Interestingly, Euros will scratch their horses if the turf is too hard, preferring to run on soft ground. Americans cancel the race if it is too soft and move it to the dirt track.

The synthetic racetracks that were installed in the U.S. in the mid-2000's (and in some cases removed) have given plenty of support to the hypothesis that more forgiving surfaces cause fewer fatal injuries, which no one can deny is a worthy goal. Unfortunately, the database is only a few years old and surfaces like Polytrack or Tapeta will hold up great in some climatic conditions and fall apart in others. If the game is to survive, tracks that limit breakdowns will have to be put in play or fans will eventually get tired of seeing the ambulance come out and the green screen go up while they euthanize a fatally injured horse.

I have been to the Kempton track in England and it works well, but the synthetic surface that was forced on Santa Anita by the state's overzealous racing commission turned out to be a disaster when the extreme heat of Southern California broke down polymers and the seasonal rains didn't drain as they were supposed to, causing holes and soft spots in the track. By 2015 all California tracks but Golden Gate Fields will have returned to traditional dirt surfaces.

Keeping in mind that horses in the U.S. usually stable at the track where they are competing, which is usually hard and fast for racing purposes, one shouldn't be surprised that they encounter frequent debilitating (although not life threatening or career ending) injuries. Bettors don't want to gamble on horses running six furlongs in 1:15, as they did on some synthetics, unless they're Arabians or Appaloosas. And the salient point is that horse racing is all about betting. No bets, no tracks.

There has been a trend over the past dozen years for top outfits to condition their horses at training centers such as Palm Meadows, Payson Park, Fair Hill, San Luis Rey Downs and others in order to avoid the tracks where a lot of racing is conducted.

Trainers like Shug McGaughey, Bill Mott and Nick Zito regularly platoon their stock in and out of the track, taking advantage of the slower, softer surfaces at the training centers between races, giving their runners a change of scenery as well as a change of pace.

My first Irish buying experience taught me that early training on forgiving surfaces equaled longer careers. We were producing over one hundred foals a year and buying racing prospects when they seemed right for the stable, so part of the program needed to be a culling process.

However, when two of the young horses that we bred and later culled turned out to be Rampage, an Arkansas Derby winner who could have won the 1986 Kentucky Derby with better luck, and Open Mind, the two-time champion and Hall of Famer, I realized it was time for a new approach.

I began sending the imperfect yearlings, those with offset knees or turned out in the ankles, to Ireland for breaking and training. Michael Osborne, architect of the Dubai World Cup Festival, was my Irish advisor and he recommended splitting the horses up, using a few conditioners to avoid losing the season if one trainer had a virus in his yard.

Con Collins, Tommy Stack, Michael Grassik and Neil McGrath all were on board with the plan to send the horses home to the U.S. after they finished their three-year-old year. We had twenty to twenty-five over there for several years, and it was amazing how many of those horses returned to the states and raced until they were seven or eight, despite crooked legs or offset knees.

One colt, a big grey that Bob named Wonderloaf after the slogan of the Brennan Bread company in Dublin ("It's the Wonder-loaf!") came home and proved the theory by winning the Talahassee Stakes and the Seminole Stakes at Hialeah for Phil Gleaves.

Through the late '80's I'm making a good number of trips to Ireland, racing and breeding there, and gain more and more respect for their horsemanship every time I go. Consider that in the U.S. the most common coin is decorated with George Washington and an eagle, whereas in Ireland, it's a horse.

Order a pint in any pub, the bartender gives you a tip in the first race. Stop at the bank to exchange currency and the teller has a cousin who grooms a horse in the third and fancies him a winner.

Everyone in Ireland, it turns out, is a lover of the horse, and they all know who's running on Irish Derby day.

Racing in Ireland, as well as Europe in general, is conducted quite differently than it is in the States. Some tracks turn right-handed, or clockwise (known in America as the "wrong way"), some are horseshoe shaped, and some courses are even straightaways of more than a mile and a half. There also are some oval tracks like ours in the U.S. that turn left-handed, but they are few and far between.

The Curragh itself, Ireland's greatest course, more resembles a huge open field than a racetrack, with a right to left stretch run up a hill to the finish in front of the stands. The configuration of the race itself depends mainly on the distance.

When you motor over the last yellow and green gorse-dotted slope nearing the race course, the green-shingled roof of the Curragh grandstand jumps out of the far hillside, perched there as it is, with a vast panorama of what Irish racing men hold dear.

For the Irish Derby, run at a mile and a half, horses traverse the horseshoe-shaped course starting nowhere near the stands, rather out by the old Main Dublin road, a good half-mile away. The conduct of the race itself is also different from American style, since riders reach to take a long hold of their mounts as soon as the field breaks from the gate, patiently settling for little better than a galloping pace in the early going.

As the finishing quarter mile at the Curragh is a stiff climb and a brutal task for a tired horse, jockeys are obliged to conserve whatever they can for the final furlong if they wish to have any chance.

Budweiser makes a big move in the mid 1980's when they take on the Guinness/Harp empire, buying sponsorship of the '87 Irish Derby. I've been making the Derby a part of my itinerary for several years, so here I am again at the Curragh, where they are handing out free Buds to a packed house of fans, many of whom come prepared with a pre-disposition toward excessive consumption.

It has to be a record heat wave at that first Budweiser Irish Derby, over ninety degrees, but Euro racing fans dress for the occasion and many wear tweeds and trilbys in spite of the temperatures.

At one point I try to get a bead on whether they would switch to Budweiser from their traditional ales and stouts, so I asked a couple of old-timers how they liked the American brew.

Says one, "Lovely, lovely."

Says his pal, "He'd drink anything, long as it's free."

There is no such thing as a boring day in Ireland, and this day is no exception after the IRA takes credit for a couple of bomb threats, timed perfectly to delay the start of the Derby, even though it is post time and the horses are a good half-mile from the stands, circling behind the gate.

We can see them in the distance as we're hustled from one of the rooms at the top of the stands -- local version of our luxury boxes -- down the stairs, up the stairs, down again, up again. Makes you respect the ladies in their stylish heels. This exercise in precaution serves to keep the Derby field waiting a good three-quarters of an hour before there is an all-clear. In the end, Sir Harry Lewis goes off the favorite and puts his American owner, Howard Kaskel, in the winner's circle.

If you take the back road from the track to the town of Kilcullen, you'll pass a small depression known as Donnelly's Hollow. Look carefully and you can see a granite monument with that designation inscribed upon it.

This is the spot where Dublin bare-knuckled fighter Dan Donnelly took on the British champ Tom Hall in September of 1814, defending Irish honor in a time of severe oppression.

Donnelly was known as a reluctant participant in the pugilistic arts, but once enlisted by a clever promoter, he beat three British champs and raised the spirits of Irishmen under the thumb of heartless colonialists.

His reputation as Ireland's greatest fighter might be considered just another bit of hyperbole were it not for the physical evidence on display at a local pub called the Hideout.

It's there that the ultimate homage to Dan's physicality could be seen for many years, displayed upon the wall. In a glass shadow box, similar to one in which some folks preserve family heirlooms, hung the mummified right arm of the mighty Mister Donnelly.

Not just any arm, this one is at least four feet long and would have enabled the champ to scratch his knees without bending over.

Leave it to the Irish when it comes to show-and-tell...

XXIV.

"THERE IS SOMETHING ABOUT THE OUTSIDE OF A HORSE THAT IS GOOD FOR THE INSIDE OF A MAN."

--WINSTON CHURCHILL

Arnold Kirkpatrick published the trade journal called the *Thoroughbred Record* and won an Eclipse Award for his writing about the game he loved. We were fast friends from the day we met and he became a mentor, introducing me to the movers and shakers in the horse game and waving me off the flim-flammers. I asked him about John Gaines and he said, "John Gaines is wiser than a tree full of owls," an assessment that was right on the money.

Gaines was one of those rare individuals sparingly referred to as a Renaissance man, versed in literature, art and science. He also possessed an essential understanding of the elements of genetics in relation to modern thoroughbred breeding.

His grandfather, who was in the feed business, developed the dog food known as Gaines-burgers and was a leader in the standardbred breeding world. John followed that pursuit until the early 1960's when he switched to thoroughbreds, naming his breeding operation on the Paris Pike outside Lexington Gainesway Farm.

Gaines perfected the art of stallion syndication, dividing his stud horses into shares among breeders with quality mares, and he stood some of the best: Lyphard, Blushing Groom, Vaguely Noble, Bold Bidder and Riverman, to name only a few.

Each stallion was domiciled in his own individual barn, designed by Gaines himself to include skylights, stained glass windows and a slate roof. The Gainesway organization was like a Swiss clock, integrating the newest technology with old time horsemanship, and the result was a parade of champions.

The achievement he is best known for, however, is the Breeders' Cup.

In 1982, using his broad reach to bring together major players in the breeding industry, Gaines formulated his idea to promote the sport of thoroughbred racing and garnered financial support, then launched what was proposed to be a championship day for thoroughbreds in November of 1984.

Most of the races would have a purse of $1 Million, the mile and a half Turf would offer $2 Million, and the Breeders' Cup Classsic would be worth $3 Million. By comparison, the purse for the Kentucky Derby that year was just over $700,000.

As envisioned by John Gaines, the Breeders' Cup was meant to create an infrastructure that would strengthen the breeding industry by rewarding breeders for excellence in producing top-class racehorses. In truth, it actually evolved into an "Owners' Cup," giving very little of the ten million in purses back to the producers of the product.

Nonetheless, the Breeders' Cup has become second only to the Kentucky Derby as the most identifiable thoroughbred racing event of the year for most sports fans and usually stamps the label "champion" on its divisional winners.

Hollywood Park in Los Angeles was picked as the site of the inaugural Breeders' Cup event in 1984, and my boss Bob Brennan grabbed the opportunity to promote his First Jersey Securities Company by putting up $1 Million to sponsor a race. The event was broadcast on NBC, and along with sponsorship came a commercial spot featuring Bob and his helicopter, urging viewers to "Come grow with us." Since it was the initial running of the Breeders' Cup and the million dollar purses were astronomical for the times, everyone with a good horse participated. As noted previously, horses follow the money.

I knew that Bob would love to have a horse in the race for a chance to get his money back, so I moved fast when my pal Woody Copeland called from Santa Anita to tip me that there was a horse for sale who could get the mile and a half trip on the grass. Woody's as savvy a horseman as you can find and he didn't call often, but when he did he was usually right on the money with his assessment of a horse.

The runner in question was a Euro-import named Raami and we bought half-interest along with the deal to run in our Due Process silks in the race. Darrell Vienna trained him and Raami was a big, good looking, rangy son of Be My Guest who liked to come from last, and he just about got the job done, finishing third by less than a length under Fernando Toro and bringing Bob back a hundred thousand of his purchase price.

From my years on the backstretch, I had direct connections with two of the horses heading to California at our farm in New Jersey. Budd Lepman was the leading trainer at Monmouth through most of the 1970's and a good friend. He rode most of my jocks during the years I was an agent and asked me if he could freshen up his good sprinter Eillo, as he wanted to give the colt a breather after Monmouth closed and before he shipped to California.

Eillo, a son of Mr. Prospector, got his name from a backwards spelling of Ollie, as in Ollie Cohen, his owner. Eillo was galloping and breezing on our five-eighths track in Colts Neck before shipping up to win a stake at Meadowlands as a prep for the Breeders' Cup Sprint. Budd's best exercise rider Bobby Velez arrived every morning to tack him up and go through his routine, and he was as fast as any horse I've ever seen going short.

Racing is an extremely competitive sport, but there's an unwritten code on the backstretch whereby everyone goes out of their way to help out each other if they can. When my pal Louie from New Orleans calls and asks if I could do the same for some guys bringing a horse named Wild Again to run in the Grade I Monmouth Handicap (now the Iselin) I was happy to oblige. Ray Beard, the Fair Grounds correspondent for *Daily Racing Form,* was close with Wild Again's trainer, Vincent Timphony, and knew Louie and I were pals. On a quiet August day in the middle of the week, a long black limo rolled into the farm and I took the owners for a tour.

Bill Allen, his wife Nina and his partner Terry Beale and Terry's wife Joyce walked through the stallion barn with me, and they couldn't resist touching the glossy lacquered knotty-pine walls and the shining brass name plates on the stall doors. What was not to like? The facilities rivaled anything they had seen in Kentucky, and I knew they had expected somewhat humbler accommodations than the 12x12 stalls in our training barn. When we finished the tour, Bill asked for a few minutes alone and he closed the door to my office.

Bill Allen was one of the coolest customers anyone ever met. He took subtlety to a new level. Bill was retired from his position as CEO of an international insurance company and horses were his lifetime passion. We later got to be great friends and spent a lot of time together on the golf course where we took advantage of my handicap and his charm to remove excess cash from the pockets of a lot of his rich pals who had more money than sense or skill.

Bill spoke quietly, in his most confidential tone, while leaning on my desk.

"This horse isn't eligible for the Breeder's Cup Classic, but I'm going to supplement him," he said, talking about Wild Again. "You should tell your boss to buy a piece from me."

It only costs $500 to nominate to the Breeders' Cup races when your horse is a foal, but if you don't do it then, you are required to put up the supplementary nomination. The supplement to enter the Classic the first year was $360,000 and the winners's share of the purse was 55 percent of $3 million. That's the same as making a bet of $360K on a 2.66 to 1 shot to net $900,000 after the trainer and jockey each get their 10 percent. It was not really a good bet since Wild Again figured to be up against Gate Dancer, Slew O' Gold, Track Barron and Mugatea, and it was more likely his price at post time would be at least 25 to 1.

The main thing you try to do when betting horses is to look for over-lays, which are horses whose odds are higher than they should be, like taking 10 to 1 on a horse you figure should be 2 to 1, not the other way around.

Factor in that Wild Again, although he had won the Oaklawn Handicap and the New Orleans Handicap, had done so both times as a longshot and had finished a well-beaten sixth at Arlington Park in his last start before coming to Jersey.

I smiled politely and told Bill I'd sure tell my boss and thanks a lot. Another crazy horse-guy. And of course, they were welcome to send the horse out for his breather after he ran at Monmouth and we'd be glad to look after him.

I kept a close eye on Wild Again at the Iselin, washy in the paddock, pressing the pace for the early part and then backing up to finish a tepid fourth among a bunch of decent horses, none of which had a chance to even make it to the gate for the Breeders' Cup Classic.

Enter Vincent Timphony, who trains *Wild Again* for Bill and was the New Orleans connection. He previously owned a restaurant, which might have been a checkered tablecloth pizza joint, and most likely was booking Bill's bets before getting hired as trainer.

Timphony calls after the Monmouth race and says he's taking a week off and asks if he can send *Wild Again* to us for his breather before running in the Meadowlands Cup. The horse shows up in a two-horse trailer, and all the groom does is walk him every day and paint his legs with DMSO.

Two weeks later *Wild Again* runs in the Meadowlands Cup against the same kind that just beat him. This time he wires the field, winning by six lengths at better than 9 to 1. I'm still scratching my head when Bill calls to thank me for taking such good care of his horse and by the way, don't forget what he said about the Breeders' Cup.

A week later *Wild Again* ships to California, and the next time I hear his name he's running in an allowance race at a mile on the grass at Bay Meadows in San Francisco. He gets dusted there, finishing third in what appeared another tepid performance. At this point it looks like he must have just liked the lights at Meadowlands.

I had a lot of things going on at the time, building out the new farms we had in Florida and Kentucky, so I pass on the trip to California to take care of business. On November 10 I'm on my way home from Lexington, changing planes in Washintgon, D.C., when I pop into an airport cocktail lounge and asked the barkeep to switch the TV to the Breeders' Cup.

He found the channel just in time for me to watch Pat Day squeeze *Wild Again* between Gate Dancer and Slew O' Gold and get the money at odds of 31 to 1. It was something more resembling a street fight than a horse race, and they'd have taken him down if he weren't a head shorter than the other two in the mugging. But they didn't, and there was my man Bill in the winner's circle, holding up the Classic trophy.

What I'd failed to realize was that Bill was discounting the supplementary fee as part of his cost of doing business and actually considered his horse an overlay. He was just looking for an opportunity to bet his lungs, as I later learned he'd done at Oaklawn and in New Orleans, where he filled the trophies with hundreds of thousands in cash.

I later asked Bill how he acquired Wild Again. He told me that he'd always been an admirer of the horse's sire, Icecapade, and when a trainer he knew was off to a yearling sale he told the guy to buy all the Icecapades, knowing that five of them might be bums, but one might be a good one.

Obviously he was right...

XXV.

"WHAT ENTHRALLS THESE CROWDS ARE MASTERS, MAN AND HORSE."

--EDWARD L. BOWEN FROM *MASTERS OF THE TURF*

For many years North American thoroughbred breeders produced an annual "crop" in excess of twenty-five thousand foals, the majority of them born in Kentucky, Florida and Louisiana, plus the ten thousand or so foaled in other countries. This makes it fairly easy to acquire those horses whose principal purpose is racing, at which point they arrive at a trainer's barn in one of several ways.

"Home-breds" are horses raced by their breeders, often not offered for sale to anyone else. Prominent racing families like the Phippses,

Vanderbilts and Whitneys have passed their broodmare bands of super-lative pedigrees from generation to generation and send the offspring directly to their private trainers, eschewing any notion of selling to anyone other than family. A prized possession of any breeder is a "Blue Hen" mare, the one which produces superior runners and passes that ability on to her daughters, thus providing the foundation for a family line for years to come.

Claude "Shug" McGaughey has proven his worth as one of the finest trainers ever, developing many divisional champions for the Phipps family, overcoming stables that have two or three times as many horses. His barn is stocked almost solely with such "home-breds" as those that he devel-oped into champions, like Hall of Famers Easy Goer and Personal Ensign. My long-time contention that Shug is the best trainer of Thoroughbreds in America was borne out in 2013, when he won the Kentucky Derby with a colt named Orb, another "home-bred" for the family partnership of Stewart Janney and Dinny Phipps.

While other great trainers like D. Wayne Lukas and Bob Baffert have won many more Kentucky Derbies, they have the advantage of running multiple horses which would obviously increase their chances. Shug, who deals exclusively with the progeny of the Phipps family broodmare band, doesn't have to guess which of his horses might be the best. He knows. He let the horse take him to Kentucky, passing plenty of other opportunities to take a shot, patiently waiting until he had the goods.

For the others, public auction is the source of thoroughbreds, sold ei-ther as foals, yearlings or two-year-olds in training. The principal venues in the U.S. for such sales are the Keeneland Sales Company in Lexington and the Fasig-Tipton Sales Company, which has its principal place of busi-ness in Lexington but also operates in Florida and Saratoga Springs, New York. There are a few other auction houses, like the Ocala Breeders in Florida and Barretts in California, but Keeneland and Fasig-Tipton sell the most and the best.

Europe has its own major sales, like the Tattersals venue at Newmarket, England, the Goffs in Ireland, and Deauville in France, while the Southern Hemisphere is served by the Magic Millions sale in Australia.

Kentucky, though, is where buyers flock to yearling auctions like gold miners did to the Black Hills of South Dakota, seeking that runner that will be the best of its crop. Although young, untested horses regularly sell for six figures and many have gone for over a million dollars, every year good racehorses are plucked from yearling and two-year-old sales at bargain prices. Logic dictates that in a sales ring that offers three or four thousand horses over a couple of weeks, some are sure to be overlooked.

The great Seattle Slew is most notable as an auction pick, bringing only $17,500 at the Fasig-Tipton sale in July of 1975 and going on to distinguish himself as the only undefeated Triple Crown winner and one of the most influential stallions of modern times. Slew's nine champions include Kentucky Derby winner Swale and Horse of the Year A.P. Indy.

Less notable was a Northern Dancer yearling sold for a record $10.2 million at Keeneland in 1983. Later named Snaafi Dancer, he never raced and proved useless as a stud.

The breeding game is not unlike racing in that it is comprised mainly of well-heeled competitors vying for that vicarious thrill one gets from owning a good horse. The stakes are high, and some are better at the game than others.

Legendary horse traders such as John E. Madden of Hamburg Place (referred to as the "Wizard of the Turf"), "Bull" Hancock of Claiborne Farm and Leslie Combs of Spendthrift Farm were among the visionaries who realized that keeping the best stallions in Kentucky would be the way to establish a permanent home-ground advantage as purveyors of horseflesh.

Racehorses are referred to as "bloodstock" and the principal element necessary to produce the best horse is pedigree, referred to in Thoroughbred terms as "blood." If you keep the best blood, you've invented the best mousetrap, and as the saying goes, the world will beat a path to your door.

Since a unique requirement for certification as a thoroughbred pre-cludes artificial insemination, the mating process necessitates that the mare and stallion actually have intercourse. There are two principal rea-sons for this, the first being that it limits the number of possible offspring, thus creating a control in supply and demand, and secondly that it creates a market for the stud service price of the best stallions. Otherwise it makes no sense at all.

During the '80's, stud fees soared in relation to yearling prices. Northern Dancer and his son Nijinsky sired the babies that brought the most when their fees reached $1 million for a "no-guarantee" breeding, wherein the purchaser paid his money with no assurance of a pregnancy. This insanity only lasted a few years, but nonetheless illustrates the type of behavior delineated in a book written in 1841 by Charles Mackay called *Extraordinary Popular Delusions and the Madness of Crowds*, citing similar irrational behavior among buyers and sellers in the Dutch tulip market of the early 1700's.

Sales companies go to great lengths to protect the integrity of their enterprise and drum out the cheaters, but it's the nature of the game to contain some degree of corruption when huge sums of cash money are in-volved. Since owners in general are compelled to rely on bloodstock agents to do their purchases, kickbacks and cash payoffs may have been occasion-ally responsible for increasing the price of some individual horses.

As it is for the most part an unregulated industry, thoroughbred pro-duction and sales have made it a great place for conniving, collusion and various degrees of legerdemain. This is not to say that the nature of the business is corrupt, but rather that individuals prone to illicit behavior have always found such unregulated situations as a wonderful opportunity to cheat and deceive.

"New money" is always easy to spot in the racing game. The big play-ers immediately attract the attention of industry media looking for a fresh story. When they are quoted and have their photos splashed all over trade journals like the *Blood-Horse,* the *Paulick Report* or the *Thoroughbred Daily News,* this places a target squarely on their backs.

Roger King, the billionaire owner of King World Productions, produced a plethora of lucrative television shows including *Oprah* and *Jeopardy.* He loved the horse game and delighted in going to auctions, sitting in the first row and waving his hand in the air to make sure everyone in the room knew he was bidding. Sellers loved him and Roger didn't seem to care that they ran him up, since he'd get his picture taken when he signed for the sales topper.

Had I been possessed of a larcenous nature, I could have made hundreds of thousands at the sales with Bob Brennan. He used the media better than anyone, and recognized the value of those photos for self-promotion, knowing that buying the sales-topper would not only get attention from racing trades, but would be picked up by *The Wall Street Journal, Forbes* and *Business Week* as advertising for his First Jersey Securities.

The first sale I attended with Bob was at the old arena on the backstretch of Hialeah where they sold yearlings in mid-February. There were probably as many people clocking us as there were timing the horses.

One of the best known sales agents of the day, who later became a Florida fixture and a principal in another sales company, took me aside and quite bluntly offered me ten percent on anything Bob bought from his consignment as if it were a foregone conclusion that I knew the standard operating procedure.

I told him "thanks anyway" and steered clear of his horses in the future. Over the years I probably had twenty offers like his to take six-figure kickbacks. It's a great way to figure out who the rats are. That was their family business, and his son handled the sales as well as being a trainer. I bought one from his son years later at a two-year-olds in training sale, and it soon after broke down. My vet was convinced the horse had been operated on before the sale, confirming once again that some rotten apples don't fall far from the tree.

The surest way to make money on a horse at auction is to have a specific buyer definitely willing to raise their hand for a higher price than the horse is likely to bring. Then it's just a matter of getting an "under-bidder," someone to provide that penultimate bid to get the intended buyer/victim to his maximum. Sales consignors typically charge the person who owns the horse five percent for preparing and bringing the animal to the auction ring. Many a horse worth twenty thousand has brought twenty times that at auction as the agents arrange the bidding strategy beforehand with the consignor and get paid off later as a "finder's fee."

The most easily facilitated ploy that requires the co-operation of the seller is a pre-sale sale. The seller agrees to take a set price, usually the amount that he thinks is his best possible outcome and then splits anything over that with the agent, who guarantees his client will be the ultimate winning bidder. It's a sure bet that the agent has a pigeon in tow who he can push to a significantly higher number, basically working both ends of the deal. For example, you're the seller and hope to get $200,000 for your yearling and the agent shakes on that price, knowing that he's convinced his buyer to give $400,000. You get $300,000 and he pockets $100,000 and another 5 percent of the total for a takedown of $120,000. The buyer's none the wiser.

Utilization of assumed names is another ploy that has always been a clever way for agents to work both ends of the sales game, since the breeder of the horse is a matter of public record, and since a lot more horses fail than succeed, the smoke and mirrors setup is rarely detected. Thousands of horses have been registered over the years with made-up names and sold at auction to unsuspecting buyers sitting next to the actual breeders.

My friend Philip Myerscough has probably sold off a billion dollars in horseflesh over the years as head auctioneer for Goffs and Tattersals and seen it all, including some spectacular blunders by inept would-be crooks. He told me the story of a yearling that topped one of the European sales after the two sellers tricked themselves while trying to run up the price on a determined bidder. It seems the pair had worked out that one would sit near the prospective purchaser (victim) and the other at some distance.

The second man would keep bidding until the first took off his glasses to signal when he felt the last bid was made. Unfortunately, when the announcer reeled off some facts about the horses' pedigree, the bid-pusher put his glasses back on and the second man threw in another (and winning) bid. The colluders were stuck with their yearling and two years later were still trying to peddle it, alas for a much lower price they'd have gotten had they not gotten greedy.

Jess Jackson of Kendall-Jackson Wineries fame came into the thoroughbred industry like the proverbial bull in a china shop, spending a couple of hundred million at the sales and buying 2007-2008 Horse of the Year Curlin and 2009 Horse of the Year Rachel Alexandra in private deals along the way. His Stonestreet operation quickly became one of the major forces to be reckoned with and he built a broodmare band second to none.

Once he became savvy to the horse business, Jackson realized he had been taken advantage of more than a few times. He tapped his background as a lawyer to inflict financial and emotional revenge on those who'd victimized him.

His personal effort to clean up the game went a long way towards raising awareness of the unethical practices. He did succeed in prevailing over a lot of agents and trainers who had chopped him up during his shopping spree, but unfortunately Jackson used a shotgun approach and sued everyone in sight, bullying a considerable number of innocent bystanders along the way. A good result of Jackson's campaign was to make the sales companies aware that unethical behavior could no longer be tolerated and over the past several years they have gone to great lengths to police their industry.

XXVI.

"THE RACE IS NOT ALWAYS TO THE SWIFT, NOR THE BATTLE TO THE STRONG, BUT THAT'S THE WAY TO BET."

--DAMON RUNYON

By the late '80's Due Process Stable is running at all the major tracks in the U.S. with nearly a hundred runners trained by Reynaldo Nobles, Phil Gleaves, Doc Fisher, Bobby Connors, Eddy Colletti, Frank Alexander, Gene Navarro, Billy Burch, Oscar Barrerra, Darrell Vienna and Carlos Garcia. There were another twenty-five in Ireland with four different trainers: Con Collins, Michael Grassik, Neil McGrath and Tommy Stack.

We participated in the yearling and breeding stock sales in Kentucky at Keeneland and Fasig Tipton and our stallion Deputy Minister was drawing the attention of the top breeders on both sides of the Atlantic. Besides Deputy Minister, we owned a bunch of stallion shares from a list that included Spend a Buck and Affirmed in Kentucky and Sadler's Wells, El Gran Senor and Be My Guest overseas.

Part of that game is simply "horse-trading" or trying to swap-up for more value than you start with. You can breed your own mares or sell the breeding at a "live-foal" fee, when the mare he covers has to produce a foal that stands and nurses, or you can do a "no-guarantee" deal which is just that -- put up the money and take your chance. The only thing for sure is that the stallion and the mare have had horse sex.

At the height of the craziness in the late '80's Due Process bought a breeding for Northern Dancer for a stud fee of $1 million. We bred champion It's in the Air to him, but she didn't get in foal right away so we had to keep trying.

Northern Dancer stood at Windfields Farm in Maryland and they were our partners in Deputy Minister, so they really didn't want us to come up empty and kept the breeding shed open until August so we could have one more chance. Most breeding operations open on February 1 and close the stud barn doors around the Fourth of July, due to the fact that thoroughbreds have an eleven-month gestation period and a universal birthdate of January 1.

That means if your foal is born in December, he's already one year old on January 1, a considerable disadvantage when he begins racing.

It's in the Air gets in foal from the August breeding and eleven months later, on the Fourth of July, we have a lovely filly born at the farm in Colts Neck. Brennan names her Air Dancer. Due to her late foaling date we don't even saddle break her until she's two, basically treating her like one of the following year's crop.

Dr. J.R.S. Fisher had a barn at the new Fair Hill training center where they jog the horses through the woods and train on a wood chip track.

Jimmy Edwards rode some winners for Doc when I was his agent and I had always admired his style. I figured we need to win with Air Dancer the first time she ran in order to enhance her value, since it's going to take a while for her to catch up to her age group. I also know Doc is another 'old schooler,' using long gallops and hacks through the woods as thorough preparation before his horses run, and he has the patience needed for a little filly up against the calendar.

Fisher had her tuned up to run at the end of the Garden State spring meet when Racing Secretary Eual Wyatt put up a maiden special weight at a mile on the grass for three-year-old New Jersey-bred fillies. Air Dancer won in a gallop, outclassing the field even though she was six months younger than anything else in the race.

Since Northern Dancer stood for stud duty in Maryland, Air Dancer was eligible for a $100,000 stakes race on the Maryland Million program. She won that, too, so the lesson learned was that patience and persistence can occasionally reward you when you have the right ammo.

Because we owned more than half the syndicate shares in Deputy Minister, I traded the breedings like baseball cards. The hot stallion and superstar of the future is obviously Alydar, who sired a fistful of graded stakes winners right out of the box and looked like the successor to Northern Dancer as king of the yearling sales. Alydar may have run second to Affirmed in the Classics, but in the breeding game he was going to win by a mile. Affirmed was becoming more than a decent stallion, but Alydar was the star of Calumet Farm.

I've been to most of the great stud farms, like Windfields, Gainesway and Spendthrift, but the drive from the entry on Versailles Road that winds to the farm office of Calumet Farm reeks of class and history.

William Wright founded the farm in 1924 as a nursery for his standard-bred horses, naming it after his Calumet Baking Powder Company, and his son converted the operation to thoroughbreds in 1932. Employing trainer Ben Jones and later his son Jimmy, Calumet bred and raced eight Kentucky Derby winners, including Triple Crown winners Whirlaway and Citation.

I was on a visit to our Due Process farm in Lexington when I made my first stop at Calumet one morning with my friend John Sikura of Hill'n Dale Farm. John was well acquainted with Calumet's general manager, J.T. Lundy, and thought it was a good idea that we should do some business.

Calumet Farm sits across the street from the Bluegrass Field Airport, and if you're flying in or out of Lexington you can't help but admire the rolling paddocks surrounded by white fences, the white barns trimmed in red. The farm stayed in family hands, passing finally to founder Wright's great-granddaughter Cindy, who possessed all the qualities of a potential old maid, save the massive fortune. She hooked up with a farm hand named J.T. Lundy when she was sixteen and married him a year later, probably her best chance to avoid being a spinster.

Never accepted into the family by his mother-in-law, Cindy's J.T. scratched out a living off a small farm he bought with his wife's money for twenty years until matriarch Lucille Wright Markey passed away.

Not exactly blessed with Hollywood good looks, J.T. was described by writer Skip Hollandsworth as having "a head the size of a gasoline can and a nose that looked like it had been busted and reset by a plumber."

But as the only one in the family with any knowledge of horses, Lundy was a natural for the position of president and general manager of a $100 million-plus Calumet operation. Sure.

When we entered the front office, J.T. was sitting on the bottom step of a spiral staircase with one shoe off, clipping his toenails. I'm just as glad he was distracted and we don't have to shake hands. During the rest of the visit J.T. picked, poked and prodded at various parts of his overweight anatomy, mining his ears for wax with a ballpoint pen and displaying the attention span of a second grader.

I'm no different from anyone who loves a good conspiracy theory, but some of those perpetuated in horseracing lore need to be taken with a grain of salt. Most of the time it's more important to the story that there are villains on a grassy knoll than if there's even a grassy knoll at all.

We bullshitted around for a bit, talking yearlings and complementing each other on successes, and when we got up to leave, J.T. led the way to the door. That was when John and I realized J.T. still had the blue plastic cap of a Bic pen sticking out of his ear. We managed to contain ourselves until we reach the car.

A week or so later I got a call from J.T., wanting to make a trade for some Deputy Minister breedings in exchange for an Alydar. We had plenty of good mares and I'd already contracted with him for two live-foal breedings, so I could afford to bargain. Alydar was standing for $150,000; Deputy Minister for $50,000, but he was sold out, what is referred to as "book full." J.T. couldn't get a Deputy Minister breeding anywhere else because we were part of a syndicate which limits the amount of mares the stallion can breed, while Calumet's intent was to breed Alydar to as many mares as he could cover. Calumet used him like an ATM and sold those "lifetime breeding rights" to him in order not to be restricted by the rules of a syndication agreement.

Effectively, what they were doing was selling Alydar but maintaining ownership, basically making him a high-priced hooker. Sell it, still own it, sell it, still own it.

Lundy gave me one for two, which was about a fifty grand profit up front for us, so I agreed with only one stipulation: Both stallions had to be able to perform on February 15, 1991, the day the breeding shed opened. Done deal, and we faxed the contract back and forth for signatures.

Calumet's 762 acres produced champions of all categories for decades, but it didn't come into the general public's awareness until the saga of Alydar, their best horse that didn't win a championship. Alydar ran a total of twenty-six times, winning fourteen races and earning nearly a million dollars, but he was most notable for finishing second in the 1978 Kentucky Derby, Preakness and Belmont Stakes to Affirmed, as of 2014 the last horse to win the Triple Crown.

A son of the great sire of sires Raise A Native, Alydar might not have been able to outrun Affirmed, but he had a superior pedigree, and when he went to the breeding shed his offspring quickly proved out the value of a stud fee that as high as $200,000 as he begat champions Easy Goer, Derby winner Alysheba and others, making him America's leading sire.

In the middle of the night of November 13 of 1990, Alydar shattered his right hind leg in his stall and failed to recover from surgery. First thing the next morning I got the news through the grapevine and immediately reviewed the contract I had with Calumet, mainly to rest easy that the deal is off and I wasn't liable for the Deputy Minister breedings.

Three days later I got a call from J.T., in a panic, explaining how he still needed those Deputy Minister breedings since he'd swapped them further on to some one else in another deal. I tell him to forget it, that we should just call it off, but apparently he made his other deal with some people who were not that easy to disappoint. Maybe guys who would leave a fish wrapped in newspaper on your doorstep as a message.

I knew he couldn't give me cash, and I certainly did not want to be involved as a third party in his barter deal, so I made a proposal. My friend Bill Allen was standing Wild Again at Calumet, so I told Lundy we would accept a lifetime breeding right to Allen's stallion if J.T. threw in a couple of extra breedings to shim up the deal. It was okay with him, and we were all square.

Sketchy circumstances surrounding Alydar's death and the fact that he was insured for $50 Million when the farm was teetering close to bankruptcy led to further investigations, perpetuating public opinion that foul play had been involved.

Ann Hagedorn Auerbach's *Wild Ride* and Skip Hollandsworth's *The Killing of Alydar* dissect both the facts and the heresay evidence and seemingly accept the opinion of an MIT professor that the horse was assassinated.

Unfortunately, they choose to discount the testimony of one of the world's most respected equine surgeons, Dr. Larry Bramlage, who was on the scene, operating on and eventually euthanizing Alydar. Said Dr. Bramlage, "There was a question as to whether it was possible someone could have purposely created the fracture in Alydar's limb. I didn't believe it then, nor do I today believe that's the cause. I think it was a stall accident."

My personal opinion is that J.T. himself got led to slaughter as a hapless dupe.

Slick guys from New York regularly paraded Lundy like a Shetland pony in a petting zoo. He flew all over the world in the Calumet jet he had stocked with macaroni and cheese and vintage champagne, selling breeding rights and making deals for cash at discounted prices while piling up hefty commissions.

Word was, J.T.'s favorite in-flight entertainment was a video of the Cheech and Chong movie, *Up In Smoke*. At least he got that right.

It is difficult to imagine why anyone owning a goose laying golden eggs would want to kill it, but that's the version everyone chose to believe.

There followed over the next eight months a series of toppling dominoes. Lloyd's of London refused to pay the policy on Alydar, forcing Calumet to default on a $15 million loan and plunging the farm into bankruptcy.

Frank Cihak, the vice chairman of the bank in Texas from which J.T. had been borrowing millions, was found to be involved in multiple shadow companies and kickback schemes and wound up getting 34 years in prison. Little surprise that he threw J.T. under the bus in the process.

J.T. got four years for bribing Cihak, which seems strange since the guy's past perfomance charts indicated that he didn't seem to need much convincing to engage in larceny.

I don't think anyone will ever know for sure what happened to Alydar, but if J.T. Lundy did mastermind the whole scheme, I'm pretty sure the moon over Kentucky is made out of cream cheese.

XXVII.

HORSE RACING, DEF. "THE SPORT OF KINGS."

--AS LISTED IN THE MERRIAM-WEBSTER UNABRIDGED DICTIONARY

A common trait of racing people is their tenacity, as evidenced by the countless stories of those who persevered in their pursuit of success in the face of nearly certain defeat. Seattle Slew may be the consummate example of how such tenacity sometimes pays off, as the colt plucked from a yearling sale for a bargain price, whose owners kept the faith and went on to eventually buy a bank with the profits he made as a racehorse and stallion.

But despite all the anecdotal evidence presented to make us feel that it's a sport "of the people," the truth is that horse racing truly is the "sport of kings," with the modern-day billionaires and oil rich sheikh playing the part of the regal and royal controlling the breeding industry and competing for the loftiest prizes.

Longchamps Racecourse in France was a product of the reign of Louis Bonaparte, the first president of the French Republic and the ruler of the Second French Empire.

Belmont Park is named for one of America's greatest success stories, a self-made financeer whose passion for racing was passed on through a family whose wealth could only be referred to as a "king's gold." The Belmonts and later the Carnagies, Phippses and Whitneys were all about wealth and power, so much so that even the U.S. Government came to them to borrow money when it needed to finance enterprises like the Spanish-American War.

Earlier I related stories of other individuals whose passion for racing motivated them to build some of the track facilities which stand today as testament to that passion. Among the character traits that got those individuals to positions of wealth was that same tenacity and fierce sense of competition, which occasionally translated to stubbornness and an unwillingness to negotiate. Nowhere has this been less productive than in the world of thoroughbred racing.

Until quite recently, those "powers that be" which run the major racing jurisdictions such as NYRA, Churchill Downs and Stronach/Magna were reluctant to enter into any sort of cooperative relationship, based on legal opinion of their counsel that to do so would constitute an infraction of Restraint of Trade caveats.

Thus, decades would pass with parallel business enterprises creating their annual schedules more or less in the dark and the owners of those tracks content to compete rather than co-operate even when the sport itself began to lose popularity. It was hardly the time to pull against one another, yet they all evidenced the same hubris rather than cede any ground.

Frank Stronach went on a track-buying spree in the 1990's and acquired fourteen racing facilities in North America, including three harness tracks and a dog racing park, with a public company, Magna Entertainment Corporation, created specifically for that purpose.

An Austrian by birth who emigrated to Canada and built an auto-parts empire from a tool and die shop in his garage, Frank bought his first good horse, Glorious Song, at the Windfields dispersal in the early '80's, sold half and eventually all of her to Nelson Bunker Hunt for a bunch of money. By that time Stronach was pretty much "bitten" by the game.

A tenacious businessman, Frank formed strong opinions about how he thought racing could be improved, and as his personal stables grew and he became a part of the Canadian racing scene at Woodbine, many in the establishment became concerned.

Frank was not shy about expressing himself and offended the sensibilities of the members of the Canadian Turf Club, so much so that he eventually did his version of "you can't fire me, I quit," setting out to turn the game around on his own. He resigned from the Ontario Jockey Club on the basis that a "club" concept was exclusionary and no good for the future of the sport.

Stronach's main asset, the Magna International auto parts company, was essentially an auto-building company without the brand name. They produced many of the parts for, and actually assembled from the ground up, many of the models for such brands as BMW, Mercedes, Chrysler and Cadillac.

I would run into Frank at the Keenleland sales in Kentucky several times a year, and we'd discuss breeding. He was a fan of our horse Deputy Minister, and we also shared an appreciation of Wild Again as a great outcross for the Northern Dancer line that was filling the stallion rosters. Frank knew my diverse background in racing, so when Due Process went out of business he contacted me right away and asked me to do some consulting work. Acquiring fourteen racetracks over a two-year period had been the easy part, but operating them was a daunting task for a public company whose top executives had little or no experience in horseracing and assumed their success in the auto industry would translate well.

I set out to visit his holdings, most of which I was already familiar with, including Pimlico, Laurel, Gulfstream and Santa Anita. The obvious conclusion I arrived at was that Magna had the absolute tops in track management, with Lou Raffetto in Maryland at Laurel and Pimlico, Corey Johnsen in the West at Lone Star, Santa Anita, Bay Meadows and Golden Gates, and Jim Gagliano covering the Northern and Northwestern tracks of Thistledowns, Portland Meadows plus Multnomah Dog Track in Portland. Since Gagliano went on to become president of The Jockey Club, Johnsen owns and operates the hugely successful Kentucky Downs, and Raffetto became CEO of the National Steeplechase and Hunt organization and President of the Asian racing conglomorate YUP!, I would maintain that my original assessment was correct.

Frank must have sensed that the lack of insight into such an esoteric sport as horseracing might be a handicap to his corporate execs, so the following year, 2002, he invited me to join him at Santa Anita to see his horse Milwaukee Brew run in the Big 'Cap. The good son of Wild Again won the race (as he would do again in 2003), and Frank offered me the position of Chief Operating Officer, feeling that he needed a horseman at the corporate level.

As the COO job includes an insight into the company's financial dealings and responsibility for income statements and balance sheets, I was uncomfortable with being in that role in a public company and declined. I didn't know Frank well enough to realize that he was not particularly disposed to hearing "no" as an answer.

Frank came right back and proposed that I take over as Vice President of Operations for all the North American tracks. I agreed to do so provided he would hire a capable executive to work with me as COO.

Roman Dorogniac had previously been involved with Magna International and was on the Board of Directors for a number of public companies, and his C.P.A. background made him a perfect fit. Roman and I soon teamed up to assess the situation and quickly realized we were in the middle of a dysfunctional family of the first degree. The chance our stock options would ever be worth anything was somewhere in the range of slim and none.

The turnover rate among MEC executives couldn't have been higher unless they installed a revolving door at the Magna corporate headquarters in Aurora, Ontario.

The CEO at the time of my hire was about the third in two years. His background as owner of a successful auto dealership explained his sales ability but failed to give him any insight into horse racing. Nonetheless, he was determined to lead the team despite having no idea where he was going.

In my first week there, I was subjected to multiple meetings in which marketing executives pitched their concepts to re-invigorate the sport via pie charts, but none were unable to locate the quarter-pole on a diagram of one of the company's racetracks.

I left the meeting shaking my head when one sharp guy suggested that the remedy to the problem of short fields was to combine races and mix the categories of horses. Yeah, that's the ticket! Maidens and stakes horses! Claimers and allowance conditions! Yeah, that's the ticket!

Another guy thought maiden was the term for a female horse. Oh boy...

There's a great scene in the late '70's film *Being There* when Peter Sellers' character tells the President of the United States, that in order to grow a crop, you need to "tend your garden."

When the inevitable discussion of "how do we get more people to come to the track" comes up, I hear a lot of recurring phrases which must have been taught in college Marketing and Management 101 courses, like "core-customer" and "gaming dollars" and "loyalty programs." I haven't heard anyone suggest that we go back to basics and figure out where the current "customers" came from, since there's a good chance that's probably the place to start.

As for myself, I began going to the races with my dad, well before the age I was supposed to be allowed in the track. I guess if he'd taken me to a ballpark with the same regularity, I might have ended up working there, but he liked the horses and the mental challenge of handicapping.

This taught me to appreciate four principles: quality time with a parent, the beauty of racehorses, it's usually okay to lie about your age, and the joy of gambling.

In fact, in recently conducting an informal poll, I've discovered that race-goers of my generation, as well as several to follow, all have something in common. We first came to the track with a parent or relative intent on spending the day outdoors, doing something out of the ordinary and, by the way, gambling. And we found the experience enjoyable. So enjoyable, in fact, that we continued to return to the "scene of the crime" in an effort to recapture the feeling of that first encounter.

Track marketing has occasionally sensed this de facto genesis, but never entirely zeroed in on it. They've tried mini-arcades, playgrounds and the "final furlong" game where the player rides a mechanical horse in a video race, but all those things have had the look and feel of an afterthought, shoved in a little-used corner of the facility.

Think about the ballpark or the stadium in comparison to the track. It's a place where they sell tickets to adults and market the product to kids. As soon as you walk in, the concessions offer hats, jerseys, banners, trinkets and every manner of items related to the game, be it baseball, football, basketball or hockey. When's the last time you saw a fan at the track wearing basic black and a devil's red cap while he roots for a Phipps horse?

Every restaurant offering anything short of "fine dining" will have a kid's menu with suitable fare and appropriate pricing for young ones who can't finish half a deli-style sandwich or a foot-long hot dog. Plenty of us resent having to spend the price of an exacta box on food that's going to get tossed before it's close to being finished.

Other sports involve kids between quarters or periods with some interactive game or event, usually with their life-size mascot posing with them for "photo-ops."

I've seen the bounce-ball races at Del Mar, and the Sumo wrestler suits at Lone Star, both popular and successful, but those are isolated incidents.

Del Mar also has a clubhouse where parents drop off the kids for part of the day and they are indoctrinated to the sport by playing racing related games. Seems like anything they try at Del Mar works, which may be attributable to the sea air.

I'm not suggesting that tracks should market gambling to kids. I just think tracks as they are now are uncomfortable and basically boring places for children.

The ones who love animals prefer the zoo where none of them get whipped. But that's an entirely different issue that needs addressing.

There is a good chance that those kids, when they are over 18 or 21 or whatever the legal gambling age happens to be where they live, will make a bet. If they are used to having a pleasurable experience at the track, that's where they will go. Otherwise, they'll head for a casino where the nightlife includes bright lights and beautiful people. And gambling.

To the track administrators that prefer to keep operating in the same ineffectual way they've done it for the past twenty years, Chauncey Gardner might say this: Do not be surprised when there are no new customers. It's because you forgot to water the garden.

Roman and I refused to sign on to a job-perpetuating contrivance by one of the execs known as the "Continuous Improvement Team," cleverly sold to Frank as systematic analysis of existing practices and engineered by the same type of clueless characters, and we soon joined the long list of Magna alumni. Threatened by anyone who actually knew the game and most concerned with keeping their own jobs at the expense of the company's future, those close to the Chairman continued to dismiss the most competent operators and promote those less competent but willingly complicit until the company eventually fell apart in 2009, filing for bankruptcy.

Stronach re-organized another entity with family funding and purchased the best tracks (Gulfstream, Santa Anita, Pimlico and Laurel) from the bankruptcy, and continues to work at implementing his ideas to improve the sport. He deserves a lot of credit for being one of the few individuals willing to improve facilities and promote racing in an era when it would be easier to take the money from interactive betting and let the chips fall where they may. I think Frank has always been concerned that his legacy be that of a man who was first concerned about the horse.

Other than an uncharacteristically naïve trust in incompetent management, the net result seemed to have been positive as his new company began to hire track operaters from the ranks of horsemen rather than smooth-talking auto execs.

The Adena Springs operations of the Stronach empire are comprised of racing, breeding and training centers in Kentucky, Florida and Canada. Run by lifetime horsemen like Jack Brothers, Dan Hall and Mark Roberts, this organization has had an entirely different life than the track owning entities, producing champions like Perfect Sting, Ghostzapper and Ginger Punch and garnering Frank a dozen Eclipse Awards, eighteen Sovereign Awards, eight leading breeder titles and four titles for leading owner in North America.

XXVIII.

"There's no business like show business..."

--Irving Berlin

Although I didn't attend the first Breeders' Cup at Hollywood Park, the trips I made to buy our Due Process runner for that inaugural Breeders' Cup Turf eventually proved to be the key to another racetrack experience, one unparalleled by all the rest.

My eyes had opened to the California racing scene, and soon we had a dozen Due Process runners in training on the West Coast, some with Darrell Vienna and some with Charlie Whittingham. Reynaldo even shipped to Los Angeles for one winter meet.

Racing in any jurisdiction needs a circuit for horses to travel, moving like the circus from town to town in order that the entertainment value remains fresh for the fans.

Isolated from the rest of the racing world, California has always operated like an island, its circuit restricted to the top tier of Santa Anita, Hollywood Park and Del Mar in the south, and Bay Meadows and Golden Gate Fields in the north. When Bay Meadows was sold to developers and then closed its doors in 2008, California racing began to fly on one wing.

Given the high cost of maintaining a horse in training (nearly $50,000 a year) most owners will opt for a circuit that gives them the best opportunity to get a return on investment. I've referred to this before as "horses following the money."

Northeast racing offers the most opportunities with tracks like Aqueduct, Belmont, Monmouth, Parx, and the Delaware/Pennsylvania/West Virginia "slot tracks" as well as Laurel and Pimlico in Maryland within several hundred miles. If they can't get a race to fill at their home track, horsemen can ship their horses a few hours to another venue and even Kentucky is a only half-day van ride away. Not so in Southern California, where the only options are Golden Gate Fields or the lesser tracks in Arizona or New Mexico. Furthermore, shipping out is frowned upon by track management since there are already too few horses to fill the races.

Of course, the good news is that when you do get in a race, there's only four or five to beat.

The bad news? At least one of them is trained by Bob Baffert.

Darrell Vienna, who trained our first Breeders' Cup runner, also trained for a number of other interesting individuals. He had horses for an heiress, a porn king and an economist. He also trained for a screenwriter named David Milch.

David had a long association with the races, growing up in Buffalo, New York, and spending every August when he was a kid attending the races at Saratoga with his father. He owned a bunch of good horses over the years including Breeders' Cup Juvenile winner Gilded Time with Darrell Vienna and Breeders' Cup Mile winner Val Royal, trained by Julio Canani.

On some of my visits to Hollywood and Santa Anita I bore witness to the Milch betting dynamo. David came to L.A. from Yale in the '80's to write for the seminal cop show *Hill Street Blues* and went on to develop the award-winning *NYPD Blue* before hooking up with HBO and creating *Deadwood* and *John From Cincinnatti*.

David bets every race at the track he's attending and all of those on the TV simulcast, and he bets with both hands, like his money came from the bank on a Monopoly board. When he wins, nobody wins more. When he loses, well, it's not quite as much fun, but there was never a non-racetracker I've ever met who was more steeped in what the racetrack life is all about.

Milch and I later bought a Monarchos yearling together at Keeneland and shared the pain when the $100,000 colt proved to be slower than Vienna's stable pony.

We spoke several times about the possibility of doing a show based on the track and I told him that when he was ready to give me a call, "I'm your man."

I didn't realize that he wasn't going to call for ... twenty-five years.

Late in November of 2008 I get a call from Darrell Vienna, telling me David was starting up the racetrack story and would I be interested in speaking with him about it. David and I have a brief phone conversation and he tells me to come out to Santa Monica to his office for a meeting after the New Year, and to bring some stories I had written. He sends me the early notes and framework of what would eventually become the pilot for an HBO series, while I resurrect my collection of stories and reminiscences and began assembling what I imagined could be scenes in a script.

I fly out for a meeting in February, which turns out to be about a half-hour of conversation in the office, followed by a lengthy lunch and a trip to Santa Anita where I was once again witness to the Milch betting dynamo. After twenty-five years and little had changed, other than the selection of bets from which he had to choose, now including Pick 3's, Pick 4's and superfectas.

Watching David gamble again that day was like watching Bobby Fischer play chess on six boards at once, a feat impossible for most, but within the capacity of one who possesses a mind like a Google search engine.

Of course, the "you can beat a race, but you can't beat the races" adage applies, even to those better equipped than the rest of us, and over the next several days I watch him win, lose, win and lose like a mere mortal. At one point David tells me the writing job is mine should I wish to take a shot. I tell him that I'm going back to Florida to get my dog Oscar and some clothes and I'll be right back.

Upon my return to L.A., I was filled with the enthusiasm of a kid on his first day at summer camp, ready to grab a bat and step to the plate. Not so fast, though, as I settled in to the daily routine of the writers' room. David worked while lying on the floor, preferring to create scenes and dialogue in a free form that suited both his attitude and his bad back. I tried it for a few weeks, propping a pillow between my aching lumbar and the couch, only to quit when the posture elicited other aches and pains.

The pilot, it seems, had a basic structure established through several years of broad strokes summoned by David from his own imaginings as well as scenes he had worked through with Bill Barich, the author of the quintessential horse racing book, *Laughing in the Hills*.

Bill was no racetracker, but he was a truly gifted wordsmith, while David had enlisted me, as it turned out, to assist in fine-tuning the sounds of the track in the work, rather than reset the bedrock already in place.

For the next six months I followed the maestro from opening bell to closing curtain, many a day filled with that angst so familiar to all writers facing the blank page. A stream of actors flowed through the office daily, gladly taking the pages David fed them, and delighted to imagine themselves as the characters in the show, now referred to simply as *LUCK*.

Bill Barich returned from Ireland and *Daily Racing Form* columnist Jay Hovdey came on board. The three of us would do our best to carve out the scenes David assigned and serve them up for him to turn into art.

Later on, the three of us would be treated to working with other master screenwriters like Eric Roth, who won a Best Screenplay Oscar for *Forest Gump,* and Walon Green, fresh from the successful *Law and Order* TV franchise and best known for writing the classic Sam Pekinpah Western, *The Wild Bunch.*

It was assumed David would pick the actors the same way he did with his previous HBO masterpiece *Deadwood,* casting as he imagined them on the page and coaching them to become the pieces of this intricate puzzle, while at the same time working side-by-side with the directors to put the contents of his dream –- our dream -- on screen.

For *LUCK* he hoped to get Jack Nicholson... but no, it would be Dustin Hoffman in the key role of the Sidney Korshak-like mob fixer. Sam Shepard was at the top of his list to play the old school horse trainer at the center of the story, but no again. Nick Nolte would fill those boots.

Julio Canani, the colorful Peruvian who trained many of Milch's runners, provided the inspiration for Turo Escalante, the irascible character played so well by the talented John Ortiz. Trainer Darrell Vienna, who earned a law degree in his forties, was the model for the trainer/lawyer who counseled the Nolte character, who in turn was based on Hall of Fame trainer Jack Van Berg.

On the way to lunch one day, David exulted, "We've got Michael Mann," as if that were a very good thing. Mann was known for directing such muscular dramas as *"Heat"* and *"The Insider,"* and made his bones in TV with the iconic *"Miami Vice."* I joined in the euphoria, subscribing to the logic that the more high-priced talent that HBO was willing to put on the payroll, the better the chance of *LUCK* coming to fruition.

We still spent plenty of time at Santa Anita and Hollywood Park, continuing to do what David referred to as "research." Later, during publicity interviews for the show, Milch would say, "If I make twenty-five million off this show, I might break even on a lifetime of research."

By August he finally found enough satisfaction with the story to make the final push with the HBO executives who had hovered patiently since first authorizing the enterprise. As one learns in Hollywood, the true test of the "green light" of any project is when you first read the network's press release in *Variety* and the *Hollywood Reporter*.

Our final draft of the pilot went to HBO on August 7, 2009, and the wheels didn't actually start to turn until January of the following year, but when they started, things really got rolling. We began in April, filming the pilot that would eventually turn out to be the first episode, and by the time we "wrapped" in June word was that the budget had swelled to over $22 million. Not for the first season, just for the pilot, while individual episodes would be budgeted somewhere north of $8 million. The pilot was aired as a premiere in December of 2011 and the series began at the end of January, 2012, nearly *three years* after I began working with David.

Theories abound regarding what actually caused the demise of *LUCK*, most of them erroneously tied to PETA and the publicity campaign that sprung to life when a horse died in March of 2012 as we were shooting what would have been the second episode of the second season.

Just about anyone who has spent time in Hollywood can tell you the real reason the show was cancelled was because it wasn't the immediate financial success anticipated by HBO execs. Networks thrive on publicity, but in this case they seemed to cave in immediately to unconfirmed reports and sensational headlines on trash-talking tabloid-type TV shows.

The Paul Harvey version -- the "rest of the story" -- is always at least a dozen degrees off what the public gets fed, and this case was no different. Executives within networks are consistently in a struggle to maintain their position while chipping away at those above them in the food chain. HBO execs had divided opinion on the future profitability of *LUCK,* and those who had the most strength prevailed.

At some point it becomes more important to network execs that a predecessor's show disappear than have it become a successful legacy.

Michael Mann later did his own investigation and found that there was plenty of evidence to prove that PETA and the TV tabloid show *TMZ* had information "leaked" to them by a disgruntled former *LUCK* crewmember and their cohort on the set, two individuals bitter over not being moved up and willing to take a quick payoff for betraying their on-set family.

The HBO execs inclined to cancel on financial grounds suddenly had a justification, based on what could be considered ethical grounds, and pulled the trigger faster than Wyatt Earp at the O.K. Corral.

In all, three horses in the *LUCK* stable of equine actors did die over a three-year period, but only one as a result of a fractured leg sustained while filming a scene.

At the conclusion of the first several months of filming, we were shooting the final racing scene and I watched with a group at Santa Anita's Clockers' Corner, near the head of the stretch, aware that the pilot would be done as soon as Michael Mann said "Cut!" Instead, we shared the shock as a five-year-old gelding named Outlaw Yodler fell while galloping out on the backstretch after the cameras had stopped rolling. I hopped in a golf cart and rushed to the scene and found our two attending vets already there, as well as the film crew. The horse's rider, David Neusch, had ridden for me many years before on Due Process horses and was once the leading apprentice in the country. I asked him what had happened, and he said that the horse just took a bad step and fell, and he was fortunate to get off unscathed.

The first impression was that the horse had suffered a heart attack. I'd seen a couple do that over the years and it looked the case, but upon further inspection, when the vets tried to turn him over, it was obvious that the gelding had fractured his shoulder, not a common injury, but always a fatal one since it is impossible to repair. Suddenly the vibe changed from upbeat to downright negative.

To attribute that horse's death to neglect or abuse is specious at best, but that was what happened, led by the group ironically named People for the Ethical Treatment of Animals.

A second horse, Marc's Shadow, did suffer a fatal accident more than a year later when he fractured his radius, a highly unusual break of an upper leg bone. Due to their size and weight, and stress on joints during exercise, horses are susceptible to fractures and chips in their knees and ankles, but that was the only one of that type that I recall seeing in over forty years.

PETA conveniently neglected to mention that the death of the third horse, a mare named Real Awesome Jet, occurred after it had just passed its morning health inspection by two veterinarian. She was walking back to her barn under the handling of a veteran horseman when she spooked and reared, losing her footing on the dirt path, and she fell, with her poll taking the brunt of the impact. Her skull was fractured and she died almost instantly.

The poll is similar to the soft spot on top of a baby's head, a vulnerabliltly with which all horses live. The accident could have happened to any horse on the grounds, and such an incident –- although not always resulting in a fatal injury -- and is not uncommon in the equestrian world by any means.

A total of over 5,000 runs by the individual horses were staged in simulated races for *LUCK*, each one limited to three furlongs and no more than twice by any one horse in any one day. If pari-mutuel races could come to anything close to that rate of care, they would be improving their current score of injuries by about 400 percent.

I was present every day we shot at Santa Anita and never saw horses better treated. They had straw up to their knees and hayracks stuffed with the best alfalfa and were pampered like equine celebrites. After all, they were in the movies!

The rumors of animal mistreatment spread as part of the PETA publicity machine did not bear scrutiny. Interestingly, when a PETA tax return surfaced on the internet, it was revealed how 90 plus percent of the money they solicited from contributors went toward "administrative" costs, specifically executive salaries, promotion and fundraising events. In addition, rather than doing anything to improve the lives of animals, part of their funding is actually used for massive euthanasia programs, killing thousands of the dogs and cats they would have you believe they're saving. The majority of animals that come under their control are euthanized fairly quickly rather than rehabilitated or put up for adoption. In other words, PETA turns out to be a business venture with a great name, not an altruistic endeavor.

In truth, *LUCK* died for about half a dozen reasons. Milch and Mann tolerated each other, but Michael's demands for plot changes and constant rewrites made their relationship a devil's deal at best.

David has been referred to by more than one critic as "the American Shakespeare." His poetic dialogue in *Hill Street Blues, NYPD Blue, Deadwood* and *John From Cincinatti* created a legion of dedicated followers over the years, and HBO kept him on retainer to produce more of the same.

Mann was master of light, color and movement on screen, but he eschewed acquiring any understanding of the sport of racing, preferring to dazzle the viewer with spectacular shots designed to cause an adrenaline rush. When alerted to technical discrepancies, his standard reply was, "Ninety-nine percent of people watching won't know what it means anyway."

Milch, on the other hand, had hopes of writing his "love letter" to the sport that had enraptured him since childhood. As creator and director, they were about as good a match as Nancy Kerrigan and Tonya Harding.

Mann also had a reputation that he came by honestly for not only exceeding every budget he ever laid eyes on, but exceeding it spectacularly. His requirements for set originality were legend, like moving entire buildings in *Public Enemy,* and *LUCK* was no exception, requiring multiple scenes to be filmed on a yacht at $85,000 a day, even though they were interior shots and could have been staged on a re-usable set built for about $20,000.

Timing had its part in the demise of *LUCK,* as HBO was so anxious to sign Dustin Hoffman that they agreed to delay shooting the second season until he returned from a commitment in London, where he directed

Maggie Smith, Michael Gambon, Billy Connolly, Tom Courtenay and Pauline Collins in the lovely film *Quartet.*

Unfortunately, the delay from September to January waiting for Dustin required putting the rest of the cast and crew on "hold," which means they were paid not to take other work. As a result, the second season was over budget before the first scene was filmed.

In order that the lofty public image of HBO could be maintained, execs chose to appear as if they were taking the higher ground out of concern for animals. It's also likely they overreacted out of fear of looking bad before parent company Time Warner, whose corporate image with shareholders might affect the stock price.

We easily could have continued the stories without shooting another racing scene, thereby removing any chance another horse would die. But closer to the truth of the cancellation was the aversion of some of their executives to risking more dollars in what was proving to be a show that was very costly and not that popular, according to their polls. Combined with some of the high-level corporate backstabbing that goes on daily in the world of entertainment, that was enough to finish the show.

Once again, when someone tells you "it's not about the money," it's usually about the money.

XXIX.

"THOSE WHO CANNOT REMEMBER THE PAST ARE CONDEMNED TO REPEAT IT..."

--GEORGE SANTAYANA FROM *THE LIFE OF REASON*

In his 1994 Introduction to Ed Bowen's concise and wonderfully written *Thoroughbred Racing in America*, Steven Crist hit the nail on the head.

"As the nineties began, American Thoroughbred racing was facing numerous crises," Crist wrote. "Racehorse owners could not afford to run for the small purses... Tracks were presenting far too many racing dates in competition with one another... A lack or uniform rules from state to state made regulation an elusive goal. Amid these grave issues, those who cared deeply... were calling for the creation of a new body, or perhaps a national czar, to supervise the teetering sport."

Even more prescient, Crist continued: "Whoever writes the introduction... in 2004, celebrating its first two centuries, is welcome to recycle the preceeding paragraph. Every word of it applies as much to the 1890's as it does to the 1990's, and it is 3 to 5 on the morning line that it will be just as valid in the good old 2090's as well."

Crist effectively predicted the battle lines drawn in 2012 between those convinced that a "zero tolerance" attitude toward medication -- most precisely the permitted diuretic Lasix or the equine version Salix -- was the only valid path to follow in "cleaning up the game."

Attempting to implement such a program, the governing body of the Breeders' Cup (self-dubbed "Racing's Championship Day") barred the use of Lasix in the 2012 events for two-year-olds. Unfortunately, the can was kicked down the road for future interpretation of the outcome when the Breeders' Cup backed off earlier assurances that no medications at all would be permitted in 2013 and decided to maintain the identical rule of "no lasix" for juveniles only.

Since the competitors in that initial experiment were not subjected to a compulsory endoscopic examination to detect any levels of bleeding, data that might have provided useful for those attempting to come to conclusions on the topic was never available.

Instead, horse racing once again proved its consistent commitment to inconsistency. The two-year-olds racing Lasix-free in the Breeders' Cup went on to race the following season as three-year-olds on the Triple Crown trail, and all of them were given Lasix.

In my opinion —- which I feel allowed because of the experiences included on these pages -- there will be no valid concensus on the topic of an issue like medication until the sport itself embraces the concept of a single leader, a racing "czar" or commissioner, heading a national office empowered to make and enforce a single set of rules and regulations for all states where the sport is offered.

Unfortunately, this concept has been unacceptable to racing's final arbiters, the track owners themselves. If they remain unable and unwilling to make any compromises, they will have surrendered their role as policymakers for the sport to the various state agencies and politicians who are more than willing to accept the status quo in return for the tax dollars that flow from the track accounts.

Racing, being such a rich international sport, deserves the same consistency of rules and regulations as found in soccer, gymnastics, skiing, hockey, golf, tennis or Formula One auto racing. But alas, no. Vested interests have provided enough incentive over the years for horse racing to have different medication rules from state to state and even different interpretations of the rules for conduct within a race. In some jurisdicions, the stewards are compelled to disqualify a horse which impedes another horse in any way. In others, the rules dictate that the foul only requires disqualification if it affects the outcome of the race, and what stewards interpret as "the best horse" should be awarded the win.

Imagine if golf, tennis or soccer each had different rules from country to country, or for that matter state to state. But that's horse racing.

Still, I'm going to be an optimist. After all these years in the game I truly can be nothing else and my greatest hope is that cooler heads prevail in future policy making decisions. I've seen plenty of what I would think was the best of racing, but the influx of bright young people still willing to seek a career in the sport makes me believe there's a chance that even better days lie ahead for the sport we love so much.

(And if anyone knows of a nice yearling we can get at the right price...)

Made in the USA
San Bernardino, CA
05 September 2016